T0301937

Understanding Financial Reporting Standards

A Non-Technical Guide

Understanding Financial Reporting Standards

A Non-Technical Guide

Roger Hussey
University of Windsor, Canada & University of the West of England, UK

Audra Ong
University of Windsor, Canada

NEW JERSEY • LONDON • SINGAPORE • BEIJING • SHANGHAI • HONG KONG • TAIPEI • CHENNAI • TOKYO

Published by

World Scientific Publishing Co. Pte. Ltd.
5 Toh Tuck Link, Singapore 596224
USA office: 27 Warren Street, Suite 401-402, Hackensack, NJ 07601
UK office: 57 Shelton Street, Covent Garden, London WC2H 9HE

Library of Congress Cataloging-in-Publication Data
Names: Hussey, Roger, author. | Ong, Audra, author.
Title: Understanding financial reporting standards : a non-technical guide /
Roger Hussey, University of Windsor, Canada & University of the West of England, UK,
Audra Ong, University of Windsor, Canada.
Description: New Jersey : World scientific, [2024]
Identifiers: LCCN 2023031249 | ISBN 9789811275531 (hardcover) |
ISBN 9789811275548 (ebook for institutions) | ISBN 9789811275555 (ebook for individuals)
Subjects: LCSH: Financial statements--Standards.
Classification: LCC HF5681.B2 H848 2024 | DDC 657/.3--dc23/eng/20230814
LC record available at https://lccn.loc.gov/2023031249

British Library Cataloguing-in-Publication Data
A catalogue record for this book is available from the British Library.

For any available supplementary material, please visit
https://www.worldscientific.com/worldscibooks/10.1142/13389#t=suppl

Desk Editors: Balasubramanian Shanmugam/Lai Ann

Typeset by Stallion Press
Email: enquiries@stallionpress.com

Printed in Singapore

Preface

Companies are very important to the way we live. They provide food and drink, clothing, transport, entertainment and influence other aspects of our lifestyle. The larger companies usually have the price of their shares listed on the London Stock Exchange and are known as Public Limited Companies (PLCs). These companies are required to issue annual company reports on their financial position for their shareholders and these are available publicly. The reports are lengthy and provide much more than just financial information. The disclosures of these companies make must comply with accounting standards that have been issued.

This book explains the requirements of all International Accounting Standards (IASs) and International Financial Reporting Standards (IFRSs) that have been issued and are still in force. We explain the development of corporate financial reporting from its very early days to the present debate on sustainability. These financial reporting standards cover a wide range of subjects and our explanations help students understand how companies operate. We also include some extracts from the Annual Report and Accounts of major UK companies to illustrate how the standards are being applied.

We would like to give special thanks to our teaching assistant, Griffen Kane, from Odette School of Business (UoW), who assisted in the preparation of PowerPoint material for each chapter. Griffen's attention to detail is much appreciated. The PPT materials (available online to lecturers) summarise key points that students find challenging into a more user-friendly perspective. A testbank is also available for lecturers online. Students will also find review exercises at the end of each chapter to consolidate their learning.

Our aim in writing this book is to present financial reporting standards in a clear, concise and engaging style that will empower and encourage students to understand corporate information and apply this knowledge in the real world. We hope that you enjoy *Understanding Financial Reporting Standards* and find this book a valuable resource!

About the Authors

Roger Hussey, PhD, MSc, FCCA is a fellow of the Association of Chartered Certified Accountants and received his M.Sc. in Industrial Relations and Ph.D. in Financial Communications from the University of Bath, U.K. He has taught in Australia, Canada, China and the U.K. Roger has written more than 40 books, some of which have been translated into other languages. Roger worked in industry for several years before moving to the Industrial Relations Unit at St. Edmund Hall, Oxford University, as Director of Research into employee communications. For many years, Roger was a member of the Financial Reporting Committee of the Institute of Chartered Accountants in England and Wales. He was later appointed as *Deloitte & Touche* Professor of Financial Reporting at the University of the West of England (UWE). Roger has also served on the advisory group on IFRS adoption in Canada. He was previously Dean of the Odette School of Business at the University of Windsor (UoW), Canada. Roger is now professor emeritus at both UoW and UWE.

Audra Ong, PhD, MBA is a professor of accounting at the University of Windsor, Canada. Prior to teaching in Canada, Audra taught at the Royal Agricultural University at Cirencester and Bath Spa University. She received her PhD in Accounting from the University of the West of England, her MBA from the University of Wales, Cardiff, and her BSc (Hons) in Accounting from Queen's University, Belfast. Audra has published in academic journals and is the co-author of several books including *A Non-Technical Guide to International Accounting Standards, A Guide to the New Language of Accounting and Finance and Pick a Number: Internationalizing U.S. Accounting* published by Business Expert Press, USA.

Contents

Chapter 1

The Growth of Financial Reporting

Structure of Chapter 1

Section title	**Main content**
A quick starter	A quick introduction to financial accounting and reporting.
A brief history of financial accounting	Problems of using financial measurement: the international need for numbers for various activities; the need for financial information.
Keeping financial records	There are many ways of describing the activities of a business and using financial measures is the foundation.
Double the work	The use of money as a measure and an explanation of double-entry bookkeeping.
Setting the Rules	Ensuring that all companies are using the same reporting regulations.
International Standards	Encouraging companies worldwide to use the same accounting methods.
Double-entry bookkeeping	Making certain that the "left hand agrees with the right hand."
Just a minute	The different methods of financial measurement.
Does thinking help?	The attempts to identify and explain accounting concepts.

A Wider View	An introduction to the concept of Environmental, Social and Governance (ESG) behaviour and sustainability reporting.
Telling it as it is	An explanation of the meaning of accounting terms and the purpose of financial reporting.
The Reporting Package	Tesco PLC shows its Financial Statements and Other Information content.
Chapter Review	

Most of us, at some stage in our life, are interested in a company's financial information. It may be because we are going to work for them, buy products from them, sell them our own goods or just for general interest. Unless you have substantial inside knowledge, one of the best sources of information is the corporate financial reports issued at least annually by a company. These are usually lengthy but should contain the following financial information:

statement of cash flows,
statement of financial position also known as the balance sheet,
income statement also known as the profit or loss account,
statement of changes in equity.

If a company is listed on the London Stock Exchange, it will publish these reports. You can have confidence in the information they provide because the reports will comply with International Financial Reporting Standards and be "approved" by an independent firm of auditors. In subsequent chapters, we explain the requirements of all the standards that currently apply. We also discuss the international perspective and the various complexities of setting and applying accounting standards.

We set the scene in this chapter by describing the development of financial accounting and reporting. This provides a platform for a more detailed explanation of financial reporting standards in our subsequent chapters. We establish the basis of recording financial transactions and introduce the advent of financial record keeping. This has the objective of providing useful information to the owners and investors in a business. They are also of interest to many others, including students seeking employment. For several centuries, this preoccupation with identifying the monetary value of items and activities was unresolved. One reason was the problems in identifying financial transactions and determining values. The best method for recording business transactions also presented challenges which were resolved by the advent of a method known as double-entry bookkeeping which we discuss in this chapter.

The introductory review of financial accounting history is followed by a discussion of the concepts accountants now use to bring validity and consistency to financial reports. We explain the dilemma of whether accountants should follow strict rules in conducting their work or if the application of basic principles is more useful. The final section before our conclusions looks at the very important and still unresolved issue which is the impact of inflation on identifying, measuring and recording financial transactions. We also look at the "darker" side of financial transactions and some of the major frauds that have taken place.

The section entitled "A Wider View" explains the role of the Financial Reporting Council in the UK. In the chapters following, we explain the particular requirements, known as International Financial Reporting Standards, that certain companies should follow when issuing financial reports. If a company wishes to be listed on the London Stock Exchange, it must issue annual reports that comply with IFRSs. There are approximately 2,000 companies listed on the London Stock Exchange.

A Quick Starter

It is useful to start by explaining the financial information required of companies and to briefly review the reporting of limited liability companies in the UK, particularly Public Limited Companies (PLCs) which have their shares listed on the Stock Exchange. A PLC is owned by its shareholders not by its managers, although some managers may have shares. The shareholders will receive an annual report from the company in which they have invested as they will wish to know how well the company is progressing financially as this can affect the share price. In addition to issuing a lengthy document, a company will hold an Annual General Meeting (AGM). At that meeting, the Directors will explain to shareholders how well financially the company has done or otherwise. The shareholder will consider not only the financial information given by the company but also the share price on the stock market. If you buy a share at a low price but now the price on the stock market has increased significantly, you may wish to sell the shares.

In addition to the annual meeting, a company will usually have a website and will also issue the following reports to the shareholders:

Preliminary Profit Announcements: In the UK, companies listed on the stock exchange must issue a preliminary statement of their annual results and dividends.

Interim Financial Reports: These are required at semi-annual intervals. There is International Accounting Standard (IAS 34 Interim Financial Reporting) that sets out best practices, and we discuss this standard in Chapter 10.

Regulatory News Service: The London Stock Exchange has a website which regularly provides detailed information of interest to investors and companies.

The printed annual report is very comprehensive, with some companies being over 300 pages long. The document will provide not only the financial information but also other details that may be of general interest. This may include several aspects of the company's various activities. For example, the annual report for 2022 for Tesco plc has several pages of detailed financial information and also includes the following:

Climate;
Task Force on Climate-related Financial Disclosures;
Non-financial information statement.

This takes up the first 100 pages plus other information which gives you an annual report on financial issues which is well over 200 pages in length.

With most companies, the easiest way to obtain an annual report is to go to the company's website. Failing this, or if the annual report you require is some years old or otherwise unobtainable, there are several websites offering access to the annual reports of companies. If you have a historic interest in a company and want annual reports from some years ago but it is difficult to trace financial information, you will find that the following website https://www.gov.uk/file-your-company-annual-accounts is an excellent source.

A Brief History of Financial Accounting

Financial transactions

Every day we enter into some form of financial transaction. You wake up in your home (rented or owned), take a shower (heated by a water company or an electricity company), eat your breakfast (cereal and milk purchased from a supermarket) and take a ride to college or work (pay fare or costs of your own bicycle or car). All of these activities will usually require you to make some form of payment. Even walking requires you wear clothes or shoes that somebody has paid. Regularly you entered into numerous financial transactions even if you make no other record than counting the small amount of cash remaining in your pocket and wondering what you have spent your money on.

In studying financial accounting and reporting, you must remember that profit is not the same as cash. Business transactions take various forms. We suspect that you know this but it explains the reason companies are required to produce a Statement of Comprehensive Income which shows a company's profit or loss for the financial period and a Statement of Cash Flows detailing the movements of cash. The differences between the timing of cash movements and profit gains can roughly be based on three different types of financial transactions.

You can have "cash up front" where you need to pay for the goods or services before you receive them. Mail-order businesses usually operate on this basis, and you have to send the money with your order for the goods. Even buying a plane seat or going to a music concert will usually require you to make your payment first. This is a good method for the company as they receive the cash before they have to provide the goods or the service so they do not have the immediate costs of fulfilling their side of the transaction. If there are large amounts of cash, they can be invested to earn interest.

There is "cash on delivery". A simple example is when you have a meal in a restaurant or buy goods from a shop. You pay when you have it. But the provider of the meal or the goods you purchase has incurred costs in obtaining them.

The third method of "cash in arrears" is not so good for the provider. They have to supply you with the goods or services and may not receive payment for some time after.

Few of us make a record of our daily financial transactions, although we may do with the more important ones. Organisations, of all types, must keep some form of records to ensure they are financially managed appropriately and to be able to provide information to organisations such as the government, tax authorities, shareholders, lenders and others with a right or an interest in receiving such information.

There are well-defined stages of accounting for economic financial transactions. Both large and small organisations go through the same process. Depending on the size of the company and the nature of its business transactions, some stages may be more troublesome than others. But the entire process attempts to capture and record business transactions.

Recognition

Accounting is concerned with the economic transactions and events that are undertaken by businesses or that affect them in some way. Economic transactions usually cause few problems because they are mainly the day-to-day operations of the business. Raw materials are purchased, the workforce is paid and sales are made. There may be payments for insurance, rent and advertising.

Economic events can be varied and outside the control of the company. One of the office buildings burns down and it is uninsured. The national currency weakens against the currencies of the business's trading partners, inflation is on the increase and the Chairman of the company unexpectedly resigns without explanations. Many of these events may affect the share price of the company, but the question arises as to how, and whether, we account for them.

Recognition is not only about whether there is an economic transaction or event but also about identifying in which financial period it took place. That is essential for calculating the profit or loss for the period and understanding the financial position of the company at the end of the period.

Financial period

The accounting of economic transactions is a continuing operation, but the reporting of that financial information normally takes place at set periods. In considering those reports that are intended for those external to the organisation, it normally takes place at set times. The period is usually 12 months interval at the maximum, but many organisations, particularly those whose shares are quoted on the stock exchange, may issue quarterly or half-yearly reports.

Initial measurement

We may have been able to recognise our economic event or transaction but the next question is whether we can measure it in financial terms with reliability. Traditionally, accountants have used a method known as historical cost accounting to record the value of items in the accounts and this is still the dominant method. The value of the economic transaction or event at the time that it took place is the value that is used and, with some exceptions, stays at that amount in the accounting records. This method has the great advantage of being very reliable (you know what was paid and should have documentary evidence). Unfortunately, this method has some weaknesses if the information is used for decision-making.

Imagine that you purchased a computer and a house on the same date five years ago. It is definite that the value of your computer will be a lot less than what you paid for it as developments in technology will have made it obsolete. On the other hand, it is likely that the value of the house has increased if you have a property market which is extremely active with many buyers. In both cases, the historic cost is different from the present value of the items and, therefore, of limited value for any decisions you wish to make now.

With some transactions and events, we may have great difficulty in measuring the current value. For example, if you have purchased the right to drill for oil and you have struck lucky, how much is that oil worth? It's obviously worth less while it is still in the ground, but how much less? Another example of difficulties in measurement is with brand names. Many of us will purchase clothes or equipment because it has a "brand" name. If that name attracts us to buying the item, then that brand must have value for the company that owns it. But how do we measure that value? In subsequent chapters, we explain the requirements of regulations which are known as accounting standards and set out the methods to be used for various events and financial transactions.

A word of caution! There are approximately 60 standards that explain the requirements for different accounting transactions and events. To make life more difficult, the first 41 standards were named International Accounting Standards (IASs). Some of these standards, for example, IAS 29 Financial Reporting in Hyperinflationary Economics, are of no interest to us and we do not discuss them. After the 41 standards had been issued, there was a change in approach, and new standards being issued were named International Financial Reporting Standards (IFRSs) with 16 being issued to date. Both the IASs and IFRSs are current ones, and in the following chapters, we have selected to explain which we consider most important.

Subsequent measurement

The problem of the lack of relevance with historic cost accounting for decision-making has resulted in some relaxation for certain assets where companies can remeasure (value) them. Subsequent measurement is the later determination of the monetary amount of economic transactions and events which will change the amount of initial measurement. This will be discussed in the following chapters, but a major issue is the method to be used for assessing the current values of the items.

Recording

Economic transactions and events must be recorded if we are to have confidence in our books of account and be able to produce information that is reliable. The usual method for recording transactions is known as double-entry bookkeeping. This method was developed in the 14th century and a book written by Luca Pacioli explaining its use was published in Venice in 1494. The same principles are still used today whether a manual or computerised system is employed.

Reporting (Disclosure): This is the communication of financial information to those who have a right to receive it or have an interest in the activities of the organisation.

Keeping Financial Records

The practice of keeping some form of record of financial transactions and calculating wealth at one point in time has a long history. Gradually, standard coinage developed in Europe, but it raises accounting measurement problems. Currencies are subject to change and the concept of measurement using the assumption of a stable homogenous coinage as a measuring unit is inadequate. The problem is that, as the amount identified does not have the same purchasing power over time, it is difficult to make a comparison of financial values in the past with present financial values. We discuss the impact of inflation and the accounting standard setters' attempts to resolve this issue in a later chapter.

Another problem is that counties use different coinage. For example, dollars in the US, pounds in the UK and franks in France. As international trade increased, the need to resolve the matter became essential. Accounting standard setters have issued a document that sets out the method that companies should use and we discuss this in Chapter 3. Unfortunately, as we will explain in that chapter, the rapidity of currency values changes so quickly that decision-making in international trade needs to be treated with caution.

A third major issue is that different types of money are now recognised as mediums of exchange. These new currencies include commodity money, representative money, the new cryptocurrency and fiat money. These "monies" frequently appear in digital form as well as physical tokens, such as coins and notes. Assessing the stability and values of these various and determining their appropriate use are not accounting issues. However, difficulties arise and the most appropriate methods for measuring and recording these transactions are being examined currently.

Accounting relies on financial measurement to determine the value of objects and the performance of businesses. Unfortunately, the concept of monetary value can depend on the circumstances. Water in the desert is worth much — a burst water pipe in your kitchen is a pain.

Record keeping, both financial and sustainable, is not an abstract subject separate from our daily lives. We list in the following some "numerical measurements" that show the size and impact of corporate activities both financial and sustainable on countries and people. These rankings may change as the importance of industries changes, and similar details of different activities are available on the Web:

- The companies making most cars are Toyota, Volkswagen and Hyundai.
- The organisations with the highest number of employees are Walmart, China railways and McDonald's.
- The countries cutting down most trees are Honduras, the Philippines and Nigeria.
- The countries with the highest mining rates are China, US and Russia.
- The companies owning most other companies are Procter & Gamble, PepsiCo and Mars Inc.
- The countries with the highest death rates are Bulgaria, Ukraine and Latvia.
- The countries with the highest inflation rates are Venezuela, Zimbabwe and Sudan.

Although some may disagree with the rankings, it is evident that human activities not only generate the incomes, goods and services we require but also present sustainability issues. In this chapter, we concentrate on the financial issues but we also introduce the sustainability aspects of human activity.

Most books you read on recording financial information spend most of the time on the "how" and very little on the "why". This results in very detailed and informative books on accounting procedures and methods (the how), often referred to as accounting standards. But if you do not know the reasons for recording the information (the why), you have no guide as to the amount and type of information to be included. We can suggest various possibilities for the use of information.

***To manage an organisation*:** Financial accounting is the term that is usually used for identifying and recording business transactions. The information can be used to report to various people and organisations the activities of a business. However, such information is not useful for managing large organisation on a daily basis. For this activity, we need to use a separate discipline called management accounting. This specifically sets out methods for collecting financial information and describes various methods and techniques for managing an organisation. There is no legal requirement for companies to use management accounting but there are several useful guides to its application.

***To calculate the taxes required by the government*:** This is not the most rewarding exercise and not acceptable by itself for regular management information. Most countries have their own tax regulations which differ from the financial accounting regulations. A certain number of adjustments have to be made to the calculated profit using financial accounting regulations to arrive at a figure that is acceptable to the tax authorities.

***To enable charities to continue their work*:** Charities provide support for various members of the community and rely on donations to do this. The funding raised by charities can be very large. For example, the US charity "Feeding America" noted in its 2020 Annual Report that the total public support and revenue for that year was $3,644,826. The financial statements of the organisation have been properly audited and the auditors state that they comply with "the accounting principles generally accepted in the United States". Note that the auditors refer to the country because different countries may have different accounting practices. These international differences can be frustrating and we explain in Chapter 2 the present position.

***To inform the owners or financial contributors of a "for profit" organisation*:** Understandably, owners may consider that calculating their profit is possibly the best reason for having accounting regulations and recording financial transactions in an appropriate way. With companies listed on a stock exchange, the owners are the shareholders. However, there are many different types of organisations conducting very different types of businesses from manufacturing articles to offering a service. There may also be different types of owners or participants requiring different financial information.

To overcome the issue of the various organisations and their financial disclosures, it is easiest when establishing financial accounting regulations in a country to identify and focus on the business entity. The underlying concept considers that the business is separate from the owner(s) and the purpose of the entity is to make a profit. Financial statements are prepared to reflect the activities of the business and not the activities of the owners. Although the concept is simple, there are inter-country differences and some examples where "special" business entities exist. These will be explained later in this chapter.

Why financial reports?

Starter companies need finance and established companies sometimes need more finance to expand their activities. Loans, hopefully, can be obtained from the bank or an investment company. Alternatively, a company can issue share to the "investing" public. The purchasers of the shares obviously want a financial reward. This is achieved by the company using the profits it makes to pay dividends to the shareholders. The company belongs to the shareholders and they expect to get some benefits from the investment they have. When a company issues an "Annual Report and Accounts" to the shareholders, it is showing them what profit "their" company has made. A company will hold an annual general meeting which shareholders can attend and they will vote on the proposals from the board of directors of the company.

Double the Work

It's only money

We expect that you have already in your studies tackled the mechanics of double-entry bookkeeping but we will refresh your memory in this section. The following two examples are designed to demonstrate how business activities are recorded using double entry and the main financial statements constructed. This process is now usually computerised but it is very helpful to understand the basics and the relationship between the process of recording financial transactions and the financial statements that are constructed from the information. In real life, the financial statements of a large company may, at first, look very overwhelming but the same principles are followed as in the following examples.

Example 1

John Helmet decides to buy and sell, at a profit, fishing baskets. He starts the business with £500 of his own money. In January, he buys with cash 20 baskets for £100 each from his supplier, although by the end of the month, he still owes the supplier for three baskets. Of the 20 baskets, he sells 17 of them at £150 each but has five customers who have not yet paid for each of their statues.

To calculate the profit, we look at the transactions regardless of any cash paid or received. The results are shown on the following profit statement.

Profit statement for the month of January

Sales (17 statues at £150 each)	£2,550
Less costs of sales (17 statues at £100 each)	£1,700
Profit	£850

You can do a simple check on the above statement. On each statue, a profit of £50 was made. As 17 statues were sold with a profit on each statue of £50, the total profit is £850. John may be pleased with this profit, but how much cash does he have? He has sold 17 statues but has only received payment for 10 of them. He has paid his supplier for 17 statues at £100 each. We now need to draw up a cash statement to show the amount of cash he has.

John Helmet
Cash statement for the month of January

Investment by John	£500
Payment received (10 × £150)	£1,500
Cash in hand	£2,000
Payment to supplier (17 × £100)	£1,700
Cash surplus	£300

Note that with both statements and particularly with the cash statement, we are showing John separate from his business. The two statements show us that John made a profit, but he cannot afford to repay himself fully for the cash he invested of £500. If we want to understand John's business, we need both a profit statement and a cash statement. But even that does not tell us the complete story. We also need to know how John stands now and a balance sheet, also known as a statement of financial position, will give us the answer.

In the following, we have drawn up a two-sided balance sheet as this gives an immediate link to all the transactions. You will find that most companies present the balance sheet in a vertical format. It contains the same type of information as the horizontal format which we show in the following.

John Helmet
Balance sheet at the end of January

Assets		**Liabilities**	
3 statues worth £100 each	£300	Owing to supplier (3 × £100)	£300
Customers owing (7 × £150)	£1050	Investment by owner	£500
Cash in hand	£300	Profit retained	£850
£1650		£1650	

You will note that the balance sheet differs from the other two statements. The balance sheet can be thought of as a snapshot at the end of January. The other two statements show events for the entire month. These three statements are very simple examples of those constructed by all companies. They provide a good illustration of the financial activities conducted by John. The business made a profit of £850 which was good, but the cash position was less favourable. The company cannot afford to pay John the full profit it made in the period. It cannot repay him the investment he made and can just pay the suppliers. John can take action to improve the situation but he needs the three separate statements to obtain a full picture. By drawing up these three financial statements, we have a better understanding of how the company is performing. To improve our investigations, it would be helpful to have the results for several financial periods. We can then analyse where there are financial problems that require attention. A quick note to add to this example. In the real world, there are four financial statements and we will explain these in Chapter 2.

Setting the Rules

If we allowed every company to prepare its own financial statements, we would possibly have some very different statements which do not provide us with the information we need. To overcome this problem, in various ways, countries have issued regulations that required companies to account for their business activities. In most countries, there are usually regulations that specify the types of organisations that must produce financial information. Obviously, tax authorities will want full financial information and the owners of companies want to know the financial progress. Some countries develop their own accounting standards to provide guidance to the information to be disclosed but several countries have adopted International Financial Reporting Standards. The UK is one among them.

These accounting standards are concerned with specific economic transactions, arrangements and events conducted by a business. For example, you will have one standard that is concerned only with identifying and measuring the revenue that a company receives. Another standard will set out the procedures for purchasing buildings and machinery. Other standards apply to such topics as accounting for valuing goods you have in stock and recording transactions in a foreign currency. An accounting standard usually focuses on the following three topics:

1. Recognition: This specifies the transactions and events that should be incorporated into the financial statements. The Chief Executive having a heart attack may be interesting and impact the share price of the company, but it is not shown on the financial statements. The factory burning down will be.

2. Measurement: This is the method used to determine the financial value of transactions and events. This can be tricky. Everything a company does has to be converted into financial measures. With many items, there are no problems, but we need to know how entities do their calculations and to have confidence in their methods. Accounting standards provide this reliability. With some transactions and events, there must be estimations and we will discuss these when we consider the individual standards.
3. Disclosure: Companies do not "open their books" to anybody who asks. Not only are there concerns over privacy, but the volume of information is huge. Information must be extracted and disclosed in a useful way. There is a standard that specifies the content and structure of the main financial statements and we discuss this in Chapter 2.

Initially, countries developed their own financial reporting standards and, although national regulations for financial accounting greatly improved financial reporting in one country, if you wanted to do business, buy shares or make loans with a company in another country, it was difficult to refer to its nationally produced financial statements. When countries use different accounting standards, there is difficulty for investors and financial lenders in comparing a company in one country with one in another country. As businesses and investors have become more international in their activities, this has caused problems. In 1973, the national accountancy bodies, not governments, from Australia, Canada, France, Germany, Mexico, the Netherlands, the United Kingdom, Ireland and the United States met and agreed to form the International Accounting Standards Committee (IASC). This was to be based in London, UK, with the task of establishing international accounting standards. The intention was that these would be used by companies, whatever their country of origin is.

After much discussion at the international level, an International Accounting Standards Committee was formed. It was very active and issued several International Accounting Standards (IAS) which still apply. After many years, an International Accounting Standards Board (IASB) was formed that would replace the IASC. The IASB kept several of the IASs issued by the IASC and commenced issuing its own standards entitled International Financial Reporting Standards (IFRSs) starting with IFRS 1 *First-time Adoption of International Financial Reporting Standards* followed by *IFRS 2 Share-based Payments.* Not all countries have adopted international accounting standards and the Financial Accounting Standards Board (FASB) in the US has developed an Accounting Standards Codification (ASC) of its own.

In this book, we explain and demonstrate standards issued both by the International Accounting Standards Committee and the International Accounting Standards Board. All of these standards are still in effect. The numbering of individual standards is somewhat confusing. The present position is that the IASC issued 41 standards between 1975 and 2000. The standards were numbered consecutively starting with number 1. Each standard also had a descriptive title, for example, *IAS 7 Cash Flow Statements*. Most of the IASC standards are still in effect. When the IASB took over from the IASC, it "adopted" the IASs still in force and started to issue its own standards. These are named International Financial Reporting Standards (IFRSs). Once again, these standards are numbered consecutively, starting with Number 1, and have a descriptive title, for example, *IFRS 7 Financial Instruments: Disclosures.*

Several countries have adopted international accounting standards. This does not necessarily mean that those countries require all companies within their borders to comply with them. Normally, it is only major companies listed on its national stock exchange that must do so. Even if a country claims it "uses" international accounting standards, caution must be used when examining the financial statements because the standards will apply only to certain organisations, that is, the large listed companies. Even where a country has adopted fully an international standard, politics, legislation, tax regulations and other pressures can lead to differences. The position at the time of writing this book was that 41 International Accounting Standards (IASs) and 17 International Financial Reporting Standards (IFRSs) had been issued. These standards are all still in force which presents a challenge to accountants preparing the financial statements of a company.

International Standards

The basis of the standards is in International Accounting Standard 1 Presentation of financial statements. The standard has been amended and revised several times. It is a surprisingly brief standard in view of the information required of companies to provide. The reason for the brevity of the standard is that it concentrates on the presentation of the four financial statements and not issues of recognition, measurement and detailed disclosure requirements which are covered in the separate standards which we discuss in later chapters.

Recognition and measurement are two key concepts in constructing financial statements. The four financial statements to be drawn up are as follows:

- **Statement of Financial Position**: This is also known as the balance sheet.
- **Statement of Comprehensive Income**: This can take the form of one statement or be separated into a profit and loss statement and a statement of other income, including property and equipment.
- **Statement of Changes in Equity**: Also known as a statement of retained earnings, this documents the company's change in earnings or profit for the given financial period.
- **Statement of Cash Flows**: This report summarises the company's financial transactions in the given period, separating cash movements into operations, investing and financing.

In Chapter 2, we elaborate more on IAS 1 which provides a structure for understanding all the standards that have been issued. If you examine the financial statements in other countries, you will find that mostly similar information is provided but the terms may differ. The terminology becomes more complex and the activities companies enter into can be substantial but the basic financial reporting principles remain the same.

The other important factor to note is that share prices for a company on a stock exchange do not usually match the capital or equity figure shown on the balance sheet of a company. The current share price represents the amount somebody is willing to pay the owner of the shares to obtain their interest in a company. In making this decision, they will refer to the financial statements but also make judgements on competitors, the nature of the industry and the movements in the share market.

At the international level, we have the International Sustainability Standards Board (ISSB) which published in 2022 an Exposure Draft, "General Requirements for Disclosure of Sustainability-related Financial Information". We will be explaining the work of this organisation in Chapter 12.

Double-Entry Bookkeeping

The term double-entry bookkeeping is usually associated with the Franciscan friar and teacher of mathematics, Luca Pacioli, who in 1494 published an instructional treatise describing the system of double-entry bookkeeping. The "double" means making two accounting entries for one process. At its simplest, you can consider those two entries as giving and receiving by the organisation. If a company purchases goods to be sold, then it will give cash and receive the goods. If it sells some of those goods on credit to a customer, then the organisation will give the customer the goods and receive a promise of payment at a later date. The process of recording these activities is known as double-entry bookkeeping.

As you can imagine, some transactions can be much more complicated, but the same principles apply, and we will set out some basic rules and provide examples. It is assumed that all the economic events and transactions will generate some form of source documents, such as an invoice or a receipt. These source documents are used by the accounting staff to record the transaction. Although all the transactions were originally made on paper, mostly the procedures are now computerised.

Although computerised systems are now used for the recording of transactions, the same principles are applied to handwritten ledgers. Each page of the ledger would represent an account. The half of the page on the left-hand side is called the debit side. The half of the page on the right-hand side is called the credit side. We show in the following simple calculations and basic accounts. If you need or, for some obscure reason, wish to know more about double-entry bookkeeping, there are many instructional books.

Name of the account

Date	Details of transaction	Amount	Date	Details of transaction	Amount

The next stage is to know the rules for the debit and credit transactions that are entered into by an organisation.

Recording assets and liabilities

The rules for recording transactions concerning assets and liabilities are as follows:

- to show an increase in an asset account, debit the account.
- to show a decrease in an asset account, credit the account.
- to show an increase in a capital or liability account, credit the account.
- to show a decrease in a capital or liability account, debit the account.

An asset is something that the business owns or over which it has control and will provide economic benefits such as premises, machinery and goods it will sell. A liability is where the organisation owes a sum of money.

Bookkeeping example

April 1: the bank lends £10,000 to the business.

The accounts will look as follows when we apply our rules for assets and liabilities. The two entries will each refer to the other account.

Loan account

		£			£
			1 April	Cash account	10,000

Cash account

		£			£
1 April	Loan account	10,000			

The above entries show that the organisation has £10,000 cash which it has received from the bank, but it owes the bank £10,000 and has presumably given an indication that it will pay the bank at some future date. On April 2, the organisation decides to purchase machinery for £4,000. The loan account will not change as there have been no transactions with the bank. However, the cash account will change as cash is being paid and we need a new account to represent the machinery that has been purchased.

We have given cash (which is an asset) so that is a credit entry as we are showing a decrease in the asset of cash. We have received another asset in the form of machinery and that is a debit entry as we are showing an increase in an asset. The loan account remains the same but the cash account shows a credit for the machinery we have paid. This reduces the total of the loan account to £6,000 but opens a new account, the machinery account to register the purchase.

Cash account

		£			£
1 April	Loan account	10,000	3 April	Machinery account	4,000

Machinery account

		£			£
3 April	Cash account	4,000			

The above example can be continued until we have hundreds if not thousands of entries. With asset and liability accounts, it will always be the same system. If revenue and expense transactions are to be recorded, the rules are as follows:

- to show a decrease in an expense account, credit the account.
- to show an increase in a revenue account, credit the account.
- to show a decrease in a revenue account, debit the account.

An increase in a revenue account occurs when the company makes a sale which is a credit to the revenue account. An increase in an expenses account occurs when a company incurs expenses and this will be a debit entry.

Other financial activities by the company follow the same debit and credit entries. Purchases are recorded as a debit entry in the purchases account and a credit entry to the cash account. When the business sells the goods, they are not shown as a credit entry in the purchases account for two reasons. First, the purchases account records what the goods cost. The goods will not be sold at the price for which they were purchased, as the business adds a mark up in order to make a profit. The second reason is that at the end of a financial period, it is likely that there will be some unsold goods remaining i.e. closing inventory.

Periodically, and at least at the end of a financial period, a company closes or balances its accounts and constructs a trial balance. This is a list of all the closing balances on the accounts of an organisation with debit balances in one column and credit balances in another. If the double-entry bookkeeping has been done properly, the two totals should agree.

Double-entry bookkeeping ensures that the transactions are recorded, but they do not necessarily reflect changes in the level of activity and the changes in costs due to increases in property values and decreases due to inflation. The answer, of course, is to apply financial measures that recognise these changes. As we discuss later, when we consider the subject of the principles versus rules in financial accounting, this has proved very difficult.

Just a Minute

To complete this section on recording and reporting financial transactions, we need to discuss the way we should measure financial transactions and report them, and there are various conflicting methods. In this section, we explain the main methods, starting with the one that is currently used, but subsequently, we examine other methods, some of which may appear more useful than the one currently applied.

Historic cost: Traditionally, this has been the approach favoured by accountants. When using this method, assets, which are the items that the company owns, such as buildings and machinery, are recorded at the amount paid for them at the time of their acquisition. Liabilities, the amount the company owes to others, such as its suppliers, are recorded at the amount of proceeds received in exchange for the obligations or the amount of cash to be paid to satisfy the liability in the normal course of business.

The great advantage of historical cost is its reliability. You know exactly how much was paid for the asset and there will in all probability be a paper trail that can be used to verify the cost. You know how much you have to pay to settle any liability you have incurred. The disadvantage of the historic cost approach is the poor input that the information gives to users for decision-making, particularly after the passing of time. Companies may have acquired premises, land and machinery over the years. If these purchases were recorded at historic cost, they will remain in the records at that amount. After several years, because of changes in prices, the values the assets are shown at a "written down value" will be out of date. Some companies still have properties in their accounts that were purchased over 100 years ago, and this original cost is still used in the reports by several companies.

Current cost: This is sometimes referred to as replacement value or current entry value. For assets such as machinery and buildings, it is the amount that would have to be paid if the same or similar asset was acquired currently, in other words, how much it would cost to replace that asset.

Realisable value: This is sometimes known as current exit value. Assets are shown at the amount that could be obtained if the assets were sold in an orderly disposal i.e. not in a bankruptcy. Liabilities are valued at the amount of cash that would be needed to settle the liability.

Present value: This is sometimes known as value in use. Assets are shown in the balance sheet at the discounted value of the future cash flows that the asset is expected to generate in the normal course of business. Liabilities are carried at the present discounted net value of the future cash flows expected to be required to settle the liabilities in the normal course of business.

Example — Differences in value

Company A needs a loan but the only asset it has is a machine that is used in production. The company knows that the bank manager will want to use the machinery for security and will ask about its value. The company has managed to obtain the following information:

Historical cost
The machine costs £250,000 five years ago and is expected to continue to produce for a further five years. The machine will have no scrap value at the end of that time.

Current cost
As prices have increased over the last five years, it would cost £300,000 to replace the machine. This would be basically the same model.

Realisable value
As industry is booming and the machine has been well maintained, the company is confident that it could sell the machine for £175,000.

Present value
The company believes that, after deducting all costs of running the machine, it will receive £100,000 in cash each year for the next five years from the output it will sell.

The problem is to decide what the value of the machine is. If we use historic cost, we have a reliable purchase cost of £250,000, but the machine is halfway through its useful life. The company will depreciate the machine annually, so the amount shown in the company's accounts is likely to be £125,000. They will have written off half of the cost of the machine over the last five years and will write off the remaining half over the next five years.

But the amount of £125,000 is not intended to show the "value" of the machine but is an indication of the proportion of the original cost that has been already written off in the financial statements. The current cost is the value of a new machine, but the machine the company owns is five years old. We could arrive at a calculated, but arbitrary, value by taking just half of the value of the new machine to reflect the age of the old machine. This gives a value of £150,000. Do we really, or more importantly the bank, believe this is the current value? The realisable value of £175,000 looks like a useful guide to the value. Of course, there are often many circumstances where the company is unable to sell the machine. Also, how confident are we that there are likely purchasers willing to complete the transactions? This also poses the question as to why does the company not sell the machine as it would receive £25,000 more than the amount it has in its books. The answer is in the final method of measurement which involves calculating the future benefits to be enjoyed.

By keeping the machine and continuing to sell the output, the company should receive a cash surplus of £100,000 for the next five years. It is obviously better for the company to keep the machine rather than to sell it. There is one refinement that we need to make to his amount and that is the calculation of the present value of the future cash flows known as "discounting". This involves calculating the current value of predicted future cash flows.

Does Thinking Help?

The search for concepts

The financial reports of an organisation may be required by the owners, tax authorities, banks and other lenders of finance, other companies that do business with it and there may be others, such as current employees. The desire to record and report the many financial transactions of an organisation leads to the question of how it is best done and to ensure that everyone uses the same method. The task is to determine how to measure business activities, often of a very different nature, and give the financial results to those who require the information.

The need for accounting concepts is not a recent concern but had been evident for many years. There have been many articles written on the subject. Although we do not usually give references, we will recommend only one, which is an article by Badua (2019) entitled "Lies, Sex, and Suicide: Teaching Fundamental Accounting Concepts with Sordid Tales from the Seamier Side of Accounting History". This identifies the need for identifying concepts. However, reaching an agreement on what those concepts are and how they should be applied in recording accounting transactions has not been easy and the debate continues.

Over the years, certain assumptions or concepts have been developed to identify, define and categorise which financial transactions and events should be recorded and how. In addition to identifying the concepts, it has been found necessary to formalise them so that accountants use the same basis in preparing financial statements, and the users of those statements can better understand the information that is being communicated. There are many concepts which are also referred to as assumptions, conventions, principles and axioms. Some of these concepts are known as "qualitative characteristics". These are the attributes that information should have in order to make it a valuable communication. For example, you would not expect the information to be biased or so incomplete that you might misinterpret it.

It was evident that accountants would be the most appropriate group to develop concepts for financial transactions, but on a global basis, it is not simple. There have been differences between the approaches to the task by the Financial Accounting Standards Board in the United States and the International Accounting Standards Board. Given the differences between the two main accounting standard setters and the conflicting opinions and changes of view over time by anyone involved in the subject, we hesitate to attempt to offer a firm and comprehensive guide to accounting concepts. Therefore, we list in the following what we consider are some of the main concepts but warn you that this list could be lengthened and changed depending on the books and articles you choose to read.

Business entity concept views the business as separate from its owner as far as its financial transactions are concerned.

Going concern assumes that the financial statements are prepared for an organisation that is going to continue in business and is not going to close in the foreseeable future.

Matching concept accounts for the expenses it has incurred in a financial period and matches them with the revenue generated in that same period.

Consistency requires the same accounting treatment to be used from one accounting period to the next unless there is a very good reason to change.

Money Measurement assumes that only the items that are capable of being measured reliably in financial terms are included in the financial records.

Historical cost values assets on their original cost, which is when the transaction or event originally took place. No adjustments are made for subsequent changes in price or value although depreciation will be deducted annually.

We would emphasise that these are some of the concepts that underpin the recording and reporting of financial transactions. To understand the financial reports by any organisation, it is necessary to be familiar with the concepts that have influenced the construction of the financial statements. It is also necessary to know if the standard setters, no matter in which country they reside, have adopted a principle or rules-based approach which we explain in the following section.

Underlying assumptions

In addition to the above concepts or assumptions, there are two that are fundamental to accounting: the accruals concept and the going concern concept. These are so important that the International Accounting Standards Board (IASB) included them in a pronouncement entitled "Framework for the Preparation and Presentation of Financial Statements". This is an old document, also known as the Conceptual Framework, that was published in 1989, and in March 2018, a revised Conceptual Framework was published by the IASB. It is important to remember that a Conceptual Framework, whether issued by FASB or the IASB, is not a standard. It is the basis on which standard setters develop their individual standards. If a company enters into a transaction or there is an event where no standard exists, the company can refer to the Conceptual Framework for guidance. Some critics may argue that this would provide information but not clarity on some of the conundrums experienced by accountants. Accounting regulations are not carved in stone but reflect the business activities, experiences and knowledge at a particular stage in the development of society. If we look at the world in a different way, then accounting may change. In the following chapters, we base our explanations on the approach of the International Financial Reporting Board. They have a very useful website if you want more information.

A Wider View

Financial and sustainability reporting

The financial report forms a substantial part of a company's annual report and accounts. These documents may be well over 200 pages in length and those for major companies can be found on their website. These reports are prepared initially by qualified accountants for the owners of the company. For companies "listed" on a stock exchange, these would be the shareholders. Even with small companies, not listed on a stock exchange, there are other potential users of the annual report such as banks and other lenders who wish to see the Annual Report containing a firm of accountants' name before agreeing to any loans.

The annual report and accounts, in addition to containing the financial information, will also contain a substantial amount of narrative information about many aspects of the company's activities. Such information may be very closely linked to sustainability. The following segment is from the annual report and accounts of Microsoft:

> *Many of our shareholders are increasingly focused on the importance of the effective engagement and action on ESG topics. To meet the expectations of our stakeholders and to and maintain their trust, we are committed to conducting our business in ways that are principled, transparent, and accountable and we have made a broad range of environmental and social commitments. From our CEO and Senior Leadership Team and throughout our organization, people at Microsoft are working to conduct our business in principled ways that make a significant positive impact on important global issues. Microsoft's Board of Directors provides insight, feedback, and oversight across a broad range of environmental and social matters. In particular, among the responsibilities of the Board's Regulatory and Public Policy Committee is to review and provide guidance to the Board and management about the Company's policies and programs that relate to CSR.*

The term ESG refers to **Environmental, Social and Governance** behaviour and we discuss this at length in later chapters concerned with sustainability.

To be listed on a stock exchange, a company must produce financial reports which comply with accounting standards and are approved by auditors. The majority of companies listed on a stock exchange are now publishing reports that provide substantial information on their own sustainability efforts. There are also several companies and associations that are producing sustainability reports that are not directly linked to financial reports. The following example is just a small part of a report by American Beverage Association https://www.innovationnaturally.org/plastic/:

> Our plastic bottles are made to be remade. We are carefully designing them to be 100% recyclable — even the caps. Our goal is for every bottle to become a new bottle, and not end up in oceans, rivers, beaches and landfills. And that means we are using less new plastic.
>
> That's why America's beverage companies have launched a new initiative to get *Every Bottle Back*. This unprecedented commitment includes:
>
> - Working with World Wildlife Fund through the *ReSource: Plastic* initiative to reduce our plastic footprint.
> - Partnering with The Recycling Partnership and Closed Loop Partners to improve recycling access, provide education to residents and modernize the recycling infrastructure in communities across the country.
> - Increasing awareness about the value of our 100% recyclable plastic bottles.
> - Introducing a new voluntary on-pack message to promote the recyclability of our plastic bottles and caps.

Similar sentiments and awareness of the sustainability responsibilities are shown in a 56-page document by Associated British Foods plc and an extract is shown in the following:

> A growing global population needs more accessible, ethical and affordable food and clothing but with less cost to our planet's finite resources and climate. We are meeting people's present needs but also helping to shape a more sustainable future with them. This means cutting carbon emissions in our manufacturing operations, making them more energy efficient, and using resources such as water in more circular ways to reduce the impact of serving our customers.
>
> ---
>
> Associated British Foods plc Responsibility Update 2021. Responsibility update 2021.pdf.downloadasset.pdf.

Information by companies on their sustainability efforts is not restricted to only US and UK companies. Numerous examples are available on the Web and we show in the following extracts from the Chinese company *Kweichow Moutai (600519.SH)*:

> Since 2012, the company states that it has donated 100 million yuan each year to help 140,000 poor students in total enter colleges and universities. It has earmarked 50 million yuan annually to participate in the ecological protection and environmental management of the Chishui River basin. https://www.imsilkroad.com/z/191028-1/#g309050=1.

There are several websites providing corporate examples and commenting on the progress being made in different countries. We will be looking more closely at sustainability reporting in later chapters. At this stage, we would suggest that financial reporting is well established and that international standards are accepted in several countries. The position with sustainability reporting is that considerable concern is being expressed around the world, and many companies are publicising their efforts to pursue sustainability. However, corporate efforts are diverse and there are efforts to establish standards for sustainability reporting similar to financial reporting. We examine these efforts in later chapters.

The need for information

Companies have shareholders and lenders of finance, such as banks, to conduct their businesses. Investors and lenders need financial information about a company before any investment is likely to be made. Even a one-person business requiring a loan from a bank will be required to provide financial information to obtain the loan. When investors are buying company shares, they want to look closely at the financial benefits of doing so. There is the risk that the providers of information, those wanting the loan, will select the information that it provides to the potential investors. To prevent this, there are standards drawn up by accounting organisations that establish the financial information that should be disclosed.

Essentially, there were the following three financial statements which have been in existence for several years:

- the income statement that shows the profit or loss for a financial period,
- the statement of cash flows that shows the cash that has been given and received for the financial period,
- the statement of financial position, also known as the balance sheet, which shows the assets owned by the amounts that it owes.

We explain these three financial statements in the following chapters. A fourth statement was introduced by the International Accounting Standards Board in 2007 known as the statement of changes in equity, and we discuss this statement in a later chapter.

Telling It as It Is

The language of accounting

As with most disciplines, accounting has words and phrases that are specific to their particular activities and interests. The main terms you encounter are as follows:

Terms	Simple explanation
1. Revenue 2. Turnover 3. Sales	These are the economic inflows, usually payments or promise of payment, that an entity receives in a financial period.
1. Non-current assets 2. Long-lived assets 3. Fixed assets	A resource controlled by an entity that is expected to provide future economic benefits and that will be kept in the business for a long period. Examples of these resources are land, buildings and machinery.
1. Accounts receivable 2. Debtors	People or other groups that owe money to the entity.
1. Accounts payable 2. Creditors	People or other groups that are owed money by the entity.
1. Shares 2. Stock	Money invested in the business in the form of risk capital.
1. Finance leases 2. Capital leases	A financial agreement entered into by an entity for the use of an asset which appears on the balance sheet as an asset and a liability.
1. Profit and loss account 2. Income statement 3. Statement of financial performance 4. Statement of comprehensive income	A financial statement giving the financial performance of an entity over a period of time. There are several variations on this term which we discuss in later chapters.

The purpose of financial reports

All types of institutions prepare some form of annual financial report, not only the profit companies with shares listed on a stock exchange but also charities and other types of smaller organisations. Even the owners of your local businesses want to know if they are making a profit or a loss. In this chapter, we explain the types of financial reports prepared by large companies that usually have shares listed on a stock exchange. There are two main purposes of these reports:

1. providing reliable information on the financial position and performance of a company. This information is contained in financial statements, the content of which is controlled by financial accounting standards;
2. the results of the stewardship and accountability of management for the resources entrusted to it by shareholders and lenders, such as banks.

There are generally considered to be two main models for financial reports. These are usually referred to as the decision model and the stewardship model. To a large extent, they are incompatible and it is extremely difficult to prepare general-purpose financial statements that achieve both objectives.

To explain the arguments, we will summarise them into two extreme viewpoints although there are various ranges of opinion. It is considered that the decision model must provide information that is relevant and the most interested users would be the providers of capital being individuals and institutions that financially support the company, usually by purchasing shares. The purpose of financial reports is to assist them in making decisions regarding their financial relationship with a company. The stewardship model argues that there is a moral, if not a legal, obligation for entities to provide information to a wide range of users who may be interested in its activities. Increasingly, interest has been concerned with the impact of a company's activities on the world in which we live and this falls under the general heading of sustainability which we discuss in later chapters.

The givers and users of financial reports

The givers of financial reports: In this book, for simplicity, we use the term business entity and this encompasses any type of organisation whose main purpose is to make a profit. This means that we are not including such organisations as charities, government agencies and social clubs which have their own regulatory requirements. We assume that the business is separate from the owner(s) and the actual business and its owners are treated as two separately identifiable parties. Financial statements are prepared to reflect the activities of the business and not the personal activities of the owners. Although the concept is simple, there are inter-country differences and some examples where "special" business entities exist. In reading or compiling financial statements, it is useful to think of the business as an "entity" separated completely from the owner or owners. Entities listed on stock exchanges are frequently labelled as Groups, that is, a number of separate companies either wholly owned or partly owned by a holding company. As users of financial statements, we are usually interested in seeing the financial statements for the group and that is our reporting entity.

The users of financial reports: We tend to think of the annual report and accounts that companies listed on a stock exchange publish as a company's financial reports. However, there are many different types of organisations and there are many types of users of the financial information they generate. We list in the following the possible users of financial reports and the types of information they may use.

Shareholders: There are three basic types of decisions taken by shareholders who invest in a company. They wish to know whether to buy more shares, hold on to all the shares they already own or sell part or all of the shares they own. In making these decisions, the investor will be considering not only the potential future of an individual company but also the prospects for the stock market. In trying to predict the future, the shareholders will have one or both of the two objectives. One is to achieve a regular and attractive income through the dividends received from the company. The other is to achieve a capital growth in shares where the company becomes successful, and therefore its share price on the stock market increases. The owner of the shares can sell these shares at a profit. Of course, companies do not have any specific knowledge on the aims of the shareholders and therefore apply a general approach. The details of this approach are set out in financial reporting standards which we discuss later.

Employees and their trade unions: Generally, these possible users wish to assess the security of their jobs, employment opportunities and the security of their pensions. From the unions' position, they will be attempting to negotiate pay increases and other benefits for their members. Knowledge of the financial status of the company will be invaluable in these negotiations as the trade union wishes to evaluate the company's "ability to pay". Individual employees may be interested in their career prospects and security of employment within the company. Obviously, the future looks more attractive to an employee in a financially successful company.

Lenders: These wish to assess whether their loans and the interest charges involved will be paid. If the loan is short term, it is likely the lender is interested in the current cash position of the company and how likely it is to change in the future. Long-term lenders will need information on the future stability of the company and the probability of the interest on the loan being paid and the loan principle being repaid at the end of its term. The long-term lender may also wish to assess the probability of the loan being repaid in full if the company goes bankrupt.

Suppliers and other trade creditors: These are clients, customers and others who wish to know whether they will be paid and if the entity is likely to be a long-term customer. Some suppliers are particularly dependent on one or two large customers. If those companies go out of business, then the supplier will go out of business. If the customer is expanding, the supplier can feel confident about the future.

In addition to these main users, there may be many others with their own information needs. Customers want to know about the future of the entity, particularly if they have warranties or may require replacement parts or repairs in the future. Governments and their agencies need to regulate and collect tax from business entities and use company information in national planning and statistics. The public is often affected by the activities of large entities, whether it is the donations the entities make to charities, the training they offer, their involvement with community activities or the pollution they cause. This will lead us into discussing the subject of "Sustainability" in later chapters.

Students: If you are going for "job" interviews, it is sensible to read the annual reports of the prospective employer and remember a few helpful comments you can make in the interview.

General public: Companies are extremely important aspects of our lives. They provide work, products and services and generally are an active part of our environment. Most of us have some knowledge of the most important companies because of their importance in our lives. Some guide to their importance is provided by the number of employees the companies have worldwide. Compass Group has approximately 596 thousand employees. Tesco has 295 thousand, and HSBC Holdings has 235 thousand employees. We would not be surprised if these numbers have increased since we wrote this book.

The financial information a company generates usually complies with "standards" set by an accounting organisation. In many countries, there are accounting standard setters working within a coalition of interests including reporting organisations, shareholders, the media, political groups and others. The powers of these interested parties differ, and the need and desire of the accounting standard setters to gain the support of particular factions also vary. Because of these different needs and information availability, the practice was for individual countries to set their own accounting standards which were usually set by a professional accounting body within that country. Over the years, this led to some problems.

In the latter half of the 20th century, there were some highly publicised examples of companies in Europe that were very profitable and wanted to list shares on the New York Stock Exchange (NYSE). To do so, the profitable company had to redraft their financial information to comply with the US accounting standards, known as Generally Accepted Accounting Principles (GAAP). The result sometimes was that the previously declared profit for a company calculated according to their own country's accounting standards became a loss when redrafted to comply with US GAAP as required for a listing on the New York Stock Exchange. We had arrived at the unhappy position where financial accounting and reporting financial results differed depending on the country in which a company was operating.

This problem of the appropriate treatment of accounting recording being country specific had been recognised earlier. In 1973, national accountancy bodies from Australia, Canada, France, Germany, Mexico, the Netherlands, the United Kingdom and Ireland and the United States established the International Accounting Standards Committee (IASC). These countries agreed that the IASC would formulate and publish, in the public interest, accounting standards to be observed in the presentation of financial statements and to promote their worldwide acceptance and observance. This was to be achieved by ensuring that published financial statements issued by companies complied with International Accounting Standards (IASs) in all material respect. It only needed to persuade governments, national standard-setting bodies, authorities controlling securities markets and the industrial and business communities that published financial statements that should comply with IASs. A daunting task!

In 1995, the IASC embarked on an ambitious program to issue a set of core standards entitled International Accounting Standards (IASs). This was completed in 1999 with 15 new or revised standards which reduced the number of alternative methods available to companies and established benchmark treatments and permitted variations. Although the IASC was successful in the core standards project, in retrospect, it is easy to see that the work it was attempting to undertake was impossible because of the way that the organisation was structured and resourced. The IASC did not have the resources for establishing standard regulations for worldwide accounting and did not have the power to enforce them. The only way forward was to establish a more powerful and better-funded organisation. The International Accounting Standards Board (IASB) was established formally in April 2001, but it took many years to arrive at that point. It subsequently changed its name to the International Financial Reporting Standards Board. We are now in the position where we have to issue some of the International Accounting Standards (IASs) and also the International Financial Reporting Standards (IFRSs). We explain all of these standards in subsequent chapters.

The Reporting Package

Although we focus in this book on the financial statements issued by the company, their annual report and accounts go far beyond these boundaries. We show in the following the contents of the Annual Report and Accounts for 2022 issued by Tesco plc:

Contents
Strategic report
Introduction
2022 highlights
Tesco at a glance
Our purpose
Our purpose in action
Chairman's statement
Group Chief Executive's review
Our market context
Our strategic priorities and performance framework
Key performance indicators
Our business model
Our colleagues
Engaging with our stakeholders
Section 172 statement
Financial review
Principal risks and uncertainties
Longer term viability statement
Climate
Task Force on Climate-related Financial Disclosures
Non-financial information statement
Corporate governance Chairman's letter
Compliance with the UK Corporate Governance Code
Board of Directors
Executive Committee
Division of responsibilities
Board leadership and company purpose
Board activity
Composition, succession and evaluation
Nominations and Governance Committee
Corporate Responsibility Committee
Audit Committee
Directors' remuneration report
Directors' report
Financial statements and other information
Index

The last section headed Financial Statements and Other Information starts on page 105 and the detailed contents of those pages are as follows:

Financial statements and other Information
Independent auditor's report
Group income statement
Group statement of comprehensive income/(loss)
Group balance sheet
Group statement of changes in equity
Group cash flow statement
Notes to the Group financial statements
Tesco PLC — Parent Company statement of changes in equity
Notes to the Parent Company financial statements
Related undertakings of the Tesco Group
Other information
Supplementary information (unaudited)
Glossary — Alternative performance measures
Five-year record
Shareholder information

The last page was numbered 216.

In this book, we are going to concentrate on financial information, particularly financial information which is disclosed. This information is regulated by independent financial accounting standard setters and we commence our explanations in the following chapter.

Chapter Review

The growth of businesses required some accurate and acceptable methods for recording financial transactions. At the very beginning, it was very basic but the introduction of double-entry bookkeeping was a major move to the use of financial accounting in a structured way. Accounting standards for recording business activities are well established and you need to understand them if you are studying accounting, if you invest in shares or if you work in a large company. International accounting standard setters and national standard setters determine the information to be provided in financial statements that are available to those investing in the company or doing business with it. Financial reporting to those who are outside the company has grown extensively and most companies have websites that provide substantial information and analysis.

In most countries, tax authorities will have their own rules to establish the amount of profit on which tax should be paid. Also, lenders of finance usually request more information when contemplating the request from a company for a loan. As for running a company, the directors will rely on regular management accounting information generated internally. This is not a criticism of the present method of financial accounting standards, but it has focussed mainly on the perceived needs of investors in the financial markets and not others affected by a company's activities.

In subsequent chapters, we explain reporting financial information by companies, both at the country level and also internationally. We explain the details of accounting standards requirements relating to various activities. However, interest and publicly voiced concerns have moved away from only financial reporting to promote sustainability reporting. In later chapters, we will describe the developments that have taken place and we also discuss the role and governance of sustainability standards and reporting.

CHAPTER 1 The Growth of Financial Reporting

Review Questions

1. Which of the following statements best describes the term "going concern"?
   a. The ability of a business to continue into the foreseeable future.
   b. When current assets minus current liabilities give a negative figure.
   c. Where the income less the expenses of a business is a negative amount.
   d. The business is likely to be taken over in the next 12 months.

2. Which one of the following is the best description of "reliability" in relation to information in financial statements?
   a. Understandable for users.
   b. Does not contain any material error.
   c. Includes a substantial amount of caution with the information disclosed.
   d. Information is easily understood by readers.

3. What is the main financial information provided by the Statement of Comprehensive Income and the Statement of Cash Flows and how do they differ?

4. State the three different methods for settlement of financial transactions.

5. Which two concepts apply when constructing financial statements?

6. When a company is identified as a PLC, what does that mean?

7. Which method do accountants usually use to record business activities?

8. Which two concepts apply when constructing financial statements?

Chapter 2

Broadening the Reporting Agenda

Structure of Chapter 2

Section title	Main content
Information reported	A broad review of the information a company may issue.
The need for information	Companies require information on their operations, and also investors and lenders require information for decision-making, and increasingly employees and other groups also need information.
IAS 1 Presentation of financial statements	The standard sets out the overall requirements for the presentation of financial statements, guidelines for their structure and minimum requirements for their content.
Advances in Reporting	Financial information issued by companies has increased substantially both in the content and in the detail.
A conceptual framework	Standard setters and information recipients require some analysis of the entire financial operations of a company.
Extending the reporting agenda	Originally, financial information was only for the owners of a company, but increasingly many other groups are requiring and receiving information.

The four financial statements	A brief description of the four financial statements that companies issue.
The accounting standard setters	An explanation of the different accounting standards that can be applicable in the UK and the emphasis that we give to international standards.
Chapter Review	There has been significant growth in both the scope and details of financial disclosure.

The financial report forms a substantial part of a company's annual report and accounts. These documents may be well over 100 pages in length and for some companies these reports could span 200 or 300 pages. Those for major companies can be found on their website and downloaded. These reports are prepared initially by qualified accountants for the owners of the company. For companies "listed" on a stock exchange, these would be the shareholders. Understandably, the managers of the company, employees and other companies trading with it may have an interest. Even with small companies not listed on a stock exchange, there are other potential users of the annual report such as banks and other lenders who wish to see the annual report containing a firm of accountants' name before agreeing to any loans or other financial transactions.

Information Reported

Originally, financial reports were intended mainly for existing shareholders. It is important to remember that shareholders are the owners of the company. With large companies, they are available to anyone interested and are best obtained from the company's website. The annual report and accounts, in addition to including the financial information, will also contain a substantial amount of narrative information about many aspects of the company's activities. This can mean that it is a lengthy document. In the following, we show the index of the 2021 annual report for Tesco plc. We doubt if it is the longest report, but it does demonstrate the amount and nature of the communications made.

Strategic report:
3 2021 highlights
4 Tesco at a glance
5 Chairman's statement

The above list of disclosures by Tesco plc may look overwhelming, but, in future chapters, we concentrate on the information provided by companies as required by the financial reporting standards. One issue we mention at this stage is the Independent Auditor's Report. The financial statements should be accompanied by an auditor's report. Remember that shareholders would have held discussions with the directors and managers of the companies before the auditor's report is issued. There are several types of audit reports and the main ones are as follows:

Unqualified opinion — Clean report: An unqualified opinion is known as a clean report. Companies hope that they will receive this type of report. The report states that the auditors are satisfied that the company is operating. This is the type of report that auditors give most often. This is also the type of report that most companies expect to receive. An unqualified opinion doesn't have any kind of adverse comments and it doesn't include any disclaimers about any clauses or the audit process. Essentially, the auditors are stating that the company complies with governance regulations and any applicable laws.

Qualified opinion — Qualified report: This is a note to shareholders that the auditor is not confident about the company's treatment of a specific process or transaction. In this event, a clean report cannot be issued or the auditor may choose to issue a qualified opinion. Investors don't find qualified opinions acceptable, as they project a negative opinion about a company's financial status.

Disclaimer of opinion — Disclaimer report: When an auditor issues a disclaimer of opinion report, it usually means that they have not been able to see all the information they want. This may be because the company limited the number of investigations that the auditor wished to examine or the financial accounting system was suspect. Such a report will be read with concern by the shareholders.

Adverse opinion — Adverse audit report: If auditors are not satisfied with the financial statements or discover a high level of material misstatements or irregularities in the accounting systems of the company, they will state this in their report which will be read by shareholders. Such an audit opinion is serious and financial institutions, investors, major customers and suppliers will take this opinion seriously. The result may be that the company has to close.

Fortunately, most companies have a clean audit report and we show in the following the opening paragraph of the Auditor's Report for Tesco

> "– the financial statements of Tesco PLC (the 'Parent Company') and its subsidiaries (the 'Group') give a true and fair view of the state of the Group's and of the Parent Company's affairs as at 26 February 2022 and of the Group's profit for the year then ended; – the Group financial statements have been properly prepared in accordance with United Kingdom adopted international accounting standards; – the Parent Company financial statements have been properly prepared in accordance with United Kingdom Generally Accepted Accounting Practice, including Financial Reporting Standard 101 'Reduced Disclosure Framework'; and – the financial statements have been prepared in accordance with the requirements of the Companies Act 2006, which is a UK expression and, to our knowledge, not used in other countries."

The full auditors' report covers pages 106–115 and is very specific in the statements it makes. Although the company's directors will find it of interest, the report is for the shareholders who are the owners of the company. The auditors will have had lengthy discussions with the directors of the company to ensure the information and statements in the financial report are "true and fair". If the auditors consider that they have found a defect in the financial statements, they will bring that to the attention of the shareholders.

The auditors' report

This is not just a two-liner stating that the auditors are satisfied with the financial statements. It is a lengthy statement and a significant and important part of the, usually, very lengthy annual report and accounts issued by a company. The auditor's report for Tesco was a lengthy statement and covered pages 107–115 of their annual report and accounts and we show the report in the following. The auditors were Deloitte plc.

Report on the audit of the financial statements:

1. "**Opinion In our opinion**: – the financial statements of Tesco PLC (the 'Parent Company') and its subsidiaries (the 'Group') give a true and fair view of the state of the Group's and of the Parent Company's affairs as at 26 February 2022 and of the Group's profit for the year then ended; – the Group financial statements have been properly prepared in accordance with United Kingdom adopted international accounting standards; – the Parent Company financial statements have been properly prepared in accordance with United Kingdom Generally Accepted Accounting Practice, including Financial Reporting Standard 101 'Reduced Disclosure Framework'; and – the financial statements have been prepared in accordance with the requirements of the Companies Act 2006. We have audited the financial statements which comprise: – the Group income statement; – the Group statement of comprehensive income/(loss); – the Group and Parent Company balance sheets; – the Group and Parent Company statements of changes in equity; – the Group cash flow statement; and – the related Notes 1 to 37 of the Group financial statements and Notes 1 to 15 of the Parent Company financial statements. The financial reporting framework that has been applied in the preparation of the Group financial statements is applicable law and United Kingdom adopted international accounting standards. The financial reporting framework that has been applied in the preparation of the Parent Company financial statements is applicable law and United Kingdom accounting standards, including FRS 101 'Reduced Disclosure Framework' (United Kingdom Generally Accepted Accounting Practice)."

You will note that the auditors have used the term "true and fair". This is the phrase that everyone is looking for if they are interested in a company, but it is not part of our common everyday language. The Financial Reporting Council (FRC) states that the "true and fair" concept has been a part of English law and central to accounting and auditing practice in the UK for many decades. There has been no statutory definition of "true and fair". If you wish to pursue the concept and meaning of the statement, we recommend that you visit their website: https://www.frc.org.uk/accountants/accounting-and-reporting-policy/true-and-fair-concept.

The Need for Information

In the first chapter, we introduced the International Accounting Standards (IAS) and International Financial Reporting Standard (IFRS) issued by the International Financial Reporting Board. The standards that are currently in force are IAS 1–IAS 41 and IFRS 1–IFRS 17. From this, you may conclude that all countries use the same accounting standards. That is not the case and the companies in any one country may not follow the same standards as others. Although we use the term "company" in the UK, there are companies, particularly those quoted on the stock exchange that follow IFRS, and there are smaller UK companies that follow Financial Reporting Standards as issued by the FRC in the UK.

The number of organisations now involved in setting standards and monitoring companies is substantial and acronyms are mostly used in discussing their activities. The following list should assist you in studying this topic:

- International Accounting Standards Board (IASB) is an independent group of individuals responsible for the development and publication of IFRS Accounting Standards, including the *IFRS for SMEs* Accounting Standards.
- EFRAG is the European Financial Reporting Advisory Group that advises the European Commission on IFRS in Europe.
- Financial Reporting Council (FRC) is UK based and regulates auditors, accountants and actuaries. It also sets UK's Corporate Governance and Stewardship Codes. In January 2022, it issued the present editions of UK and Ireland accounting standards.
- IAS stands for International Accounting Standards.
- The International Financial Reporting Interpretations Committee (IFRIC) was developed by the IFRS Interpretations Committee and was issued after approval by the IASB.
- IFRS stands for International Financial Reporting Standards. IFRS Foundation is a not-for-profit, public interest organisation established to develop high-quality, understandable, enforceable and globally accepted accounting and sustainability disclosure standards. The standards are issued by two standard-setting boards: the IASB and International Sustainability Standards Board (ISSB).

Before discussing the details of reporting, we emphasise that the financial reports prepared by accountants for a company are intended primarily for the shareholders, in other words, those who have invested money in the company and are the "owners". Certainly, the annual reports of companies are easily available to anyone. However, the owners of a company are the shareholders and they decide at annual general meetings the policies a company should follow. The individual on the streets does not have this authority although they can decide not to use a company's products or services if they are displeased with the company's operations.

Companies rely on shareholders and lenders of finance, such as banks, for finance to conduct their business. Investors and lenders need financial information about a company before any investment is likely to be made. Even a one-person business requiring a loan from a bank will be required to provide financial information to obtain the loan. When investors are buying company shares, they want to look closely at the financial benefits of doing so. There is the risk that the providers of information, those companies wanting the investment, will select the information that best meets their objectives. To prevent this, there are standards drawn by accounting organisations that establish the details of the financial information that should be disclosed. Essentially, there are three following financial statements which give detailed information that have been in existence for several years:

- the income statement that shows the profit or loss for a financial period,
- the statement of cash flows that shows the cash that has been given and received for the financial period,
- the statement of financial position, also known as the balance sheet, which shows the assets owned by the amounts that it owes.

We explain these three financial statements in the following chapters. A fourth statement was introduced by the IASB in 2007 known as the Statements of Changes in Equity and we discuss this statement later in this chapter.

In conducting an analysis of an organisation's financial statements, some degree of caution should be exercised. Capturing all of an organisation's activities in financial terms and explaining them in a structured manner is a difficult task for the company's accountants. There is always the possibility of errors occurring and, in some cases, fraud. When the financial statements are being drawn up, all the relevant information will not be available. The company may have not received an invoice from the local supplier of electricity. The company will make the best estimate, but it may be somewhat later before you know the actual amount. Another possibility is the uncertainty over the amount. For example, a customer is refusing to pay the full amount for the service they have received and wants a 25% discount. The matter is still unresolved. What do you put in your financial statements at the end of the financial period?

Accountants have to make the best estimates in these circumstances and are guided by the requirements of financial accounting standards. This does mean that the financial statements that you examine may not have the 100% strict accuracy that you believe but the information they provide is in the opinion of accountants "true and fair". Taking a company's activities and describing them in financial terms have difficulties and errors may occur. In subsequent chapters where we discuss individual chapters, we will discuss the disclosure requirements in detail.

One issue not usually discussed in books on accounting is the fact that we rely on money measurement. That has its disadvantages as we illustrate in the following simple example: You decide to buy a pair of Jeans. They are very good, and after two years, you decide to purchase a new pair exactly the same. You are the same size as you were two years ago, so you do not expect to have any difficulties. You go back to the same clothes shop and you are delighted that they still sell the same type of jeans. You go to pay the cashier and are astounded that the new jeans are more expensive than the original pair. You ask why this is so and the reply is "Well, it's inflation". This raises in your mind the important issue that we use money as a measure of value but it increases because of inflation.

We do not have any suggestions on how to solve the problem but you should keep the difficulties in using money as a method of measurement when you are looking at a long time period. None of the accounting standards that have been issued tackle this difficult problem.

IAS 1 Presentation of Financial Statements

This standard became operative for periods beginning on or after 1 January 1975, and over the years, there have been many amendments and some are still taking place because economic factors and corporate alterations affect the standard. In this section, we discuss the main content of the version issued in 2007 which is concerned with general-purpose financial statements. The standard sets out the overall requirements for the presentation of financial statements, guidelines for their structure and minimum requirements for their content and applies to all general-purpose financial statements that are prepared and presented in accordance with IFRS.

The standard IAS 1 defines key terms as follows:

Equity shows the owners' interests in the company. It is calculated by adding reserves shown on the balance sheet to the share capital amount, including share premium.

Revaluation reserve reflects any gains made where non-current assets have been revalued. It is reasonable for companies to revalue some of their assets, particularly land and buildings. However, it is not a gain made from its trading activities and cannot be added to the profit reserves of the business.

Retained earnings are the total of all the profits and losses made by the business since its incorporation and that have not yet been paid to shareholders as a dividend. This amount is of obvious interest to shareholders as it represents their wealth as shareholders.

The importance of IAS 1 is that it highlights for the user of financial information the factors which caused a change in owner's equity during the accounting period. The statement of changes in equity provided by a company can be very complex and lengthy. We show in the following an example from Unilever of the notes that supported their lengthy financial statements.

"Example from Unilever plc 2020

(a) Repurchase of shares reflects the cost of acquiring ordinary shares as part of the share buyback programmes announced on 19 April 2018 and 6 April 2017.

(b) During 2019, 254,012,896 NV ordinary shares and 18,660,634 PLC ordinary shares were cancelled and in 2018 122,965,077 PLC ordinary shares were cancelled. The amount paid to repurchase these shares was initially recognised in other reserves and is transferred to retained profit on cancellation.

(c) Includes purchases and sales of treasury shares, and transfer from treasury shares to retained profit of share-settled schemes arising from prior years and differences between exercise and grant price of share options.
(d) The share-based payment credit relates to the non-cash charge recorded against operating profit in respect of the fair value of share options and awards granted to employees.
(e) 2020 includes €163 million paid for purchase of the non-controlling interest in Unilever Malaysia. 2018 includes a €662 million premium paid for purchase of the noncontrolling interest in Unilever South Africa from Remgro.
(f) As part of Unification (see note 1 for further details), the shareholders of NV were issued new PLC ordinary shares, and all NV shares in issue were cancelled. The net impact is recognised in retained profit.
(g) Includes the reduction of PLC's share capital following the cessation of the Equalisation Agreement. Prior to Unification, a conversion rate of £1 = €5.143 was used in accordance with the Equalisation Agreement to translate PLC's share capital. Following Unification, PLC's share capital has been translated using the exchange rate at the date of Unification. To reflect the legal share capital of the PLC company, an increase to share premium of €73,364 million and a debit unification reserve for the same amount have been recorded as there is no change in the net assets of the group. This debit is not a loss as a matter of law.
(h) Consideration for the Main Horlicks Acquisition included the issuance of shares in a group subsidiary, Hindustan Unilever Limited, which resulted in a net gain being recognised within equity. See note 21 for further details."

Do not worry about understanding all the detail in the above statement. In this chapter and the following ones, we concentrate on the main purpose of a standard and the most important disclosures that have to be made:

- a statement of financial position at the end of the period;
- a statement of profit and loss and other comprehensive income for the period. Other comprehensive income is those items of income and expense that are not recognised in profit or loss in accordance with

IFRS Standards. IAS 1 allows an entity to present a single combined statement of profit and loss and other comprehensive income or two separate statements;
- a statement of changes in equity for the period;
- a statement of cash flows for the period;
- notes comprising a summary of significant accounting policies and other explanatory information;
- a statement of financial position at the beginning of the preceding comparative period when an entity applies an accounting policy retrospectively or makes a retrospective restatement of items in its financial statements, or when it reclassifies items in its financial statements.

Information required and reported

Accounting standards are not cast in stone. They are subject to amendments resulting in changes to the information a company provides. For a company listed on the stock exchange, the most important readers are those who are buying and selling shares in the company. These shareholders are the owners of the company. The majority of companies listed on a stock exchange are now publishing reports that provide substantial information on their own sustainability efforts. In a later chapter, we explain the current debate on business sustainability and the impact it has on corporate reporting. There are also several companies and associations in different countries that are producing sustainability reports not directly linked to financial reports. These are not only by companies listed on the London Stock Exchange.

Awareness of the sustainability responsibilities is shown in a 56-page document by Associated British Foods plc and an extract is shown in the following:

> "A growing global population needs more accessible, ethical and affordable food and clothing but with less cost to our planet's finite resources and climate. We are meeting people's present needs but also helping to shape a more sustainable future with them. This means cutting carbon emissions in our manufacturing operations, making them more energy efficient, and using resources such as water in more circular ways to reduce the impact of serving our customers."
>
> — Associated British Foods plc Responsibility Update 2021.

Information by companies on their sustainability efforts is not restricted to only US and UK companies. Numerous examples are available and there are several websites providing corporate examples and commenting on the progress being made in different countries. We will be looking more closely at sustainability reporting in later chapters. Bear in mind that with our discussions and the examples we show, our main focus is those companies quoted on a stock exchange. The financial reports of these companies are very lengthy and comply with financial accounting standards.

A proportion of the information provided by companies can be somewhat technical particularly when we are looking at large sums of money. Companies need large amounts of finance to operate their business. The profit they make can be used, if required, to repay the interest on the funding they have received. Two terms in relation to funding you may encounter are equity and non-current liabilities. These are important because they demonstrate how the company has been funded which will be through various forms of equity and non-current liabilities. Each of these terms has several components which you may encounter and we list them in the following table:

Equity	**Non-current Liabilities**
Called up share capital	Bonds and bank loans
Capital redemption reserve	Borrowings
Cash flow hedging reserve	Corporate bank loans
Currency translation reserve	Derivative financial instruments
Merger reserve	Other payables
Non-controlling interests	Retirement benefit obligations
Other reserves	Provision for liabilities and charges
Own shares	Trade and other payables over 12 months
Retained earnings	
Share premium account	

The management of financial risk requires significant attention from a company and we show in the following a statement from the Annual Report and Financial Statements 2022 of J. Sainsbury plc:

"Financial risk management. The principal financial risks faced by the Group relate to liquidity risk, credit risk, market risk (foreign currency

> risk, interest rate risk and commodity risk) and capital risk. Financial risk management is managed by a central treasury department in accordance with policies and guidelines which are reviewed and approved by the Board of Directors. The risk management policies are designed to minimise potential adverse effects on the Group's financial performance by identifying financial exposures and setting appropriate risk limits and controls. The risk management policies also ensure sufficient liquidity is available to the Group to meet foreseeable financial obligations and that cash assets are invested safely. Financial risk management with respect to Financial Services is separately managed within the Financial Services' governance structure."

Advances in Reporting

In this chapter, we concentrate on the setting of standards that determines the content of financial statements issued by companies. However, there are other factors that influence the content as well as the requirements required by accounting standards. One of the developments has been the increasing disclosure of information other than financial information. We show in the following the content headings and page numbers of the annual report for J. Sainsbury plc for 2022:

Strategic Report 01,
Contents and Performance highlights 02,
Chairman's letter 05,
Chief Executive's Q&A 07,
Business model 09,
Our strategy 10,
Our priorities 13,
Plan for Better 24,
Engaging with our stakeholders and our Section 172 statement 30,
New KPIs 31,
Legacy KPIs 32,
Financial Review 38,
Principal risks and uncertainties 53,
Non-financial information statement Governance Report 54,
Board of Directors 58,

You may feel overwhelmed by the amount of information that is made available. The company's consolidated financial statements, which show aggregated financial results for multiple entities or subsidiary companies, do not start until page 113 and continue until page 188. Although the financial statements are still the main part of the report, other information is very important for shareholders making investments. Different shareholders will have various interests but we will explain KPIs which are key performance indicators and are increasingly being disclosed by companies. The reason that companies give this additional information is that accounting standards are intended as a requirement for all companies.

Performance indicators and measures

It is impossible to summarise all the types of voluntaries and disclosures of information that companies make in their annual report and accounts. Frequently, the voluntary disclosures are related to legally required disclosures and it is difficult to separate them. It is also difficult to deduce the intended audience for some of the information provided. The distinctly typical voluntary information is usually in the first few pages. There is normally an "overview" of the financial results. This is in a diagrammatic form and may cover several years. There may be a statement from the Chairman, although some companies prefer to use this as the lead for the strategic report.

One disclosure that has grown in importance are key performance indicators and these are an important component of the disclosures used to describe and explain a company's progress in achieving its strategy. We would emphasise that KPIs provide additional information to that found in the financial section of the annual report and accounts. But what KPIs should a company disclose?

The usual pattern is that the company identifies and explains, where relevant, the following:

(a) its definition and calculation method,
(b) its purpose,
(c) the source of underlying data,
(d) any significant assumptions made,
(e) any changes in the calculation method used compared to previous financial years, including significant changes in the underlying accounting policies adopted in the financial statements that might affect the KPI.

KPIs may include measures related to product quality and customer complaints. They may be indicators of future financial prospects and progress in managing risks and opportunities. They are mainly closely related to the industry in which a company operates. The literature is replete with suggestions and examples of KPIs suitable for a specific type of industry.

There are also KPIs for different issues. In 2012, the Department for Environment Food and Rural Affairs (Defra) commenced an informal consultation to seek views on revised guidance for how UK organisations should measure and report on their environmental impacts. The guidance sets out general principles for how to measure and report on environmental KPIs. It suggests a structured means for reporting those indicators and covers the following five areas:

1. air pollution and other emissions,
2. water,
3. biodiversity/ecosystem services,
4. materials,
5. waste.

Such measures may be named KPIs but some companies and commentators refer to them as Additional (or Alternative) Performance Measures (APMs). There are no regulations preventing companies from providing APMs as long as they have also provided, in addition, the audited financial statements complying with IFRS.

KPIs and APMs supply useful information. They usually provide data that are not easily extracted from the audited financial statements. However, the unsophisticated user may not be aware that some measures are recalculations of the profit as shown on the IFRS-compliant financial statements. They are essentially alternative performance measures. The user may also not realise that some measures, as well as not being financial but quantitative, have not been audited.

Growing financial reporting

Financial reporting is not a static subject and in this section, we consider some changes that have taken place in recent years.

Internet

One significant change in the dissemination of financial reports is the growth in the use of the Internet by companies. The present position is that most companies have a website that contains an abundance of useful and interesting information. However, the annual financial report remains the most regulated document of information. In recent years, there have been doubts expressed on the quality of the non-financial information on corporate websites as they are mostly unregulated. The position is improving as increasingly countries are requiring companies to file their financial information using eXtensible Business Reporting Language (EXRL). This format allows an analysis of large amounts of financial information and assists in comparisons to statements filed using other formats. The following extract from the annual report of Unilever demonstrates the care that some companies use in getting their message across:

> "This is a PDF version of the Unilever Annual Report and Accounts 2021 and is an exact copy of the printed document provided to Unilever's shareholders. The Annual Report and Accounts 2021 was filed with the National Storage Mechanism and the Dutch Authority for the Financial Markets in European Single Electronic Format, including a human readable XHMTL version of the Annual Report and Accounts 2021 (the ESEF Format). The Annual Report and Accounts 2021 in ESEF Format is also available on Unilever's website at www.unilever.com. Only the Annual Report and Accounts 2021 in ESEF Format is the official version for purposes of the ESEF Regulation."

Although the financial information reported by companies should comply with accounting standards, a substantial amount of other non-financial information is given in a very attractive and interesting manner. These greater disclosures of the activities of a company may be very useful, but, to a large extent, this additional information remains unregulated. This is an issue that we will consider again when we discuss sustainability reporting in later chapters.

A Conceptual Framework

As we have discussed earlier, financial accounting has its oddities and determining a standard for some of the business transactions which are conducted has been a problem. Standard setters came to the conclusion that a conceptual framework would be helpful instead of treating each issue that arises individually. The search at the international level for a Conceptual Framework has been long and exhausting and is continuing. The benefits of a CF are that it

1. assists the IASB to develop and revise standards,
2. preparers to understand standards and develops its own consistent accounting policies,
3. assists users to understand and interpret financial statements.

The International Accounting Standards Committee (IASC) published its *IASC Framework for the Preparation and Presentation of Financial Statements* (1989). The IASB adopted it in 2001 on assuming the role of the IASC. Part of the agreement between FASB in the US and the IASB was to converge their standards, which involved a joint project to construct a new conceptual framework. The two boards, not having achieved agreement, deferred the project in 2010. In 2012, the IASB commenced its own revision of the 1989 framework and in 2018, the IASB presented a revised Conceptual Framework.

The IASB regards the users of financial reports being an entity's existing and potential investors, lenders and other creditors. These groups require financial information about the reporting entity that is useful to other creditors in making decisions relating to providing resources to the entity. The financial report provides information about the reporting entity's assets, liabilities, equity, income and expenses. There have been criticisms of the document. One is the potentially limited range of users of financial reports and the reason they require the information. This dispute has been with us for many years. The Conceptual Framework from the IASB is concerned specifically with the annual financial report but companies provide substantial narrative information. They issue what is better described as a Corporate Reporting Package (CRP). Although much of the additional information varies from country to country and also within countries, it is apparent that more requirements will be issued that will refer to sustainability reporting. We can expect, therefore, the IASB to issue a revised conceptual framework in the future.

Problem terms

In accounting, as with many specialised disciplines, there are words and terms used where the meaning is not immediately clear, is ambiguous or is even controversial. These terms often came into use when considering financial reporting in the UK and may not be so appropriate at the international level. We briefly explain four of these and will be referring to them again in subsequent chapters. We emphasise that these terms have been used by the IASB and others to refer to financial reporting. Different definitions will be required when we are considering sustainability reporting in a later chapter.

Stewardship: The word stewardship is not in common usage internationally but has been used in many documents issued in the UK. Those who are responsible for operating a business are not necessarily the owners of the business and they are acting as stewards for the owners. A more frequently used term is "Directors". They are responsible for reporting the operation of the business to the actual owners. For companies listed on the stock exchange, the owners are those that hold shares in a company. The directors are responsible for running the company and they report to the shareholders by issuing an annual report and holding an annual meeting for shareholders.

True and fair view: The FRC has issued its views on true and fair as this is not a concept shared by all countries in relation to financial statements. The FRC has expressed its opinion that both the UK and the EU laws require company accounts to give a true and fair view, although it is a conceptually difficult area. Our interpretation is that an entity may comply completely with the specific requirements of an accounting standard. However, in doing so, the financial statements may not provide a full picture of the situation. In these circumstances, the company can depart from the detailed requirements of the standard to provide information that gives a "true and fair view".

Prudence: For many years, there has been argument over the use of the term "prudence" which can be understood as the use of caution in making the estimates required under conditions of uncertainty. Some argue that if the financial information is prepared so that it is "neutral", then there is no need for the concept of "prudence". Others disagree, presumably holding the opinion that directors in making their estimates and assumptions at the yearend may be overly optimistic in their report to shareholders.

Going concern: When we scrutinise financial statements, we assume that they are prepared on the basis that the reporting entity is a going concern. In other words, the entity will continue in operation for the foreseeable future. If we believed that an entity was about to become bankrupt, we may change our conclusion of the information in the financial statements. The concept has been in force for many years and was included in the 1989 Conceptual Framework.

Extending the Reporting Agenda

The financial report forms a substantial part of a company's annual report and accounts. These complete documents may be well over 200 pages in length and those for major companies can be found on their website. These reports are prepared initially by qualified accountants for the owners of the company. For companies "listed" on a stock exchange, the owners would be the shareholders. Even with small companies not listed on a stock exchange, there are other potential users of the annual report such as banks and other lenders who wish to see the annual report containing a firm of accountants' name before agreeing to any loans.

The annual report and accounts, in addition to containing the financial information, will also contain a substantial amount of narrative information about many aspects of the company's activities. Such information may be very closely linked to sustainability. The following segment is from the annual report and accounts of Microsoft:

> "Many of our shareholders are increasingly focused on the importance of the effective engagement and action on ESG topics. To meet the expectations of our stakeholders and to and maintain their trust, we are committed to conducting our business in ways that are principled, transparent, and accountable and we have made a broad range of environmental and social commitments. From our CEO and Senior Leadership Team and throughout our organization, people at Microsoft are working to conduct our business in principled ways that make a significant positive impact on important global issues. Microsoft's Board of Directors provides insight, feedback, and oversight across a broad range of environmental and social matters. In particular, among the responsibilities of the Board's Regulatory and Public Policy Committee is to review and provide guidance to the Board and management about the Company's policies and programs that relate to CSR."

The above segment includes some terms with which you may not be familiar. Possibly, ESG is a term you have not seen before. It stands for **Environmental, Social, and Governance** and we discuss this term in a later chapter. Investors are increasingly applying these non-financial factors as part of their analysis process to identify material risks and growth opportunities.

To be listed on a stock exchange, a company must produce financial reports which comply with accounting standards and are approved by auditors. The majority of companies listed on a stock exchange are now publishing reports that provide substantial information on their own sustainability efforts. In a later chapter, we explain the current debate on business sustainability and the impact it has on corporate reporting. We would emphasise that the concern over sustainability is not restricted to the UK and many countries are trying to resolve the problem. There are also several companies and associations that are producing sustainability reports that are not directly linked to financial reports. The following example is just a small part of a report by the American Beverage Association, https://www.innovationnaturally.org/plastic/.

> "Our plastic bottles are made to be remade. We are carefully designing them to be 100% recyclable – even the caps. Our goal is for every bottle to become a new bottle, and not end up in oceans, rivers, beaches and landfills. And that means we are using less new plastic.
>
> That's why America's beverage companies have launched a new initiative to get *Every Bottle Back*. This unprecedented commitment includes:
>
> - Working with World Wildlife Fund through the *ReSource: Plastic* initiative to reduce our plastic footprint.
> - Partnering with The Recycling Partnership and Closed Loop Partners to improve recycling access, provide education to residents and modernize the recycling infrastructure in communities across the country.
> - Increasing awareness about the value of our 100% recyclable plastic bottles.
> - Introducing a new voluntary on-pack message to promote the recyclability of our plastic bottles and caps."

We have shown a US example but similar sentiments and awareness of the sustainability responsibilities are shown by companies listed on the London Stock Exchange. We show an extract from a 56-page document issued by Associated British Foods plc:

> "A growing global population needs more accessible, ethical and affordable food and clothing but with less cost to our planet's finite resources and climate. We are meeting people's present needs but also helping to

> shape a more sustainable future with them. This means cutting carbon emissions in our manufacturing operations, making them more energy efficient, and using resources such as water in more circular ways to reduce the impact of serving our customers."
>
> — Associated British Foods plc Responsibility Update 2021
> Responsibility update 2021.pdf.downloadasset.pdf

Information by companies on their sustainability efforts is not restricted to only US and UK companies. Numerous examples are available on the Web and we show in the following extracts from the Chinese company *Kweichow Moutai (600519.SH)*:

> "Since 2012, the company states that it has donated 100 million yuan each year to help 140,000 poor students in total enter colleges and universities. It has earmarked 50 million yuan annually to participate in the ecological protection and environmental management of the Chishui River basin. https://www.imsilkroad.com/z/191028-1/#g309050=1."

There are several websites providing corporate examples and commenting on the progress being made in different countries. We will be looking more closely at sustainability reporting in later chapters. At this stage, we would suggest that financial reporting is well established and that IAS are accepted in several, but not all, countries. The position with sustainability reporting is that considerable concern is being expressed around the world and many companies are publicising their efforts to pursue sustainability. However, corporate efforts are diverse and there are efforts to establish standards for sustainability reporting similar to financial reporting. We examine these efforts in later chapters.

The Four Financial Statements

The requirements on which financial statements and their content are in IAS 1 Presentation of financial statements. The standard has been amended and revised several times. IAS 1 is a surprisingly brief standard in view of the information required of companies to provide. The reason for the brevity of the standard is that it concentrates on the presentation of the four financial statements and not issues of recognition, measurement and detailed disclosure requirements which are covered in the separate financial reporting standards which we discuss in later chapters.

Recognition and measurement are two important concepts in constructing financial statements. In this section, we discuss the requirements of IAS 1 regarding the content and presentation of the main financial statements.

The following short list gives the financial statements required:

- **Statement of financial position:** This is also known as the balance sheet.
- **Statement of comprehensive income:** This can take the form of one statement or be separated into a profit and loss statement and a statement of other income, including property and equipment.
- **Statement of changes in equity:** Also known as a statement of retained earnings, this documents the company's change in earnings or profit for the given financial period.
- **Statement of cash flows:** This report summarises the company's financial transactions in the given period, separating cash movements into operations, investing and financing.

In addition to these basic reports, a company must give a summary of its accounting policies. The standard requires that the financial statements should contain comparative information in respect of the preceding period. However, entities are not obliged to use the titles of the statements given in the standard and some prefer to use their own terminology.

In some books and articles, you may find the term "Balance Sheet" used instead of Statement of Financial Position. Usually, this is merely the use of the previous title and the actual contents of the statements are broadly the same. Care must be taken with the Statement of Comprehensive Income as some may use the term profit and loss account. Sometimes, these are not the same type of statements, and in later chapters, we explain the differences. The four statements required are as follows.

Statement of financial position

The alternative title of this statement was Balance Sheet, and several entities have kept that heading. In this chapter and the following ones, for reasons of brevity, we use the term balance sheet.

The information, if applicable, required by the standard is as follows:

(a) property, plant and equipment,
(b) investment property,
(c) intangible assets,
(d) financial assets,
(e) investments accounted for using the equity method,
(f) biological assets,
(g) inventories,
(h) trade and other receivables,
(i) cash and cash equivalents,
(j) the total of assets classified as held for sale and assets included in disposal groups classified as held for sale,
(k) trade and other payables,
(l) provisions,
(m) financial liabilities (excluding amounts shown under (k) and (l)),
(n) liabilities and assets for current tax,
(o) deferred tax liabilities and deferred tax assets,
(p) liabilities included in disposal groups classified as held for sale,
(q) non-controlling interests, presented within equity,
(r) issued capital and reserves attributable to *owners* of the parent.

A somewhat bewildering array of items. Entities can also include additional line items, headings and subtotals when such presentation is relevant to an understanding of the entity's financial position.

There is no particular format for the balance sheet, and usually, entities use a format with headings and subtotals based on the accounting equation or a variation. The basic accounting equation is

$$\text{Assets} = \text{Capital} + \text{Liabilities}.$$

Essentially, the assets are the items a business owns, such as buildings and equipment.

We will be discussing the $A = C + L$ equation in later chapters.

Statement of comprehensive income

The IASB made a significant amendment to IAS 1 in 2011 introducing a completely new Statement of Comprehensive Income. The format of the existing profit or loss account or income statement remains and links to the new statement. Comprehensive income recognises both realised and unrealised gains and losses that have increased or decreased the owners' equity in the business. The items that are in a comprehensive income statement but not reported in the traditional profit or loss account are such transactions as revaluations of non-current assets under accounting standard IAS 16 Property, Plant and Equipment. Two other items are gains and losses from translating the financial statements of a foreign operation (IAS 21) and the remeasurement of defined benefit plans (IAS 19). We explain the requirements of both these standards in later chapters.

There has been considerable debate on the purpose of the statement of comprehensive income and its conceptual basis. Some argue that it is difficult to understand and provides little information of value to the users. Others claim that it has information value, and preparers and users of financial data need time to become accustomed to it. IAS 1 does not define profit as a concept but as the result of a calculation. It is the total income less expenses excluding comprehensive income. This explains the mechanics of arriving at a figure of profit or loss but can be criticised for not describing the nature of profit in the financial reporting standards.

The statement of comprehensive income gives a fuller picture of the shareholders' wealth than a profit statement. Comprehensive income shows the gains and losses, both realised and unrealised and these increase or decrease the owners' equity. Thus, the value of the shares they hold should increase. One example of a non-realised gain leading to a gain in equity is a revaluation of fixed assets. For example, an entity owns the property it purchased for £1 million. The value of the property increases to £1.25 million. The entity is wealthier and using the accounting equation of assets – liabilities = capital, the shareholders are wealthier. If we have increased the assets by a quarter of a million pounds, equity must have increased by the same amount.

The main weakness of ignoring comprehensive income is that the profit statement only records profits that have been realised, in other words, the goods and services that the company has sold. An entity may own land or buildings that have increased in value. There is no recognition of that increase in a profit statement until the sale of the asset. But beware of the impact of inflation and we discuss this issue in subsequent chapters. Also, depreciation charged in the profit statement is only an allocation, on an estimated basis, of the original historic cost of an asset. The value shown on the balance sheet has no meaning. However, the profit or loss account has been an important source of information for users for many years.

A company may decide to show the Statement of Comprehensive Income in two parts: one being the profit account and the other being the loss account. The great importance of the profit or loss account is with the final entry. Using a double entry approach, at the end of the financial period, the profit and loss account needs a debit entry to close it and that amount is the profit for the financial period. The debit closes the profit and loss account and that amount is credited to the retained profit account or distributed to shareholders.

In Chapter 4, we emphasise some of the issues relating to the measurement and reporting of comprehensive income.

Statements of changes in equity

IAS 1 introduced a new financial statement in 2007 that relates to equity. The statement of changes in equity informs the users of financial statements of the factors that cause a change in the owners' equity over the accounting periods. This statement is of particular interest to shareholders wishing to assess the size of their financial interest in the entity. Shareholders, understandably, are very interested in any changes in the equity shown on the balance sheet.

There are several reasons that the amount of equity can change throughout the financial period. There are two distinct categories. First, there are the changes that occur from transactions with shareholders, such as the issue of new shares and payment of dividends. Second, there are changes that occur due to matters, such as the net income for the period and the revaluation of fixed assets.

The statement of changes in equity is a summary of the changes that have taken place during the financial reporting period. The standard requires the balances of equity accounts at the beginning of the financial period to be reconciled with the closing balances. As there is a requirement for the previous year's disclosures as a comparison, this can result in a considerable amount of information.

The statement must disclose the following information:

- total comprehensive income for the period, showing separately the total amounts attributable to owners of the parent and to non-controlling interests,
- for each component of equity, the effects of retrospective application or retrospective restatement,
- for each component of equity, a reconciliation between the carrying amount at the beginning and the end of the period, separately disclosing changes resulting from
  (1) profit or loss,
  (2) other comprehensive income,
  (3) transactions with owners in their capacity as owners, showing separately contributions by and distributions to owners and changes in ownership interests in subsidiaries that do not result in a loss of control.

Statement of cash flows

It took standard setters many years to decide, or possibly entities to accept, that the cash amount is very important to users of financial statements. Simply put, a company may report a profit, but unless it has managed its cash coming in and going out, it can go bankrupt. The introduction of a statement of cash flows was long overdue. The standard now requires the provision of information about the historical changes in cash and cash equivalents of an entity in a statement of cash flows. This statement classifies cash flows during the period from operating, investing and financing activities.

Cash flows from operating activities are a key indicator of an entity's ability to generate sufficient cash without needing external finance. Some would argue that the standard could have been tougher in its approach to the calculation of cash from operating activities. The standard setters allow a choice of two methods:

- the direct method which shows major classes of gross cash receipts and payments or
- the indirect method which adjusts the profit or loss for the period by transactions of a non-cash nature.

The package

The above description of the four financial statements simplifies the length and complexity of the documents published by large companies. We have extracted the following from the annual report of 2021 of Unilever plc. This is only an extract of the financial information in a report that is almost 200 pages in length and available from their website. You will note that several pages are given to a Strategic Report and we will discuss these reports in the later chapters of this book concerned with sustainability reporting.

Extract from the index of Unilever plc annual report
Pages 105–198 Running a responsible and effective business
Our full financial results and notes for the year 68
Corporate governance 106
Statement of Directors' responsibilities 78
Report of the Audit Committee 107
Independent Auditor's Report 80
Report of the Corporate Responsibility Committee 114
Consolidated financial statements 82
Report of the Nominating and Corporate Governance Committee 118
Notes to the consolidated financial statements 167
Unilever PLC Company Accounts and notes 84
Directors' Remuneration Report 176
Group Companies 187
Shareholder information 188
Additional Information for US Listing Purposes

We would emphasise that this is a very small part only of a report that is very lengthy.

The Accounting Standard Setters

Financial reporting can be defined as the communication of an entity's business activities to those external to the business. Decision-useful information is defined as information about the reporting entity that is useful to present and potential equity investors, lenders and other creditors in making decisions in their capacity as capital providers, in other words, providing finance to the company in some form. A substantial part of financial reporting regulation is concerned with the process of identifying and measuring the activities of an entity. This ensures that the financial reports produced are based on sound information. The regulations are issued in documents referred to as financial accounting standards.

In the UK, two financial reporting frameworks are in effect. One is based on specific company law requirements and the accounting standards are set by FRC based in the UK. However, publicly listed companies, that is, those listed on the stock exchange, are required to adopt IAS. These have been in force for many years and originally, they were known as International Accounting Standards and forty-one (41) standards were issued. The final one was IAS 41 Agriculture. There was then a name change for the standards to IFRS. The last one issued was IFRS 17 Insurance Contracts, and we can expect in future years more standards will be issued. Many companies which are not publicly listed, that is, their shares are not quoted on the stock exchange, have a choice between two frameworks. They may choose between either IAS or UK and Ireland Generally Accepted Accounting Principles (GAAP) for the preparation of their individual parent accounts.

Initially, individual countries developed their own standards, but, in 1973, the IASC was established to set standards that could be adopted by any country. There was a reorganisation, and in 2001, the standard-setting work was taken over by the IASB which is the independent standard-setting body of the IFRS Foundation. Several jurisdictions use international standards, but, to the disappointment of many, the United States uses their own system, known as Generally Accepted Accounting Principles (GAAP). Domestic public companies must use US GAAP. However, more than 500 foreign SEC registrants, with a worldwide market capitalisation of US$7 trillion, use IFRS Standards in their US filings. The outcome of these various reorganisations and name changes is that we now have the following at the international level:

- IAS starting with IAS 1 Presentation of financial statements and ending with IAS 41 Agriculture. Several of the IASs have been replaced by IFRSs but over 20 remain in force.
- IFRS starting with First-time adoption of International Financial Reporting Standards (IFRS 1) and the last one (at the time of writing) is IFRS 17 Insurance Contracts.

Various accounting organisations in different countries issue their own accounting standards but our subsequent chapters focus on IASs and IFRSs. Accounting standards are concerned with specific economic transactions, arrangements and events conducted by a business. For example, you will have one standard that is concerned only with identifying and measuring the revenue that a company generates in a financial period. Another standard will set out the procedures for recording the buildings and machinery owned by the company. Other standards apply to such topics as accounting for valuing goods a company holds and the methods used to make financial records of the activities it undertakes.

A financial reporting standard has the following three requirements to be met:

1. **Recognition** specifies the transactions and events that should be incorporated into the financial statements. The Chief Executive having a heart attack may be interesting and impact the share price of the company, but it is not shown on the financial statements. The factory burning down will be of interest and will have an impact on a company's activities that must be reported in the financial statements.
2. **Measurement** describes the method used to determine the financial value of transactions and events. This can be difficult. Everything a company does has to be converted into financial measures. With many items, there are no problems, but we need to know how entities do their calculations and to have confidence in their methods. Accounting standards provide this reliability. With some transactions and events, there must be estimates and we will discuss these when we consider the individual standards.
3. **Disclosure** requires information to be disclosed in a useful way. There is a standard that specifies the content and structure of the main financial reports. It is also the responsibility of a government to determine the amount and type of information an entity is obliged to disclose.

Chapter Review

Companies are an extremely large part of our lives, although we do not often realise that it is impossible to envisage our society without their presence. Not only do they provide employment but they also provide the general population goods and services. Obviously, those who buy shares in a company or lend it finance are extremely interested in the company's operations. Also, other companies that depend on its goods or services and the general public want to know the status of a company. Over the years, accounting standards have been developed, which companies follow and ensure that financial disclosures are acceptable. The present position is that companies following international standards should produce four financial statements. In the following chapters, we explain the requirements that companies should follow in producing these four statements.

CHAPTER 2 Broadening the Reporting Agenda

Review Questions

1. When a company purchase equipment for cash it should
   a. Credit the cash account and debit the equipment account
   b. Debit the cash account and credit the equipment account
   c. Credit the cash account and debit the equipment account
   d. Credit the cash account and the equipment account
2. Which one of the following statements is correct concerning International Financial Reporting Standards?
   a. All countries must follow them.
   b. A country can decide whether to adopt them
   c. Public limited companies can decide whether to use them
   d. A company can decide which of the standards it will follow
3. What are retained earnings?
4. What is the other term used for the balance sheet?
5. What is the basic accounting equation that refers to the balance sheet?
6. What information does the comprehensive income statement present?
7. Does a smaller UK company usually comply with International Financial Reporting Standards?
8. What is an Independent Auditor's Report?

Chapter 3

From Standards to Profit

Structure of Chapter 3

Section title	**Main content**
Back to basics	The issues of defining profit and the importance of cash and comprehensive income.
IAS 1 Presentation of Financial Statements	IAS 1 became effective from 1975. Since then, there had been numerous amendments with the latest being in 2022. The disclosures that entities must make in calculating and disclosing the figure of profit for the financial period. It requires companies to issue a statement of financial position, a statement of profit or loss and other comprehensive income, a statement of changes in equity and a statement of cash flows. The statement of financial position is also referred to as the balance sheet and we will also use that term when appropriate.

IFRS 15 Revenue from Contracts with Customers	IFRS 15 came into effect from January 1, 2018. The standard defines revenue as income arising in the course of an entity's ordinary activities and explains the methods for recognising revenue from contracts with customers.
IAS 2 Inventories	IAS 2 was first issued in 1975 as Valuation and Presentation of Inventories in the context of the historical cost system. Latest issue of the standard was in 2003 as Inventories. It is critical that companies can calculate the correct amount of profit for the period. IAS 2 explains the accounting for goods at the beginning and end of the financial period.
IAS 16 Depreciation of Property, Plant and Equipment	Certain items owned by a company have a finite life (same as with humans). Depreciation is a method for recognising this fact and affects both the Income Statement and Statement of Financial Position.
IFRS 2 Share-Based Payments Issued in 2004	Several amendments were issued with the latest in 2016. This is when an entity transfers equity instruments (usually shares or share options) in exchange for goods or services supplied by employees or third parties.
On the Dark Side	A brief reminder of the impact some unwelcome activities can have on the profit of a company.
Chapter Review	Cost of inventories and the allowance for depreciation are fundamental to accounting activities with a direct impact on the financial statements. Share-based statements involving the transfer of equity instruments are important but have a restricted impact.

The Statement of Comprehensive Income, in an earlier and simpler time, was known as the Profit or Loss Account or Profit Statement and many still use those terms. Historically, the profit or loss account was simply that. It showed the profit or loss generated by a company in a financial period. The total costs of the company were deducted from the revenue to give the profit. It did not record any cash movements but only the contracts, whether to buy or sell, that were entered into.

For those companies complying with international accounting standards, the position is more complex. The significant standard is IAS 1 Presentation of Financial Statements which became effective in 1975. There have been many subsequent amendments. The most important one was for annual periods beginning on or after 1 January 2009 which requires companies to provide a statement of profit or loss **and** other comprehensive income for the period. This information can be given either as a single statement or with the profit or loss section, showing the details in a separate statement followed by a statement presenting comprehensive income beginning with profit or loss figure for the financial period.

We emphasise that the statement of comprehensive income is not about cash. We discuss this topic in Chapter 4 when we explain the Statement of Cash Flows as required by IAS 7. In this chapter, we discuss the notion of profit and explain the standards that regulate some of the activities to be measured.

Back to Basics

Before we discuss in detail the present accounting requirements for financial reporting, it is useful to look at a few examples that demonstrate the differences between profit and cash. You may have studied some of this information before and this chapter will reinforce and expand your knowledge. To complete the various issues, we also demonstrate a simple Statement of Financial Position which you may have seen in your earlier studies but with the title of balance sheet.

Example 1: Home fire alarms

Anne Despot decides to buy and sell home fire alarms. She has some savings of her own but borrows £500 from her friend Jay with the promise to pay this back as soon as she can. She purchases 20 alarms from a supplier and pays £100 for each alarm, but by the end of the month, she still owes the supplier for three alarms. Of the 20 alarms she sells 17 of them for £150 each but she has five customers who have not yet paid for each of their alarms. The following statements show the profit for the month but do not show cash movements. To calculate the profit, we look at the transactions regardless of any cash paid or received. The results are shown in the following profit statement:

Profit statement for 3 month of December	
Sales (17 alarms at £150 each)	£2,550
Less costs of sales (17 alarms at £100 each)	£1,700
Profit	£850

You can do a simple check on the above statement. On each alarm, a profit of £50 was made. As 17 alarms were sold with a profit on each alarm being £50, the total profit is £850. Anne Despot may be pleased with this profit, but how much cash does she have? She has sold 17 alarms but has only received payment for 10 of them. She has paid her supplier for 17 alarms at £100 each. We now need to draw up a cash statement to show these transactions.

Cash statement for the month of December	
Investment (Loan from Jay)	£500
Payment received (10 × £150)	£1,500
Total cash	£2,000
Payment to supplier (17 × £100)	£1,700
Cash surplus	£300

The two statements show us that Anne's business made a profit and has a cash surplus, but Anne Despot cannot afford to repay Jay fully for the cash she invested which was £500. Presumably, she will correct this when she receives payments from her customers.

This simple example demonstrates that if we want to understand a business, we need both a profit statement and a cash statement. But even that does not tell us the complete story. We also need to know how the business financially "balances" at the end of the period. For this, a balance sheet, also known as a statement of financial position, is required. In the following, we have drawn up a two-sided balance sheet as this gives an immediate link to all the transactions. You will find that most companies present the balance sheet in a vertical format. It contains similar but much more information than the horizontal format which we show in the following.

A. Despot

Balance sheet (Statement of Financial Position) at the end of December (Year 1)			
Assets		**Liabilities**	
3 alarms worth £100 each	£300	Owing to supplier (3 × £100)	£300
Customers owing (7 × £150)	£1,050	Loan by Jay	£500
Cash in hand	£300	Profit retained	£850
	£1,650		£1,650

You will note that the balance sheet differs from the other two statements. The balance sheet is like a snapshot at the end of December. The other two statements showed events for the entire month. These three statements give a good overview of the company. It made a profit of £850 which was good, but the cash position was less favourable. The company cannot afford to pay Jay the full loan it made but can pay suppliers. This is important because if Anne does not pay the suppliers, they may well stop "supplying".

Anne Despot can take action to improve the situation, but she needs the three separate statements to obtain a full picture of how her business operates. We need individual statements to show the profit gained, cash movements and final financial position at the end of the period. By drawing up the three separate financial statements, we have a better understanding of how the company is performing. To improve our investigations, it would be helpful to have the results for several financial periods. We can then analyse whether there are any serious financial problems that require attention.

We can take this example further by looking at year 2. In that year, Anne manages to sell 20 alarms at £150 each, but the supplier is now charging £110 for each alarm and Anne pays this in full. The Income Statement is as follows:

Income statement	
Sales (20 alarms at £150 each)	£3,000
Less costs of sales (20 alarms at £110 each)	£2,200
Profit	£800

Anne is still waiting for two of the customers to pay. Remember that the Income (or profit) Statement is not about cash so the amount of profit is correct. We need the cash statement to calculate how much Anne has.

Cash statement	
Sales (20 alarms at £150 each)	£2,700 (20 alarms sold but 2 customers owing)
Less costs of sales (20 alarms at £110 each)	£2,200
Cash in hand	£500

Balance sheet at the end of December (Year 1)			
Assets		**Liabilities**	
3 alarms worth £100 each	£300	Owing to supplier (3 × £100)	£300
Customers owing (7 × £150)	£1,050	Loan by Jay	£500
Cash surplus	£300	Profit retained	£850
	£1650		£1650

This is a very simple example and possibly only a reminder of the issues you have already studied. In practice, there are four financial statements and we show in the following their proper headings together with the simpler titles frequently used in the literature. You will find that these "simple" titles are frequently used in non-official documents:

Statement of Financial Position (balance sheet),
Statement of Comprehensive Income (Income statement or profit and loss account),
Statement of Flows,
Statement of Changes in Equity.

IAS 1 Presentation of Financial Statements

This standard was first issued in 1975 and there have been several amendments since that date, the most recent at the time of writing this book was in 2020. The standard establishes the requirements for financial statements, including how they should be structured, the minimum requirements for their content and the overriding concepts, such as going concern, the accrual basis of accounting and the current/non-current distinction.

IAS 1 is very specific on the disclosures that entities must make in calculating and disclosing the figure of profit for the financial period. However, entities may in addition to the required statement provide a further "Income Statement" calculating other measures of profit for the period using different calculations. There are no regulations preventing entities from providing information additional to that required by a standard. The additional profit measures provided are usually named by the company as underlying or sustainable earnings. This is calculated by taking the profit figure and then adjusting it by any costs that the entity considers are unusual, non-recurring or misleading. The aim is to demonstrate a performance measure that gives the user information on performance in normal conditions. There is the valid argument that additional information provides the users of financial statements with a better understanding of the performance of the particular entity over a prolonged period. This assists users in making predictions. However, there is the concern that the entity may enhance the profit figure and mislead the user by "managing" the amount of profit disclosed.

Profit management can be defined in two ways:

- POSITIVE, where the application of judgement, experience and decision-making is used to report the desired level of earnings without contravening financial accounting regulations,
- NEGATIVE (fraud), where there is purposeful manipulation of the financial statement to report a level of earnings that would mislead the users of the financial statements.

In spite of the requirements of accounting standards, there is considerable scope for entities to manipulate, without infringing the regulations, the amount of earnings they report. In a country where there is quarterly reporting, such as the US, the pressures to demonstrate a steady but modest profit increase in the first three quarters ending with a final flourish in the last quarter are understandable. Investors make decisions mainly based on their predictions of future company performance. Sound, if modest, profits in each quarter might suggest to the owner that the financial results for the entire year will be very good. High profits in the early quarters followed by a dismal final performance would be a great disappointment.

In addition, entities are aware that towards the year end, analysts are publishing their profit expectations. If an entity fails to meet these, the share price most likely will drop. Half-yearly reporting of profit may therefore be cautious so as not to overexcite the expectations of the market. Even if there is no intent to deceive, the current mood of the economy and that of managers can influence the financial statements. In making their estimates and assumptions, management may be optimistic or they may be cautious. The following worked example of a hypothetical company demonstrates that even minor changes to the revenue and costs figures increase the profit.

In the following table, we show the original figures of revenue and costs to arrive at profit figure of £20,000. Accepting that it is inevitable that estimates and as sumptions must be made in constructing the financial statements, we show in column 2 a modest increase in revenue and in column 3 a modest decrease in costs.

	Original £000	**Revenue increase £000**	**Cost decrease £000**
Revenue	360	**370**	370
Costs	340	340	**330**
Profit	20	30	40

We do not wish to overemphasise the application of doubtful adjustments to financial statements and the auditors will be alert to these, but the following practices can be applied and sometimes are.

1. **Real earnings management:** This takes place when managers deviate from optimal business decisions with real business activities. For example, management may decide to cut discretionary expenses such as research and development and training to achieve current earnings targets. Such reductions in some of its cost activities may have adverse effects on future performance.
2. **Accrual earnings management:** With this technique, managers use discretionary accruals, to increase earnings in the current period by shifting anticipated earnings from future periods. Some accruals depend on estimates and assumptions that can be reassessed. Depending on the need, management can shift earnings from the current period to future periods thus decreasing current period earnings.
3. **Classification shifting:** This does not have an impact on net income for the period but consists of the misclassification of items in the financial statement. For example, management may move charges from operating expenses to non-recurring expenses. Although net income is not affected, the user of financial statements may draw different conclusions about the financial performance of the company

and its future prospects. If the users believe it is a non-recurring expense, they will assume that there will be no impact on profits in future years. A normal operating expense will also appear as a charge against future profits.

In this chapter, if we concentrate on the topic of negative earnings management, we may both exaggerate the amount of financial fraud that does take place and ignore the considerable accounting problems that exist in recognising, measuring and reporting the line items on the profit or loss statement. To remedy this, we explain the legitimate problems facing company accountants in constructing a financial statement that complies with financial reporting standards.

The present standard requires that, with the two statements' presentation, the separate statement of profit or loss immediately precedes the statement presenting comprehensive income. The comprehensive income statement must begin with the figure of profit or loss shown in the separate profit or loss statement. Comprehensive income includes the net income and unrealised income, such as unrealised gains or losses on hedge/derivative financial instruments and foreign currency transaction gains or losses. A useful example is taken from the published annual report by Vodafone.

The Vodafone example

Vodafone's lengthy annual report of over 200 pages, freely available on the Internet, contains substantial information. For the Consolidated Income Statement (the old profit and loss account) for the year ended 21 March 2021, details are given. We emphasise that we are showing only the details below the main part that explains the profit for the period:

	2021	**2020**	**2019**
Profit/(loss) before taxation	4,400	795	(2,613)
Income tax expense	(3,864)	(1,250)	(1,496)
Profit/(loss) for the financial year from continuing operations	536	(455)	(4,109)
Loss for the financial year from discontinued operations	7	—	(3,535)
Profit/(loss) for the financial year	536	(455)	(7,644)

Immediately below this statement is the Consolidated Statement of Comprehensive Income. This contains all the figures given in the first statement but has the additional information required by the standard. The amounts are in pounds per million:

	2021	**2020**	**2019**
Profit/(loss) for the financial year	536	(455)	(7,644)
Other comprehensive income/(expense) Items that may be reclassified to the income statement in subsequent years			
Foreign exchange translation differences, net tax	133	(982)	(533)
Foreign exchange translation differences transferred to the income statement	(17)	(36)	2,079
Others, net tax	(3,743)	3,066	243
Total items that may be reclassified to the income statement in subsequent years	**(3,627)**	**2,048**	**1,789**
Items that will not be reclassified to the income statement in subsequent years:			
Net actuarial (losses)/gains on defined benefit pension schemes, net tax	(555)	526	(33)
Total items that will not be reclassified to the income statement in subsequent years	**(555)**	**526**	**(33)**
Other comprehensive (expense)/income	(4,182)	2,574	1,756
Total comprehensive (expense)/income for the financial year	(3,646)	2,119	(5,888)
Attributable to:			
Owners of the parent	(4,069)	1,696	(6,333)
Non-controlling interests	423	423	445
	(3,646)	**2,119**	**(5,888)**

Above are only small extracts from financial statements that are supported and explained by many pages of comments. Undoubtedly, the second statement provides a substantial amount of information. We would suggest, however, it is not easily understood by the casual investor looking to make a "quick buck".

Extraordinary items

One statement in the accounting standard that applies to all companies and is extremely important is that for extraordinary items. The regulation is that an entity shall not present any items of income or expense as extraordinary items in the statement(s) presenting profit or loss and other comprehensive income or in the notes. An extraordinary item is an unusual or unexpected one-time event, such as major employee redundancies, burning down of the factory or expensive lawsuits. Before the revisions to IAS 1, entities showed these events outside the calculation of profit. The argument was that shareholders were better informed on the continuing trend of profit and therefore were more able to predict future profits. Extraordinary items being one-off events distorted that trend and it was more sensible to exclude them.

The problem was that there was no specific definition of what comprised an extraordinary item. Some entities were continuously omitting expenses, such as redundancy payments from the main body of their profit or loss statement. As some of these expenses were occurring reasonably frequently, the suspicion was that it was merely a device for not reducing the amount of profit. The IASB considered that this procedure was misleading, hence the paragraph forbidding this practice.

When you look at the financial statements of major companies, there is a limited amount of detailed information. This is because the information disclosed is complex and the details are in the notes to the accounts which cover many pages. You should refer to these notes to ensure that a particular item has been treated properly. Although we would all want the financial statements to give an accurate picture of the financial activities that took place during the year, we must accept that there are problems for companies in providing detailed information. To demonstrate this, we show in the following an extract from the **352-page** annual report of British Petroleum plc. One can only admire the effort and time taken by the company's accountants in collecting all the relevant information to prepare the financial statements for a large company.

Significant accounting policies: use of judgements, estimates and assumptions Inherent in the application of many of the accounting policies used in preparing the consolidated financial statements is the need for bp management to make judgements, estimates and assumptions that affect the reported amounts of assets and liabilities, the disclosure of contingent assets and liabilities, and the reported amounts of revenues and expenses. Actual outcomes could differ from the estimates and assumptions used. The accounting judgements and estimates that have a significant impact on the results of the group are set out in boxed text below, and should be read in conjunction with the information provided in the Notes on financial statements. The areas requiring the most significant judgement and estimation in the preparation of the consolidated financial statements are: accounting for the investment in Rosneft; exploration and appraisal intangible assets; the recoverability of asset carrying values, including the estimation of reserves; supplier financing arrangements; derivative financial instruments; provisions and contingencies; and pensions and other post-retirement benefits. Judgements and estimates, not all of which are significant, made in assessing the impact of the COVID-19 pandemic, and climate change and the transition to a lower carbon economy on the consolidated financial statements are also set out in boxed text below. Where an estimate has a significant risk of resulting in a material adjustment to the carrying amounts of assets and liabilities within the next financial year this is specifically noted within the boxed text. Judgements and estimates made in assessing the impact of climate change and the transition to a lower carbon economy Climate change and the transition to a lower carbon economy were considered in preparing the consolidated financial statements. These may have significant impacts on the currently reported amounts of the group's assets and liabilities discussed below and on similar assets and liabilities that may be recognized in the future.

IFRS 15 Revenue from Contracts with Customers

This is an important accounting standard effective from 1 January 2018. It replaces IAS 18 which dealt with revenue from construction contracts. It also replaces the requirements in IFRIC 13, IFRIC 15, IFRIC 18 and SIC-31. IFRS 15 sets out the methods for recognising revenue from contracts with customers. The standard defines revenue as income arising in the course of an entity's ordinary activities. The objective of the standard is to ensure that entities report useful information to users of financial statements about the nature, amount, timing and uncertainty of revenue and cash flows. It seeks to achieve this by requiring that revenue calculations recognise the transfer of promised goods or services in an amount that reflects the consideration expected in exchange for the goods or services transferred. This is not a complex standard and the requirements should not prove a challenge to you.

Revenue is measured at the fair value of the consideration that is received or receivable. The title of the standard with the word "contracts" may be misleading and, in fact, the standards cover all accounting for revenue from sales of goods and rendering of services to a customer. There are also other revenues, such as from dividends received, which would be accounted for by reference to other standards we explain later in this chapter. The contract with a customer must have commercial substance, the parties have approved it, the rights of the parties regarding the goods or services to be transferred and the payment terms can be identified, and the parties are committed to perform their obligations and enforce their rights and it is probable that the entity will collect the consideration to which it is entitled.

The standard defines various terms and the three important definitions are as follows:

Income

This is increases in economic benefits during the accounting period in the form of inflows or enhancements of assets or decreases in liabilities that result in an increase in equity, other than those relating to contributions from equity participants e.g. purchasing more shares in the company.

Performance obligation

This is a promise in a contract with a customer to transfer to the customer either

- a good or service (or a bundle of goods or services) that is distinct or
- a series of distinct goods or services that are substantially the same and that have the same pattern of transfer to the customer.

Transaction price

This is the amount of consideration to which an entity expects to be entitled in exchange for transferring promised goods or services to a customer, excluding amounts collected on behalf of third parties.

The details of what a "contract" is can be complicated, but essentially, the most basic example is when a customer goes into a shop and purchases an item for cash. The shop will record that as revenue. If the customer does not pay immediately, the shop still records the outstanding revenue using the accruals concept. It also records a trade receivable or debtor for the amount outstanding. The standard identifies five stages that lead to the recognition of a sale. These are as follows:

1. Identify the contract with a customer. It is the contract that creates enforceable rights and obligations between the entity and its customer.
2. Identify the performance obligations in the contract. Each promise to transfer to a customer a good or service that is distinct is a performance obligation and is accounted for separately.
3. Determine the transaction price. The transaction price is the amount of consideration to which the entity expects to be entitled in exchange for transferring promised goods or services to the customer. It could be a fixed or variable amount or in a form other than cash. If the consideration is variable, the entity must estimate the amount to which it expects to be entitled but recognises it only to the extent that it is highly probable that a significant reversal will not occur when the uncertainty is resolved. The transaction price is adjusted for the effects of the time value of money if the contract includes a significant financing component.
4. Allocate the transaction price to the performance obligations in the contract. The transaction price is allocated to each performance obligation on the basis of the relative stand-alone selling prices of each distinct good or service promised in the contract. If a stand-alone selling price is not observable, an entity estimates it.
5. Recognise revenue when (or as) the entity satisfies a performance obligation. Revenue is recognised when (or as) the performance obligation is satisfied and the customer obtains control of that good or service. This can be at a point in time (typically for goods) or over time (typically for services). The revenue recognised is the amount allocated to the satisfied performance obligation.

To the reader, the five steps may seem over complex if you are only a small shop selling cups of coffee or a local store with a limited customer base. For many businesses, the identification of a sales transaction is an everyday, automatic practice that causes few problems. However, there are several businesses where sales transactions are more complex.

Example 1: Revenue recognition before cash flow differences

The local college has a financial year end on 30 June. It commences a new course on 1 March 2022 with 10 students undertaking a six-month course in International Accounting. The tuition fee for each student is £3,000 for the six-month course. Students should pay the full amount on 1 March, and eight students paid in full. With the two remaining students, one paid half the fee and the other paid one third of the fee.

For the year end 30 June 2022, we need to calculate the amount of revenue we should recognise. Remember we are using the accruals assumptions so whether the students have made payment does not matter. There are 10 students and the total fee for the six months is 10 × £3,000 = £30,000. As the year end of the company is 30 June 2022, only four months of the six-month course will have been provided. The amount of revenue to be recognised is £30,000/6 × 4 = £20,000. The remaining £10,000 will appear on the profit and loss statement for the year end 30 June 2022.

These calculations are for the income statement. The amount of cash the company receives by 30 June 2022 is calculated as follows:

Cash paid by students before 30 June is as follow:

8 students × by £3,000 each	£24,000
1 student by half fee	£1,500
1 Student by one third of fee	£1,000
Total cash received	£26,500

Although the income statement will show a revenue amount of £20,000, the cash statement will show an input of £26,500 which will be shown on the statement of cash flows. We discuss this issue in a subsequent chapter.

Example 2: Cash before revenue recognition

Devon Farms orders two separate supplies of food materials from Speedy Supplies plc. Both companies have a year end of 31 December. Devon Farms pays £100,000 and requires one delivery to be made in November 2022 and the next delivery to be made in February 2023.

(*Continued*)

> Under IFRS 15, Speedy Supplies must recognise the revenue separately for the two supplies of food materials at the dates they are delivered to Devon Farms. This is the case even when, in addition to the main activity which generates income, an entity may receive revenue from interest, royalties and dividends. There are two criteria that apply. There are probable economic benefits and there is reliable measurement of revenue.

Depending on the product, a large company may allow customers to defer payment for one or two years. Sometimes, the company may claim that the payment can be made at a later date and the sale is "interest-free". In these cases, the fair value of the consideration that is receivable for the goods is actually less than the amount of cash the company will receive in two years' time as the company has to bear the interest costs. We demonstrate the importance of distinguishing between the delivery of a good or service and the timing of actual performance. See the following two example.

There are other complications that can be involved with the sale of a product or the conduct of a service. The Standard includes application guidance for specific transactions, such as performance obligations satisfied over time, methods for measuring the progress of performance obligations, sales with a right of return, warranties, principal versus agent considerations, customer options for additional goods or services, non-refundable upfront fees, bill and hold arrangements and customers unexercised rights, licensing, repurchase agreements, consignment arrangements and customer acceptance.

In addition to the main activity which generates income, an entity may receive revenue from interest, royalties and dividends. There are two criteria that apply. There are probable economic benefits and there is a reliable measurement of revenue. The standard explains the proper accounting method to be applied for the following transactions:

- **revenue interest** on a time proportion basis that takes into account the effective yield,
- **royalties** on an accruals basis in accordance with the substance of the relevant agreement,
- **dividends** when the shareholders' rights to receive payment are established.

In studying this section, it is important to appreciate that the goods and services being negotiated are likely to be extremely large. Salespeople, who may be on a high commission, can spend several weeks or months in negotiations. External legal fees may be required. The salespeople may incur other legitimate costs in attempting to secure the contract. The standard allows capitalisation of the incremental costs of obtaining a contract if the entity expects to recover these costs. These costs can appear on the entity's balance sheet as an asset.

These costs can only be capitalised if the contract negotiations are successful. For example, salespeople may receive a basic salary irrespective of the success of negotiations. If the negotiations do not prove successful, the salespeople do not receive a commission. There can be some costs incurred in trying to obtain a contract regardless of whether the contract negotiations are successful. These costs cannot be capitalised unless they can be classified as fulfilment costs. Of course, as the entity will be showing these costs as an asset on the balance sheet, they must be amortised on a systematic basis. The period of amortisation would be consistent with the pattern of transfer of the goods or services to which the asset relates. If the amortisation period is less than 12 months, the standard allows the charging of the expenses to the profit or loss statement.

IFRS 15 Revenue from contracts with customers is not such a difficult standard as you, at first, may suspect. The purpose of the standard is to recognise the differences that can exist in the timing of the actual delivery of a good or service and the date that payment is made. Obviously, where a customer pays for a good or service when supplied, there is no need to refer to IFRS 15. Unfortunately, there is revenue fraud committed by companies to enhance their business. Some examples of the methods used are prebilling for goods that have not yet been sent and billing more than once for the same sale.

IAS 2 Inventories

IAS 2 Inventories applies to a company's goods and products that are ready to sell, along with the raw materials that are used to produce them. The standard sets the appropriate accounting requirements for inventories which are those goods that are held and have not yet been sold. The supplier of goods usually will have a holding of the goods so that delivery can be made immediately. A record will be maintained, but usually, at the end of a financial period, there will be a store of goods that will, hopefully, be sold in the next financial period. Using the accruals basis, the supplier will record its sales and purchases of goods. At the end of the financial period, there will be some goods unsold — the closing inventory. This is a critical item in arriving at a soundly based figure of gross profit. The purpose of IAS 2 is to explain the treatment of closing inventory, that is, the goods that remain in store but, hopefully, will be sold in the next financial period.

An entity can only record a profit on goods that it has sold. However, to arrive at the cost of the goods sold in the financial period, we deduct the closing inventory at the end of the period from the opening inventory at the beginning of the period plus the purchases during the period. This calculation gives us the value of the goods sold. We say goods sold, but some may be stolen, damaged, lost or otherwise "disappeared". The entity has to bear these costs. The calculations of inventory values ensure the correct accounting treatment. We provide a simple example in the following to demonstrate the calculation:

Closing inventory

Empties Company is based in the UK and buys plastic buckets from various suppliers in different countries. The baskets are then sold to various stores and shops. The records for the first year show the following:

Purchases	5,500 buckets at £5 each = £27,500
Sales	5,200 buckets at £10 each = £52,000

The Managing Director works on the basis that that each bucket makes a profit of £5. He calculates the profit for the period as 5,200 × £5 = £26,000 deducted from £52,000. The records in the store confirm that there are 300 buckets that can be sold in the next financial period.

When the end of the year count of inventory takes place, it is found that there are only 200 buckets remaining. The other 100 have been stolen, lost or were damaged and could not be sold. The correct calculation to calculate the profit is as follows:

	£	£
Sales for the period		52,000
Purchases	27,500	
Less closing inventory (200 × £5 each)	1,000	26,500
Profit for the period		25,500

The actual profit of £25,500 is lower than the expected profit of £26,000 because of the missing 100 buckets valued at £5 each. The error of the Managing Director was the calculation of the value of closing inventory. The problems of closing inventory can be much greater than those illustrated in our simple example. IAS 2 is an important guide for companies so that they can calculate the correct amount of profit for the financial period and show the value of the current asset of inventory on the balance sheet.

Of course, for established companies, the closing inventory at the end of one period is the opening inventory for the next period. Opening inventory plus purchases and deducting inventory at the end of the period give the cost of goods sold. It is critical to calculate the correct value of inventory. It can also be very difficult in practice. IAS 2 resolves the problems by first defining what is meant by inventories. IAS 2 states that Inventories are assets:

- held for sale in the ordinary course of business,
- in the process of production for such sale,
- in the form of materials or supplies to be consumed in the production process or in the rendering of services.

Inventories are finished goods but also include work in process and raw materials that are being held for subsequent production. In our simple example, the plastic buckets are held as finished goods and no further production takes place in the UK company.

IAS 2 excludes certain inventories from its scope and these types of inventories are covered by other standards. The main ones, which we discuss in later chapters, are as follows:

- work in process arising under construction contracts — IAS 11 *Construction Contracts*,
- financial instruments — IAS 39 *Financial Instruments: Recognition and Measurement*,
- biological assets related to agricultural activity and agricultural produce at the point of harvest — IAS 41 *Agriculture*.

IAS 2 Inventories has been in effect for many years, and there are few problems in its application, but conducting an inventory valuation in a company at the financial year end can cause some major problems. These can be both practical and conceptual in nature. The standard requires all costs that have been incurred in bringing the product to its present location and condition to be included in the calculation of inventory. This includes costs, such as transport, import duties and production overheads. It excludes factors, such as selling costs, abnormal waste, general expenses and storage costs.

The type of material could be fabric, metal, powder, gas or liquid. A company may have several types of materials all requiring valuation. There is also the issue of the stage of completion in the manufacturing process. Where there is only raw material or finished products, the problem is not challenging but when the material is part way through the manufacturing process, it becomes more difficult to determine the value.

The requirement to include all the expenditure in bringing the product to its present location and condition is also challenging. This requirement includes costs, such as transport, import duties and production overheads. It excludes things like selling costs, abnormal waste, general expenses and storage costs. However, companies develop a system that complies with the standard and can be managed efficiently.

As closing inventories may not be substantial in some types of companies, the issue may not be regarded as too important. However, the correct valuation of inventories is critical for arriving at a figure for the cost of goods sold and, therefore, the profit or loss for the financial period. Auditors need to ensure that the inventory exists and, more challengingly, whether the valuation placed on it by the company is acceptable. Auditors must rely on the accuracy of the entity records and statistical sampling to conduct their investigations.

Inventory valuation

The valuation of inventory can be a major issue, particularly for manufacturing organisations. There will not only be raw materials but also work in progress and finished goods. The following example is an extract from the 2020 annual report and accounts of Aston Martin Lagonda Global Holdings Plc. This is a British manufacturer of luxury sports cars and grand tourers. The company is traded at the London Stock Exchange. In 2003, it received the Queen's Award for Enterprise for its outstanding contribution to international trade. Financially, the company has had some troubled times but has survived a number of bankruptcies.

16 Inventories	2021 £m	2020 £m
Parts for resale, service parts and production stock	115.5	80.9
Work in progress	29.8	43.9
Finished vehicles	51.5	82.6
	196.8	207.4

These are substantial amounts and it is obvious that, at the year end, it is not possible for an auditor to visit the company and individually count and value all the inventories. The company must keep comprehensive accounting records and the auditors will ensure that the financial records are sufficiently comprehensive to reflect the actual position with inventories.

The inventory can be of several types. There may be a range of different raw materials. Calculating the value of work in progress, which can be substantial, is extremely challenging. The company must have a very sound system in place to capture the values of partly finished products. Even finished goods present their own problems. Given the high values of these inventories, correct valuation is essential both for calculating the profit and for disclosing the value of current assets on the balance sheet.

Under the standard, inventories must be valued at the lower cost and net realisable value (NRV). We examine NRV later, but the following list demonstrates what is included in the cost:

- costs of purchase (including taxes, transport and handling) net of trade discounts received,
- costs of conversion (including fixed and variable manufacturing overheads),
- other costs incurred in bringing the inventories to their present location and condition.

Although not addressed in the standard, there is an argument that the inclusion of fixed overheads should not be included in inventory costs. These overheads relate to a period and should not be attached to the closing inventory and therefore carried forward to the next financial period.

The phrase "to their present location and condition" is very important. It establishes the limits to the costs of inventory. The following items cannot be included in the costs of inventory:

- abnormal waste,
- storage costs,
- administrative overheads unrelated to production,
- selling costs,
- foreign exchange differences arising directly on the recent acquisition of inventories invoiced in a foreign currency,
- interest cost when inventories are purchased with deferred settlement terms.

Valuation methods

There are three main methods for valuing inventory. There is another method in the US known as last in, first out. The IASB does not allow this method. The three main methods for inventory valuation acceptable internationally are FIFO (First In, First Out), weighted average and retail method.

FIFO: This method assumes that the items of *inventory* that were purchased or produced first are sold first. The items remaining in inventory at the end of the period are those most recently purchased or produced and will be valued at that closing figure.
Weighted average: The cost of each item is determined from the weighted average of the cost of similar items at the beginning of a period and the cost of similar items purchased or produced during the period. The company can elect to calculate on a periodic basis, for example, each month, or as each additional shipment is received.
Retail method: This is a technique used to estimate the value of closing inventory using the cost-to-retail price ratio.

The following examples demonstrate the application of the use of FIFO and weighted average methods on the value of inventory. These examples are followed by an explanation of the retail method:

First In, First Out Method

Date	Received	Issued	Calculation	Total Inventory valuation
January 1	5000 at £1.80 each		5,000 × £1.80 = £9,000	£9,000
January 15	5,000 at £18,500		5,000 × £1.90 = £9,500	£18,500
January 25		8,000	5,000 × £1.80 = £9,000	
			3,000 × £1.90 = £5,7000	(£14,700)
January 26				£3,800

The issue of inventory of 8,000 units on January 25 using FIFO was 5,000 units purchased on January 1 and 3,000 units purchased on January 15. Closing inventory is 2,000 units purchased on January 15 at £1.90 each.

Weighted Average Method

We are using the same data for the number of units received and issued, but we are calculating the weighted average values.

Date	Received	Issued	Calculation	Total Inventory valuation
January 1	5000 at £1.80 each		5,000 × £1.80 = £9,000	£9,000
January 15	5,000 at £1.90 each		5,000 × £1.90 = £9,500	
January 15			10,000 × £1.85	£18,500
January 25		8,000	8,000 × £1.85	(£14,800)
			2,000 × £1.85	£3,700

The above examples demonstrate that the two methods give different values for the closing inventory. This not only gives a different amount for the balance sheet but, more importantly, also gives a different figure in calculating gross profit. It is essential therefore to comply with the following requirements of the standard:

- An entity should apply the same method for all inventories having a similar nature and use to the entity. For inventories with a different nature or use, an entity can apply different methods.
- The entity should use the specific, individual cost of items that are not ordinarily interchangeable and goods or services produced and segregated for specific projects.

The retail method, as its name suggests, is only relevant to certain types of trading activities. The method requires a company to

1. determine the retail value of goods available for sale during the period by adding the retail value of the beginning inventory and the retail value of goods purchased,
2. subtract total sales during the period from the retail value of goods available for sale,
3. calculate the cost to retail price ratio using the formula we show in the following,
4. multiply the difference obtained in second step and the cost to retail ratio to obtain estimated cost of closing inventory.

The cost-to-retail ratio is calculated using the following formula:

Cost to retail ratio

$$= \frac{\text{Cost of beginning inventory and purchases during the period}}{\text{Retail value of beginning inventory and purchases during the period}}$$

Net realisable value

An entity must value its closing inventory at the lower of cost or net realisable value. Net realizable value (NRV) is the estimated sales value of the goods minus the additional costs likely to be incurred in completing production, if necessary, and any other costs necessary to make the sale. The net realisable value can be lower than the original cost because of the following reasons:

- The inventories have been damaged while in store.
- The inventories have become obsolete.

- The selling prices have declined below the original cost.
- The cost of completing production or making the sale has increased.

Although an entity may purchase or manufacture goods with the intention of selling them at a profit, this may not happen. In some industries, or with certain goods, or in certain economic climates, the amount an entity could achieve by selling its inventory is lower than what it costs them originally. Examples are fashionable goods, such as certain clothing items, or consumer technology, such as cell phones. If the demand for these items falls, shops will have to lower their prices considerably to sell their goods. The selling price could even be lower than the original cost. In this instance, any closing inventory must be valued at the net realisable value.

It is important to include the estimated costs of completion or the estimated costs to be incurred to make the sale in the calculations. We illustrate this in the following example:

Example — Closing inventory valuation

Pretties Company imports ceramic pots and pans for use in the home. At the year end, it calculates that the closing inventory using FIFO is as follows:

- 50 saucepans costing £90 each
- 25 baking pans costing £75 each
- 40 boiling pots costing £45 each

The company conducts a physical inspection of its inventory and discovered that some items need repairs before they can be sold. The standard states that the NRV is the estimated sales value of the goods minus the additional costs likely to be incurred in completing production. The company constructs the following table:

Type of pot/pan	Selling price	Repair cost	NRV
Saucepan	£160	£30	£130
Baking pans	£110	None	£110
Boiling pots	£60	£28	£32

Applying the rule of net realizable value or cost, the total value of the company's inventory is as follows:

50 saucepans at FIFO valuation £90 each = £4,500
25 baking pans at FIFO valuation £75 each = £1,875
40 boiling pots at NRV £32 = £1,280

It is important to note that it is only the additional cost required to sell the inventory and not the costs that are normally incurred in the business that is deducted from the selling price.

In our example, we have given low-value figures to make the calculations easy to follow. However, in many companies, the amount of inventory and the value can be very high. In the following, we show an extract from the financial statements of Sainsbury plc. These are large figures and demonstrate the nature of the company's operations when you next do your shopping:

Accounting policies Inventories comprise goods held for resale and are valued on a weighted average cost basis and carried at the lower of cost or net realisable value. Net realisable value represents the estimated selling price less all estimated costs of completion and costs to be incurred in marketing, selling and distribution. Cost includes all direct expenditure and other appropriate attributable costs incurred in bringing inventories to their present location and condition. 52 weeks to 5 March 2022 £m 52 weeks to 6 March 2021 £m Gross finished goods 1,930 1,751 Inventory provision (133) (126) Inventory recognised on Group balance sheet 1,797 1,625 The amount of inventories recognised as an expense and charged to cost of sales for the 52 weeks to 5 March 2022 was £22,499 million (2021: £21,459 million). Inventory losses and provisions recognised as an expense for the year were £511 million (2021: £500 million).

The company has clearly labelled its inventory losses and provisions for the year. The size of the amount would be a surprise for many people.

Inventory fraud

It is easy to forget how important the valuation of the closing inventory is in calculating profit. Our basic calculation is Sales – Cost of goods sold = profit. A key figure is the cost of goods sold. This is usually calculated by taking the cost of goods when purchased and, at the year end, deducting the value of goods remaining to give the cost of the goods sold as shown in the following simple example:

Sales		£5,000
Goods purchased		£4,000
Less closing stock	£1000	£3,000
Profit		£2,000

The value of closing inventory is obviously important in calculating the profit for the financial period. If you were to claim that the value of closing stock was £1,500, then the cost of goods sold would be £2,500 instead of £3,000 and the profit would jump to £2,500. It is mandatory for companies to conduct physical verification of inventory at a reasonable interval. Accordingly, the value of inventory is recorded on the basis of these counts. The management can manipulate accounting records by simply falsifying the inventory count figure. Also, they can add fictitious items to inventory through journal entries, shipping and receiving reports or purchase orders. Another method is not to write down the value of closing stock which has been damaged or is past its "sale by date".

If you are interested in this subject (and who is not interested?), there are numerous cases of fraud listed on the Internet.

IAS 16 Depreciation of Property, Plant and Equipment

A major cost shown on many companies' statements of financial position is depreciation. The standard covering this subject is IAS 16 Depreciation. There have been a number of changes to the requirements of the standard over the years. The most recent amendment effective from 1 January 2022 prohibits deducting from the cost of an item of property, plant and equipment any proceeds from selling items produced while bringing that asset to the location and condition necessary for it to be capable of operating in the manner intended by management. The entity must recognise the proceeds from selling such items, and the cost of producing those items, in profit or loss.

Depreciation affects two of the main financial statements. It is a charge to the Statement of Income, thus reducing the profit figure and also reducing the value of assets shown on the Statement of Financial Position (balance sheet). The amount of depreciation recorded on the financial statements is therefore of considerable importance, and the standard defines the depreciable amount of the asset as the original cost of the asset less what can be expected to be received when the entity disposes of it i.e. its residual value also known as salvage or scrap value.

If an entity purchases a machine for cash, the initial accounting is simple. There is a credit to the cash account and a debit to the machinery account. At the year end, the asset appears on the statement of financial position, but non-current assets do not last forever. They have finite useful economic lives. The entity will use the machine to generate profits. It seems sensible that the cost of the machine is shown as a cost on the statement of comprehensive income. However, it would be misleading to users of financial statements if the full cost was shown in the year of purchase. If the entity considers that the machine has an economic useful life of five years, it makes sense to spread the initial cost or depreciable amount over the five years profit or loss accounts.

Example

On 1 January 2020, Equip Company purchases equipment for £26,000. It is expected to have a life of 3 years and a residual value of £2,000. The following table shows the amount of depreciation charged to the statement of comprehensive income and the carrying amount shown on the statement of financial position at the end of each of the three years. The annual depreciation charge is

$$\frac{£26,000 - £2,000}{3\,\text{years}} = £8,000 \text{ each year}$$

Year	Charge to profit or loss £	Cost of asset £	Accumulated depreciation £	Carrying amount on balance sheet
1	8,000	26,000	8,000	18,000
2	8,000	26,000	16,000	10,000
3	8,000	26,000	24,000	2,000

The amount of depreciation shown on the financial statement is the depreciable amount of the asset, spread over the asset's expected useful life. The standard has the following two definitions of useful life:

1. the expected period the asset is available for use,
2. the expected number of production or similar units the asset will generate.

The depreciation charge for a financial period is subject to a significant amount of estimation. An entity buying a non-current asset using the expected period the asset is available must estimate how long the asset will be used by the entity and what will be the amount received when the asset is finally sold or scrapped, possibly in several years' time.

The estimation of the expected life of the asset has a direct impact on the charge to the income statement and is possibly not so accurate as one would think as the following example shows. An entity purchases some new machinery for £250,000. One engineer considers the machinery will last for 12 years and is likely to have no value when it is finally disposed of by the entity. The annual depreciation charge is

$$\frac{£250{,}000}{12\,\text{years}} = £20{,}833$$

Another engineer estimates a useful life of 15 years and a residual value of £10,000. The annual depreciation charge is

$$\frac{£250{,}000}{12\,\text{years}} = £10{,}000 = £16{,}000$$

If 12 years is selected, the annual charge to the Income Statement will be higher than the 15-year option thus reducing profits, and the value of the assets shown in the statement of financial position annually will reduce quicker. However, if the 15-year option is chosen, the income statement will have a lower charge of £16,000 thus helping profits, and the assets on the statement of financial position will be higher. It is now for the person responsible for compiling the financial statements, usually the chief accountant, to decide which of these alternatives should be shown. Certainly, the trustworthiness and experience of the two engineers will be taken into consideration. However, there may also be the opinions of the board of directors to be taken into account. A difficult decision and the best procedure is not covered by IAS 16.

Of course, both estimates may be incorrect. It is essential, therefore, for entities to revisit the calculations and estimates as the machine is used. The standard requires entities to review the residual value and the useful life of an asset at least at each financial year end. If there are differences between the previous and current estimates, the differences are accounted for as a change in estimate under IAS 8.

Depreciation has an effect both on the statement of financial position and the statement of comprehensive income account. Depreciation has no effect on the statement of cash flows. The only cash movement is when an entity makes the original payment for the asset. On the statement of financial position, the annual depreciation charge reduces the carrying amount of an asset. On the statement of comprehensive income, it is an expense reducing the amount of profit.

Throughout IAS 16 and its Basis for Conclusions are various paragraphs that set out the general principles in applying the standard. We have summarised these and the following notes illustrate the processes:

1. Once there is recognition of an item of property, plant and equipment, an entity should disclose it at its cost less any accumulated depreciation and accumulated impairment losses.
2. The depreciation charge commences when the asset is available for use. It continues until derecognition of the asset. This is regardless of periods of idleness. However, in some instances, the depreciation charge constitutes part of the cost of another asset and is included in its carrying amount.
3. If an item of property, plant and equipment has separate parts with differing useful lives, the entity should depreciate each part separately. The standard gives the example of an aircraft and the separate depreciation of the airframe and the engine. A building can have parts, such as the heating system, windows and security system. These have differing economic lives and are depreciated separately.
4. Land and buildings are separable items. Land usually has an unlimited useful life and is not depreciated. Buildings have a limited useful life and are depreciated.
5. Where there are different parts of an item, it is possible that some of them will have similar useful lives and depreciation methods. In this case, the parts can be grouped together to determine the depreciation charge.

Residual values and useful life

The residual value of an asset is the estimated amount that an entity would currently obtain from disposal of the asset, after deducting the estimated costs of disposal, if the asset were already of the age and in the condition expected at the end of its useful life. Entities can determine that the amount of residual value will be zero. Even if it decides an amount for residual value, it is usually insignificant and has little impact on the calculation of the depreciable amount. There has been debate on the determination of the residual value. The calculation of the depreciable amount is the net cost of the asset i.e. the purchase price less the residual value. In times of rising prices, it is reasonably certain that the residual value will have increased. Some argue that this "economic value" or future price is the most informative as the estimated residual value.

The Board considered the arguments and changed the original definition of residual value to clarify the meaning. The residual value is the amount which could be received for the asset currently (at the financial reporting date) if the asset already were as old and worn as it will be at the end of its future useful life. Using this explanation, the expected residual value of an asset is based on past events. Estimations of changes in residual value are due to the effects of expected wear and tear and for no other reasons.

The useful life of an asset may be determined in three ways. First, the entity may have a policy. For example, all cars will have a useful life of five years. Second, the manufacturers may also suggest what the useful life will be for the asset. Third, the useful life is an estimate of the

- expected usage of the asset,
- expected physical wear and tear,
- technical or commercial obsolescence,
- legal or similar limits on the use of the asset.

The estimations required and the stipulation in the standard for the annual review of these estimations can result in changes in estimations and the annual depreciation charge. This is particularly so if the useful life is changed. The following example illustrates the accounting procedure.

Example — Change in useful life

A company acquires a non-current asset with a useful life of 10 years and no residual value for £200,000. The annual depreciation charge is £20,000 and at the end of year 4, the carrying value is £120,000. The remaining useful life is revised from 6 years to 4 years.

Original cost of asset	£200,000
Cumulative depreciation charge at end of year 4 (£20,000 × 4)	£80,000
Carrying amount at end of year 4	£120,000

$$\text{New depreciation charge} = \frac{\text{£}120{,}000}{4\,\text{years}} = \text{£}30{,}000 \text{ each year.}$$

This revision of the useful life of the asset increases the depreciation charge in the Income Statement by £10,000 and reduces the written-down value of the asset in the balance sheet.

Depreciation methods

There are different methods of depreciation and the standard identifies three:

(1) straight line method,
(2) diminishing balance,
(3) units of production method.

Deprecation starts when the asset is available for use. It continues until the sale or derecognition of the asset. Depreciation does not stop when the asset becomes idle or retired from active use unless it is fully depreciated. There is an exception to this and where the usage method of depreciation is applied, the depreciation charge may be zero when there is no production.

The straight-line method is the simplest and the following formula is used:

$$\text{Annual depreciation charge} = \frac{\text{Cost of asset} - \text{residual value}}{\text{Useful life of asset}}$$

The diminishing balance method calculates the annual depreciation charge by applying a set percentage rate to the cost of the asset in the first year. In subsequent years, the depreciation rate is applied to the carrying amount of the asset in the preceding year. This results in a decreasing annual charge for depreciation.

Some prefer the diminishing balance method and argue that as the asset ages, it becomes less productive and costs more in repairs. The depreciation charge is decreasing as the charge for repairs is increasing thus, one hopes, resulting in the total of the two charges to the profit or loss account being similar over the years.

Comparison of depreciation methods

The following example illustrates the diminishing balance method and the straight-line method. The approximate rate of depreciation required for the diminishing balance method is 33%. We have rounded the amounts to the nearest £10. The asset cost is £10,000, has a life of 4 years and has an estimated scrap value of £2,000 at the end of its useful economic life.

	Diminishing balance method (30%)		**Straight-line method**	
Depreciation method	**Annual depreciation charge to Income Statement £**	**Written-down value shown on balance sheet £**	**Annual depreciation charge £**	**Written-down value £**
Original cost 1 January 2012		10,000		10,000
Depreciation to 31 December 2012	3,300	6,700	2,000	8,000
Depreciation to 31 December 2013	2,210	4,490	2,000	6,000
Depreciation to 31 December 2014	1,480	3,010	2,000	4,000
Depreciation to 31 December 2015	990	2,020	2,000	2,000

The diminishing balance method leads to a substantial charge for depreciation in the early years and lower in later years compared to the straight-line method. Similarly, the written-down amount on the balance sheets varies. The method of depreciation will result in different profits for the year. To comply with the consistency concept, once chosen, the same method of depreciation should be used every year, unless the entity has a valid reason to change it. A further method of depreciation is revenue-based depreciation. This has been used for both tangible and intangible assets. The principle is that the asset should generate over its useful economic life a specific amount of revenue.

In 2014, the IASB issued an amendment to IAS 16 and IAS 38 explicitly prohibiting revenue as a method for depreciating property, plant and equipment. The reason is that a revenue-based depreciation method is inappropriate because factors other than consumption of an asset affect the level of revenue in a financial period. The depreciation charge and the revenue generated share some common attributes, but the IASB did not consider them intrinsically linked. They are not the same. Depreciation is an estimate of the economic benefits of the asset consumed in the period whereas revenue is the output of the asset. Revenue changes due to other factors that do not affect depreciation, such as changes in sales volumes and selling prices, the effects of selling activities and changes to inputs and processes. The IASB concluded that revenue is an inappropriate basis for measuring depreciation expense.

The amendment to IAS 38 is very similar to that for IAS 16 but the Board recognised that there could be "limited circumstances" that would permit such a depreciation method.

The standard accepts the use of the revenue generated to amortise an intangible asset when the rights embodied in that intangible asset are either

1. expressed as a measure of revenue or
2. when there is evidence that revenue and the consumption of economic benefits are "highly correlated".

A "highly correlated" outcome is only where a revenue-based method of amortisation is expected to give the same answer as one of the other methods permitted by IAS 38. One example is where revenue is earned evenly over the expected life of the asset. This results in a similar depreciation charge as the straight-line method.

IAS 16 is a substantial standard and it requires companies to provide the following information:

For each class of property, plant and equipment, we have:

- basis for measuring carrying amount,
- depreciation method(s) used,
- useful lives or depreciation rates,

- gross carrying amount and accumulated depreciation and impairment losses,
- reconciliation of the carrying amount at the beginning and the end of the period, showing factors relevant to the depreciation charge.

At this stage, we identify an issue with the "written-down amount" of an asset that has not been resolved and is sometimes misunderstood. A company calculates the amount of depreciation to be charged on an asset annually and deducts this amount from the original cost of the asset. The amount of depreciation is charged to the Income Statement and the remaining balance of the asset (the written-down amount) is shown on the Statement of Financial Position.

This amount is NOT the value of the asset, although sometimes it is referred to as the written-down value. The issue is, as the written-down amount does not refer to the current value, our balance sheet, although it balances, does not illustrate the current values of its non-current assets. We will return to this issue in a later chapter.

The IASB has amended IAS 16 to prevent the deduction from the cost of an item of property, plant and equipment any proceeds from selling items produced while bringing that asset to the location and condition necessary for it to be capable of operating in the manner intended by management. Instead, an entity recognises the proceeds from selling such items and the cost of producing those items, in profit or loss. This amendment is effective from 1 January 2022.

IAS 16, taking a quick view of the standard, appears to be dealing with very simple decisions on determining the cost of an asset. However, the cost depends, to a large extent, on the decisions of management and the practices it follows. This is an area that the auditors would be examining closely to ensure that the methods used in determining depreciation are suitable.

IFRS 2 Share-Based Payments

This standard was first issued in 2004 and there have been several changes over the years. The standard applies where the transaction is a transfer by the entity of equity instruments (e.g. share options or shares) in exchange for goods or services supplied by employees and third parties. Share-based payments are often associated with schemes for rewarding employees with share-based options, but the standard covers more than that one transaction. Other transactions included in the scope of IFRS 2 are share appreciation rights, employee share purchase plans, employee share ownership plans, share option plans and plans where the issuance of shares (or rights to shares) may depend on market or non-market-related conditions. IFRS 2 does not apply to share-based payment transactions other than for the acquisition of goods and services. Share dividends, the purchase of treasury shares and the issuance of additional shares are therefore outside its scope.

Although IFRS 2 is broad in its scope, there are some exemptions. The issuance of shares in a business combination comes under IFRS 3 *Business Combinations*. Share-based payments for commodity-based derivative contracts that may be settled in shares or rights to shares come under IAS 32 *Financial Instruments: Presentation* or IAS 39 *Financial Instruments: Recognition and Measurement*. We discuss these regulations in subsequent chapters.

The three types of share-based payments

There are three types of share-based payments:

- ***share-based payment transactions*** where payment may be made in cash on a value based on the entity's share price **or** in shares,
- ***equity-settled share-based payment transactions*** where entity issues shares in exchange for goods or services,
- ***cash-settled share-based payment transactions*** where entity pays cash to a value based on the entity's share price.

The basic principle of accounting for share-based payments is that there is the recognition of an expense in the income statement in the period in which a share-based transaction takes place. The corresponding entry will be either a liability or an increase in equity depending on whether payment is by cash or shares to settle the transaction. Where there is a choice in payment, the entity will recognise a liability if it determines that it will pay in cash. If the entity finally settles by issuing shares rather than paying cash, the value of the liability is transferred to equity.

Several entities have a policy of rewarding some employees with shares or share options. This is particularly applicable to senior managers and directors. The reason is the belief that the employee will be motivated to perform better by the share option. IFRS 2 sets out the regulations for such options, and they are recognised in the profit or loss account.

The need for a standard arose mainly because of the accounting treatment in the US for stock options. A review of the experiences in that country underlined the need for a standard to protect shareholders and illustrates the practices that may occur without strong accounting regulations.

Share options

A share option is a benefit, given or sold by one party to another (in this case, the employee), that gives the recipient the right, but not the obligation, to buy (call) or sell (put) a share at an agreed-upon price within a certain period or on a specific date. A simple example is an entity giving a director the option to purchase shares at a future date at the price when the option is first granted. Let us say that the director pays £5 for the option and the price of the share at that time is £40. If in six months' time the share price drops to £30, the director decides not to exercise the option and loses the £5. If in six months' time, the share price is £60, the director purchases the share for £40 and makes a profit, a clear incentive for the director to ensure that the share price increases.

When employees receive stock options, they usually do not gain control over the stock or options for a certain period of time. This period is the vesting period and is usually 3–5 years. During the vesting period, the employee cannot sell or transfer the stock or options. Thus, the employee is obliged to continue working for the entity to get the benefit of the stock options.

The use of stock options led to highly questionable practices in the US. In 1972, a new revision in US GAAP meant that entities did not have to report executive incomes as an expense to their shareholders in specific circumstances. This is where the income resulted from an issuance of "at the money" stock options, that is, the stock option's strike price is identical to the prevailing market price. The result was that organisations reported higher profits and directors benefitted without the full knowledge of shareholders.

The history of stock options is an area where directors may conduct questionable (or even fraudulent) activities if the accounting regulations are not appropriate. Possibly, the most publicised case of the abuse of stock options is that of Greg Reyes in 2007. Reyes was the former chief executive officer of Brocade Communications Systems Inc. Bloomberg. (BRCD). In a broad government crackdown on options backdating, Reyes was the first chief executive convicted by a jury. He lost his bid to reverse his conviction for backdating employee stock-option grants and hiding the practice from auditors and investors. Reyes received an 18-month prison sentence and £15 million fine imposed after his second criminal trial. Brocade investors lost as much as £197.8 million in 2005 when they sold shares that had fallen in value after the practice was uncovered and the entity restated financial results.

On the Dark Side

Although you may understand the requirements of the Statement of Comprehensive Income, it is useful to consider those activities that can impact the financial statements. It is important to be aware of these to gain a full understanding of the Statement of Comprehensive Income. If these activities are substantial, they usually are detected and reported widely.

The minor

Under this title, we would put "petty theft". The amounts are normally small and may not have a significant impact on the financial statements of an entity but should be investigated. The two aspects where they may have an effect are the sales figure and the closing profit amount. The sales figure can be hit in several ways. One method of increasing the final profit is the simple tactic of increasing the sales figure. A "false" sales figure can be shown by claiming high credit sales with the amount "owed" being shown as a debtor. Another method is to increase the amount shown for closing stock. This method lowers the cost of sales as the formula for calculating the cost of sales to be deducted from the actual sales is to calculate opening sales plus purchases less closing cost of sales figure which is overstated.

The major

Many examples of financial fraud are reported, but one we like because of the simplicity was the Great Salad Oil Scandal. It was a fraudulent financial scheme in the 1960s committed by executives at Allied Crude Vegetable Oil Company to exaggerate the amount of salad oil it had in stock. The salad oil stock was held in large containers and the auditors would measure the depth by inserting a measuring stick to obtain a reading. Unfortunately, most of the inventory was actually water covered with a small portion of soybean oil which stuck to the measuring stick. We have also heard (but not personally tested) that cold tea looks very, very similar to whisky. If a company is claiming to have a substantial number of bottles of whisky, it is recommended that the auditor should conduct a substantial taste test.

A search of the Internet will reveal several cases of major fraud in most countries, including the UK. Unfortunately, some can be attributed to poor accounting although we have the opinion that mostly fraud is committed with considerable thought. However, there is in the UK a Serious Fraud Office (https://www.sfo.gov.uk/) that is a specialist prosecuting authority tackling the top level of serious or complex fraud, bribery and corruption. Most countries have a similar organisation.

Chapter Review

The correct identification of the costs for a financial period is critical to calculating the profit for that specific period. To a large extent, the normal accounting procedures are sufficient. The cost is recognised for the financial period on an accruals basis. Measurement does not usually cause a problem and the transaction is entered into the accounting records. Two items of cost that can cause difficulties are closing inventory and depreciation of non-current assets.

Closing inventory is shown as a deduction on the profit or loss account which enables an entity to identify the cost of goods sold. The adjustment ensures that any losses, for any reason, of inventory are properly accounted for on the profit or loss account. IAS 2 Inventories is a well-established standard. The regulations are clear and relatively easy to understand and apply. However, we realise that for some companies, it requires a substantial amount of work to arrive at the amount. Most companies use either FIFO or weighted average. Different methods could arrive at different answers, but the requirement for consistency ensures that is not an issue. The requirement to calculate the net present value is also a safeguard against profit alterations. However, the ease of calculating closing inventory makes it susceptible to fraud and there have been many examples.

IAS 16 contains the regulations for depreciation. It is another well-established standard. Some conceptual issues can sometimes erode the usefulness of the information. Depreciation is the allocation of the original cost of the non-current asset over a period. The carrying amount of the depreciated asset, in all probability, has little relationship to its current value. The depreciation charge on a long-held asset, in all probability, has little relationship to the depreciation charge on a new asset. Despite these deficiencies, there are no indications that the IASB intends to make any amendments to IAS 16. We consider that this is an area where fraud can be easily conducted.

CHAPTER 3 From Standards to Profit

Review Questions

1. A company has an opening inventory of £2,000 and during the period purchases £5,000 of goods. At the end of the period, it calculates that the value of the goods sold amounts to £5,000. What is its closing inventory?
   a. £2,000
   b. £5,000
   c. £7,000
   d. £1,500

2. A company purchase £400 of goods during the financial period. Its opening inventory is £100 and its closing inventory is £50. What is the initial cost of the goods that it has sold?
   a. £600
   b. £550
   c. £450
   d. £150

3. What is negative earnings management?

4. What is classification shifting?

5. What is an extraordinary item?

6. What is a transaction price?

7. What does net realisable value (NRV) mean?

8. What impact does depreciation have on the statement of cash flows?

Chapter 4

Cash and Income

Structure of Chapter 4

Section title	Main content
IAS 7 Statement of cash flows	This statement shows the cash the organisation generated from its operating activities and its use of its cash.
Classification of cash flows	The standard identifies cash flows under three main activities: operating, investing and financing.
Profit to cash	The calculations that are required to convert a company's profit figure to a cash amount.
The users' perspective	Although the standard has improved financial reporting, critics suggest that the standard requires improvements.
Financial failures	Entities may raise finance to make acquisitions or maybe repaying amounts borrowed. This disclosure requirement informs investors how the entity is funding its activities and reveals possible claims on future cash flows.
Statement of Comprehensive Income	The introduction of this statement caused some criticisms and we review the main issues.

IAS 21 The Effect of Changes in Exchange Rates	Recognises both realised and unrealised gains and losses that have increased or decreased the owners' equity in the business.
IAS 19 Employee Benefits	Pay and any other benefits to employees have an impact on a company's finances and should be disclosed.
Chapter Review	This review covers the main issues regarding cash transactions.

The accruals concept is used to calculate the figure of profit for a financial period, but it tells us little about the cash activities of the entity. Profit and cash movements are usually different amounts for a financial period. Experience has shown that apparently profitable entities can become insolvent and have to close for the simple reason that they have run out of cash. Although the Statement of Cash Flows will not prevent insolvency, it alerts the users of financial statements to potential cash problems. It also reveals the decisions entities make with financing and investing activities that support their operating activities. In this chapter, we examine the three separate sections of the Statement of cash flows as required by IAS 7. These are operating activities, financing activities and investing activities.

Not surprisingly, interested users of financial information want to know how much cash a company generates from its operating activities and what it did with its cash. They hope to see a surplus of cash from operating activities and will investigate carefully if there is a deficit the company has not explained. A period of negative cash flows can be a warning that the company is going to become insolvent. Both the financing and investing sections in the statement of cash flows disclose movements of cash. The financing activities section shows whether the company invested in non-current assets that would help the company grow or whether it sold non-current assets. The investing section shows whether the company has issued shares or debentures or repaid amounts of borrowings.

The first section of this chapter explains the purpose and main requirements of IAS 7 Statement of Cash Flows. We explain the three activities that structure the statement. Entities can show the cash flows for operating activities by using the direct or the indirect method. We demonstrate the disclosure of operating cash flow using both the direct and indirect approaches as permitted by the standard.

In concentrating our discussions in this chapter on one of the four main financial statements, we are only examining part of the "financial" information given by companies. The following is an extract from the 220-page annual report of Tesco. The section of financial information listed here takes up about 100 pages when explained in full.

Independent auditor's report
Group income statement
Group statement of comprehensive income/(loss)
Group balance sheet
Group statement of changes in equity
Group cash flow statement
Notes to the Group financial statements
Tesco PLC
Parent Company balance sheet
Parent Company statement of changes in equity
Notes to the Parent Company financial statements
Related undertakings of the Tesco Group
Other information Supplementary information (unaudited)
Glossary — Alternative performance measures
Five-year record
Shareholder information.

This is a formidable list and we will cover the main requirements of IAS 7 in this chapter and add further comments to the Statement of changes in equity that we first discussed in Chapter 2.

Also, in this chapter, we explain the requirements of IAS 21 The Effect of Changes in Exchange Rates and IAS 19 Employee Benefits. If we are considering large and even medium-sized businesses, they may conduct a considerable proportion of their activities with foreign countries and IAS 21 establishes the accounting procedures. Although employee benefits may not seem like an accounting issue, we have demonstrated in other chapters that some companies have thousands of employees. There are issues of pensions, sickness and redundancies. The standard resolves these issues.

IAS 7 Statement of Cash Flows

In calculating profit, the accruals concept is used. Transactions and other events are recognised as they occur and not when cash or any other consideration such as cheques is given or received.

In some instances, the actual transaction and the payment for it occur at the same time. You go into a store and buy a bottle of milk and pay for it immediately at the check-out. This is recorded as a sales transaction and the organisation has received the cash.

Compare this to a retailer who offers credit. In December, the retailer buys goods for £8,000 and sells them for £10,000. This will be recorded in the accounts and a profit on the transaction, ignoring other costs, is £2,000. However, if the customers do not pay until the following March, then there may be a substantial lack of cash in the business. This depends, of course, on whether the retailer has paid for the goods when it first purchased them.

Using the above example, let us take three scenarios where there is a difference in the timing of the cash movements:

A. The retailer and the customer have paid for the goods in the same financial period.
B. The retailer has not yet paid the supplier for the goods but the customer has paid for the goods.
C. The retailer has paid the supplier for the goods but the customer has not yet paid.

These three positions are shown in the following from the view of the retailer:

The cash position

	Scenario A	Scenario B	Scenario C
Cash from customers	£10,000	£10,000	—
Cash paid to suppliers	£8,000	—	£8,000
Cash surplus/(deficit)	£2,000	£10,000	(£8,000)

In all three situations, the retailer will record the same profit of £2,000 for the financial period. The cash position is very different.

In Scenario B, the retailer has a cash surplus because he has not paid the supplier. In C, the retailer is in an unenviable position with a cash deficit of £8,000. A manager of a business must closely monitor the cash position in the company separate from the calculation of the profit. The monitoring and control of cash are critical.

Historically, companies were only required to publish Income Statements and Balance Sheets. It became recognised that the cash position is interesting and useful information for those who are external to the business. They want to get an overview of where the cash came from, how it is spent and where any cash surplus is invested. We now have IAS 7 Statement of Cash Flows which requires that information be disclosed.

Recording cash

With normal record keeping, organisations have a cash account as part of double-entry bookkeeping. A large company may have several types of cash accounts and may also maintain accounts for transactions with any banks with which they have dealings. In this book, we use the term cash accounts to mean any type of cash or bank record that is maintained by the business. In recording cash, we are dealing with present transactions and building a historical bookkeeping record. This will allow the monitoring and control of the movements of cash.

Where actual cash is received as notes and coins, security is always an issue. At regular intervals, possibly daily, it is essential that there is a reconciliation of the physical amount of cash held, if any, and the amount shown in the records. Differences, which must be investigated, can arise for the following reasons:

- incorrect recording of the amount received or paid,
- theft or loss of cash,
- incorrect additions,
- omission of entries in the records either through error or by intent.

A company may hold a certain amount of cash, but it is usual practice to pay cash into the bank as soon as possible. The company will maintain its own records of all deposits into the bank account and any payments made from the bank account. Sometimes, items may be shown in the company's records and not the bank's or vice versa. One example is a cheque that has been received by the company and entered into its records but is subsequently dishonoured and not shown in the bank statement. Also, entries may have appeared on the bank statement, such as bank charges, direct debits and cash withdrawals, and the company has failed to record these.

One of the main reasons for company records and bank statements not agreeing is timing. For example, a cheque may have been sent by the company and entered into its records, but the recipient has not yet paid it into his bank account. Alternatively, the company has immediately recorded cheques that have been received but there has been a slight delay in recording these on the bank statement. A bank reconciliation should resolve these differences. A simple example follows.

Example — Bank reconciliation

Dave Dubs maintains a cash book for his small business. He receives some cash payments but the majority are made by cheque. He makes a few small cash payments on a daily basis, but for any significant amounts, he issues a cheque. On 31 March, the bank statement shows a balance of £5,420 and his cash book a balance of £4,540. Dave, or his accountant, should conduct a bank reconciliation to identify the reason for the difference.

Bank reconciliation as of 31 March 2022

	£
Balance shown on the bank statement	5,420
Add deposits into bank but not yet cleared	1,040
	6,460
Less cheques not yet presented by recipients	1,920
Balance as shown in cash book	4,540

The reconciliation shows that the reasons for his cash book and his bank statement were as follows:

- Dave had paid some cheques he had received into the bank. These deposits had not been cleared by the bank and therefore did not appear on the bank statement.
- Dave had issued cheques to various people who had not yet paid them into their own banks.

With the advent of electronic banking, automated payments and sophisticated cash registers, the need for bank reconciliations has diminished. However, many small business transactions are still made in cash and this is an obvious area for fraud. Although detailed records must be maintained, management usually monitors cash through regular summaries of movements over a period of time and the current cash position. These summaries are not required by any regulations, but businesses will construct one that meets their needs. This allows management to consider its cash performance in the past and its current financial position. There is a financial statement (IAS 7) that requires companies to report cash movements.

IAS 7 "Statement of Cash Flows" was first issued in 1992 and there have been subsequent amendments. The statement classifies cash flows during a period into cash flows from operating, investing and financing activities:

- Operating activities are the principal revenue-producing activities of the entity and other activities that are not investing or financing activities. An entity reports cash flows from operating activities using either
  - the direct method, whereby major classes of gross cash receipts and gross cash payments are disclosed, or
  - the indirect method, whereby profit or loss is adjusted for the effects of transactions of a non-cash nature, any deferrals or accruals of past or future operating cash receipts or payments and items of income or expense associated with investing or financing cash flows.
- Investing activities are the acquisition and disposal of long-term assets and other investments not included in cash equivalents. The aggregate cash flows arising from obtaining and losing control of subsidiaries or other businesses are presented as investing activities.
- Financing activities are activities that result in changes in the size and composition of the contributed equity and borrowings of the entity.

Investing and financing transactions that do not require the use of cash or cash equivalents are excluded from a statement of cash flows but are separately disclosed.

The standard was necessary as the Income Statement calculates the profit for the financial period but does not give any guide to the cash activities of an entity. A company goes "bust" because it has run out of money! The cash flow statement shows the inflows (receipts) and the outflows (disbursements) of cash over a period of time. The inflows of cash may occur from the sale of goods, sale of assets, receipts from debtors, interest, rent, issue of new shares and debentures, raising of loans, short-term borrowing, etc. The cash outflows are due to the purchase of goods, purchase of assets and payment of loans loss on operations. In addition, there is the payment of tax to the government and, for a successful company, the dividend to shareholders. The recording of the flow of cash is essential for the following reasons:

- Cash is crucial for survival. Companies can become insolvent even when they are making a profit. This means the company is bankrupt and out of business.
- Cash may be easier to understand by users than profit who are unfamiliar with the accruals concept applied in the calculation of profit.
- Cash is less subjective than profit for forecasting because Income Statements contain several non-cash entries, such as depreciation and provisions. The decision for the amounts to be shown for these non-cash items is largely determined by the entity.
- Loan repayments depend on cash availability so lenders can assess whether the entity is likely to repay its loans.
- Cash satisfies the stewardship function and the responsibility of managers is to maintain the assets of the entity.
- Independent auditors can physically count the cash or request a bank to confirm the amounts that it holds for the client.
- Inter-entity comparisons are more informative because cash is a definite figure regardless of the accounting regulations and practices an entity uses.

If the users of financial reports are to understand fully an entity's financial performance, they need information on cash. They require disclosures on an entity's use of cash in its operating, investing and financing activities. Such disclosures assist users of financial statements to understand the liquidity of an entity and cash itself. There are cash equivalents which are very important for understanding fully a company's cash position. Companies do not usually hold large amounts of cash, and if they have a cash surplus, it is usual practice to invest it to earn interest. This may be a long-term investment where the company commits to leave its funds, without making any withdrawals, for an extended period. A business may also decide to put part or all of its surplus funds in a short-term investment, possibly something that will mature in less than three months. Generally, three months from the date of making the investment is regarded as short term. The standard, IAS 7, considers short-term investments as the equivalent of cash.

There are situations where a company may have deposited money in an account with a bank and the bank requires it to remain there for 6 months or longer. This deposit would not be classified as a cash equivalent. Deposits tied up for a specific period are known as time deposits or fixed deposits. Usually, fixed deposits earn a better interest rate than short-term deposits.

Examples of types of cash and cash equivalents are as follows:

- cash on hand and deposits that can be withdrawn immediately in cash without suffering any penalties,
- short-term, highly liquid investments that are readily convertible to a known amount of cash and that are subject to an insignificant risk of changes in value,
- bank overdrafts that are repayable on demand and are an integral part of cash,
- equity investments if they are in substance a cash equivalent (e.g. preferred shares acquired within three months of their specified redemption date).

We emphasise that a record of cash flows is critical to all companies whatever their size. To demonstrate the cash flow statement, we show the one issued by Oxford Biomedica which has less than 1000 employees. Although it is a small company compared to the others we have mentioned, it is extremely important to all of us as it is a viral vector specialist focused on therapies for patients. In the following extract from its website, we have omitted the amounts to illustrate the structure and headings of the statement.

Statements of cash flows for the year ended 31 December 2021.

Cash flows from operating activities
Cash generated from/(used in) operations
Tax credit received
Net cash generated from/(used in) operating activities

Cash flows from investing activities
Purchases of property, plant and equipment
Proceeds on disposal of investment assets
Loan to subsidiary
Interest received
Net cash used in investing activities

Cash flows from financing activities
Proceeds from issue of ordinary share capital
Costs of share issues
Payment of lease liabilities
Interest paid
Net cash generated from financing activities

Net increase in cash and cash
Cash and cash equivalents at 1 January
Cash and cash equivalents at 31 December

Classification of Cash Flows

The statement of cash flows standard IAS 7 classifies the cash flows under three main activities: operating, investing and financing.

Operating activities, in most cases, are the principal revenue-producing activities of the entity, in other words, how the company makes its money.

Investing activities are the acquisition and disposal of long-term assets and other investments not included in cash equivalents. Aggregate cash flows from obtaining or losing control of subsidiaries should be presented separately and come under the investing activities category.

Financing activities are activities that result in changes in the size and composition of the investment of shareholders and the borrowings of the entity.

Investing and financing transactions that do not require the use of cash are excluded from the statement of cash flows but need to be disclosed. An important part of preparing a statement is identifying the net cash flows from operating activities in greater detail than shown in the above financial statement.

Operating activities

Examples of cash flows in and out from operating activities are as follows:

- cash receipts from sale of goods and services,
- cash receipts from royalties and commissions,
- cash payments to employees,
- cash payments to suppliers of goods and services.

The standard permits entities to choose one of the two methods for disclosing operating activities. There is the direct method or the indirect method. The direct method discloses the amount of cash generated by operating activities. The indirect method starts with the figure of the profit for the financial year. This is adjusted by non-cash transactions to arrive at the calculated amount of cash.

The following fictitious example is a Statement of cash flows which uses the direct method for operating activities. We have inserted amounts so that you can see what the deduction and additions are.

Cash Flows from Operating Activities

Cash collection from customers	1,100
Interest and dividends received	150
Cash paid for operating expenses such as employee salaries	(250)
Cash paid to suppliers	(250)
Cash paid for other operating expenses	(150)
Interest paid	(100)
Taxes paid	(150)
Net cash flow from operating activities	350

The above is a simplified example. In practice, you will encounter more items disclosed by an entity. The type of headings and the detail provided depend on the cash activities of the entity. There are some definitional problems associated with items, such as interest. Some entities may classify these as financing activities while others may decide they are operating activities. There is a considerable amount of evidence that all types of users of financial reports prefer the direct method because it is far more useful for forecasting future cash flows. The users of the information are interested not only in the present cash position but also in applying that information to predict the future cash position. This is also the method recommended in the standard as it shows each major class of gross cash receipts and gross cash payments.

However, the regulations permit, and many companies use the indirect method. Instead of showing detailed cash movements as in the direct method, the indirect method starts with the net profit figure from the Income Statement and adjusts this with non-cash movements, such as depreciation. This method adjusts the net profit or loss for the effects of non-cash transactions.

Investing activities

Operating activities should generate cash directly. The buying and selling of goods and services generate cash in the financial period. However, a company will purchase items so that it can operate. These may be items such as buildings, machinery or other resources. It may also sell some of those it already owns. These activities are not carried out to earn profit directly but to represent movements of cash.

We have condensed the list given in IAS 7 Statement of Cash Flows to extract the following examples of investing activities' cash flows:

- payments to acquire property, plant and equipment, intangibles and other long-term assets,
- receipts from sales of property, plant and equipment, intangibles and other long-term assets,
- payments to acquire equity or debt instruments of other entities and interests in joint ventures,
- receipts from sales of equity or debt instruments of other entities and interests in joint ventures,
- advances and loans made to other parties,
- receipts from the repayment of advances and loans made to other parties,
- payments for futures contracts, forward contracts, option contracts and swap contracts.

The investing activities section reflects an entity's strategies in its management of wealth-creating resources. If this strategy is successful, the financial performance of the entity will improve before working capital changes.

Before moving on to the final section of the Statement of Cash Flows concerned with Financing Activities, we explain the calculations required using the indirect method to ascertain the net cash flows from operating and investing activities. The general rules for the balance sheet changes reflect the accounting equation:

ASSETS = LIABILITIES + CAPITAL

As the balance sheet must always balance, that is, the sum of the assets must equal the liabilities plus capital amount, any change in one of the above three classifications must bring about a change in another. We demonstrate these movements in the following table, assuming at this stage that the changes are cash based. For example, a non-current asset is either bought which is an addition to the value of Non-current Assets a company has and decreases cash or sold in a cash transaction which increases the amount of cash the company holds.

Relationship of Assets, Liabilities and Cash

ITEM	**CASH**	
Non-current asset increases		Decreases
Non-current asset decreases	Increases	
Current assets increase (other than cash)		Decreases
Current asset decreases	Increases	
Non-current liabilities increase	Increases	
Non-current liabilities decrease		Decreases
Current liabilities increase	Increases	
Current liabilities decrease		Decreases
Equity increases	Increases	
Equity decreases		Decreases

In real life, a company would not conduct all transactions on a cash basis. An asset may be purchased with long-term borrowings. The asset would be shown on the balance sheet and so would the liabilities by the same amount. We can explain these transactions with the example of a business that commences at the beginning of year one with £120,000 in cash comprising £80,000 from the owners (known as equity) and £40,000 from the bank as a long-term loan.

Example — Cash and loans

The opening balance sheet is as follows:

Balance sheet at beginning of year

	£		£
Cash	120,000	Equity	80,000
		Loan	40,000
	120,000		120,000

The following is the profit or loss account for the first year of trading:

Profit or Loss Account year 1

	£	£
Revenue		250,000
Purchase of goods	200,000	
Less closing inventory	30,000	170,000
Gross profit		80,000
Expenses		60,000
Net profit		20,000

During the year, the company acquired equipment for £15,000 cash.

At the year end, it owed £10,000 to its suppliers and owed £32,000 to its customers.

Balance sheet at end of year

	£		£
Equipment	15,000	Equity	80,000
Inventory	30,000	Retained earnings	20,000
Accounts receivable	32,000	Loan	40,000
Cash	73,000	Accounts payable	10,000
	150,000		150,000

The cash movements are as follows:

	£	£
Opening cash		120,000
Net cash from operating activities		
Add receipts from customers	250,000	
Less amount owed	32,000	218,000
Deduct purchase of goods	200,000	
Less amount owed	10,000	(190,000)
Expenses paid		(60,000)
		88,000
Net cash flow from investing activities		
Purchase of equipment		(15,000)
Closing cash		73,000

Operating activities

Although this tends to be the shortest section of the Statement of Cash Flows for most entities, this does not detract from its importance to the user of the information. Entities may be securing finance to make acquisitions or maybe repaying amounts borrowed. Financing activities show how the entity is funding its activities and reveal possible claims on future cash flows. We have condensed the list given in IAS 7 Statement of cash flows to give the following examples of financing activities' cash flows:

- proceeds from issuing shares or other equity instruments,
- payments to owners to acquire or redeem the entity's shares,
- proceeds from issuing debentures, loans, notes, bonds, mortgages and other short-term or long-term borrowings,
- repayments of amounts borrowed,
- payments by a lessee for the reduction of the outstanding liability relating to a finance lease.

In preparing a Statement of Cash Flows from the Profit or Loss Statement and the Statement of Financial Position, we are trying to adjust our profit, which is a non-cash figure, into a cash figure.

The Statement of Cash Flows relates to the other main financial statements. Although we demonstrated that the indirect method for operating activities requires data from the income statement, the statement of cash flows links to the balance sheet. The following worked example demonstrates these relationships.

Worked example

The following is the summarised Income Statement and Balance Sheet of a hypothetical company, Pinstips plc, which complies with international accounting standards.

Income Statement for the year ended 31 December 2022

	£000	£000
Revenue		650
Purchases	70	
Employee costs	100	
Depreciation	110	280
Gross profit		370
Interest payable		30
Profit before tax		340

Balance Sheets at year ends

	2022		2021	
	£000	£000	£000	£000
Non-current assets				
Cost	1,650		1,450	
Depreciation	334	1,316	224	1,226
Current assets				
Inventory	20		20	
Accounts receivable	76		60	
Cash	368	464	94	174
		1,780		1,400

Share capital	600	600
Retained earnings	640	300
Long-term loans	400	380
Accounts payable	140	120
	1,780	1,400

As mentioned previously, the calculation of the statement of cash flows is linked to the balance sheet. This is shown below:

1. The operating profit of £370 is not a cash figure and we need to adjust it.
2. Depreciation of £110 is not a cash movement. It is added back to the net profit.
3. Accounts receivable increased by £16. We did not receive this cash and must deduct it from the profit figure.
4. Accounts payable increased by £20. This must be added to the profit figure.
5. The balance sheet shows the cost of current assets increased by £200, so that is cash going out.
6. With financing activities, we received £20 from an increase in the loan as shown on the balance sheet and we paid out £30 for interest.

Statement of cash flows for the year ended 31 December 2022

	£000	£000
Net cash flow from operating activities		
Operating profit	370	
Add depreciation	110	
	480	
Increase in accounts receivable	(16)	
Increase in accounts payable	20	484
Cash flows from investing activities		
Acquisition of non-current assets		(200)
Cash flows from financing activities		
Increase in loans	20	
Interest	(30)	(10)
Increase in cash and cash equivalents		274
Cash and cash equivalents as of 1 January 2020		94
Cash and cash equivalents as of 31 December 2020		368

Profit to Cash

The requirement that a company must produce a profit statement and a cash statement requires several calculations. It is also a popular subject with examination questions as it requires students to demonstrate their knowledge of the relationships. In the following tables, we show the main calculations made in converting a profit figure to cash. It is also a useful summary of the various transactions we have discussed in this chapter.

Movement	Reason for adjustment
Depreciation	It is deducted from the Income Statement to calculate profit but it is not cash.
Decrease in inventory	Inventory has been sold that was acquired in a previous period so we have more cash than profit.
Decrease in accounts receivable	Customers have paid from sales made in a previous period so we have more cash.
Increase in accounts payable	We have not paid suppliers fully for this financial period so we have more cash.
Increase in inventory	We have purchased more inventory so we have less cash.
Increase in accounts receivable	Not all customers have paid for the sales shown on the Income Statement so we have less cash.
Decrease in accounts payable	We have paid more to suppliers than for the period's receipts of goods so we have less cash.

The Users' Perspective

It is argued that a company goes "bust" not because of the lack of profit but because of the lack of cash. Most would agree that IAS 7 Statement of cash flows has enhanced corporate reporting. The statement of cash flows provides information value for the users. The separation of cash flows into three separate activities offers an analysis of the cash flows for operations, investing and finance activities. If we consider the history of the standard, including national requirements, there have been few changes over the years. There are some perceived weaknesses. A long-standing complaint from users is that entities can use either the direct or the indirect method. Numerous surveys over the years have confirmed that users prefer the direct approach. The IASB has given no indication that it intends to make the direct method compulsory.

The argument is that the complicated adjustments required by the indirect method are difficult to understand. It also provides entities with more leeway for manipulation of cash flows and there are well publicised examples of companies manipulating their financial statements. This is mostly where the company is trying to enhance the profit figure. This is the very figure that is used in the indirect method to calculate the net cash from operating activities. An issue for users is the abuse or confusion regarding the classifications of specific cash flows. Classification can occur within different sections of the statement. Cash outflows that could have been reported in the operating section may be classified as investing cash outflows to enhance operating cash flows.

The IASB allows some flexibility in classifications that reflects specific industry and entity practices. An entity can classify interest and dividends received and paid as operating, investing or financing cash flows. Even a single transaction may include cash flows that are classified differently. For example, the cash repayment of a loan can include both interest and capital. An entity may classify the interest element as an operating activity and the capital element as a financing activity. Some preparers and users welcome this flexibility as it permits entities to select the most appropriate activity for a transaction. Others find it disquieting and would prefer a more rigid regulation. They argue that an entity may select the activity that presents the information in the most favourable light. Critics also argue that the flexibility makes it more difficult to make comparisons with other companies.

The complexity of the adjustments to net profit before tax can lead to the manipulation of cash flow reporting. Cash flow information should help users understand the operations of the entity, evaluate its financing activities, assess its liquidity or solvency and interpret earnings information. A problem for users is that entities can choose the method and there is not enough guidance on the classification of cash flows in the operating, investing and financing sections of the indirect method used in IAS 7.

Users find the Statement of cash flows for evaluating a company very helpful as it is possible to calculate ratios that assist in the analysis of the company's performance. The formula for a company's cash ratio is as follows:

Cash Ratio: Cash + Cash Equivalents / Current Liabilities

There is no one perfect ratio and the acceptable cash ratio will depend on such issues as the size of the company, the type of industry, the profit it is making, the changes in the ratio compared to other similar companies and the movement in the ratio over a period of time.

Cash flow from operations

With any business, it is critical to determine whether it has sufficient cash to pay its current liabilities – its current debts. If not, the result could be the closure of the business. The Statement of Cash Flows contains the figure for the cash flow from operating activities. The current liabilities are shown on the balance sheet. It is best to use the average current liabilities for at least two years and calculate the average in case there are significant fluctuations in the amount. The formula is as follows:

$$\frac{\text{Net cash flow from operating activities}}{\text{Average current liabilities}} \times 100$$

It should ring alarm bells if the company does not have sufficient cash coming in to cover its current liabilities.

The Cash Flow Statement has the advantage of being relatively easy to understand as it shows the actual cash position. This allows judgements to be made on the liquidity of the company and whether there are problems which could lead to insolvency and the closure of the company. It must be remembered that the statement is about cash and does not give any guidance to the profit or loss of a company, however, it is extremely useful in gauging the financial strength of the company. One calculation that investors may use to assess the strength of the company is the cash flow per share. If a company intends to pay dividends, it needs the cash to do it. Investors may take the cash amount and divide it by the number of shares in issue. If the cash flow per share is only small, you may suspect that the company may have difficulties in paying dividends. We return to this issue in a later chapter where we explain ratio analysis.

An excellent example of the type of information some companies give is in the following summary of a cash flow taken from the annual financial report of Barrick Gold Corporation which is the largest gold mining company in the world, with its headquarters in Canada. Note that this summary is taken from their annual report for 2021 which contains

215 pages. We emphasise that this is only an extract but it demonstrates the financial information and explanations some companies provide.

Barrick Gold Corporation example

Free Cash Flow Free cash flow is a measure that deducts capital expenditures from net cash provided by operating activities. Management believes this to be a useful indicator of our ability to operate without reliance on additional borrowing or usage of existing cash. and analysts to better understand the underlying operating performance of our core mining business through the eyes of management. Management periodically evaluates the components of adjusted net earnings based on an internal assessment of performance measures that are useful for evaluating the operating performance of our business segments and a review of the non-GAAP financial measures used by mining industry analysts and other mining companies. Adjusted net earnings is intended to provide additional information only and does not have any standardized definition under IFRS and should not be considered in isolation or as a substitute for measures of performance prepared in accordance with IFRS. The measures are not necessarily indicative of operating profit or cash flow from operations as determined under IFRS. Other companies may calculate these measures differently. The following table reconciles these non-GAAP financial measures to the most directly comparable IFRS measure. Free cash flow is intended to provide additional information only and does not have any standardized definition under IFRS, and should not be considered in isolation or as a substitute for measures of performance prepared in accordance with IFRS. The measure is not necessarily indicative of operating profit or cash flow from operations as determined under IFRS. Other companies may calculate this measure differently.

Following this summary, the company provides a table which reconciles this non-GAAP measure to the most directly comparable IFRS measure.

The cash flow statement must not be confused with the funds flow statement which some companies prepare but are rarely made public. Funds Flow Statement states the changes in the working capital of the business in relation to the operations in one time period. The main components of Working Capital are as follows:

Current assets

- cash,
- receivables,
- inventory.

Current liabilities

- payables.

We explain the analysis of working capital in a subsequent chapter where we discuss ratio analysis.

Financial Failures

In the UK, the term insolvency usually applies to companies and the term bankruptcy is a legal process applying to an individual who cannot repay debts to creditors and may seek relief from some or all of their debts. The bankruptcy process will ensure that the insolvent's assets, if any, are shared among their creditors. The legal basis for an individual being made bankrupt is as follows:

- they cannot pay what they owe and want to declare themselves bankrupt,
- their creditors apply to make them bankrupt because they owe them £5000 or more. The individual should
- give the official receiver information on their finances,
- give the official receiver a full list of their assets,
- tell their trustee about any rise in income during the bankruptcy,
- tell anyone who offers to loan them over £500 that they are bankrupt,
- go to court to explain why they owe money if asked to do so.

If a firm is insolvent, it can decide to file for bankruptcy protection, which is a court order that oversees the liquidation of the company's assets. Insolvency legislation does not focus on the liquidation and elimination of insolvent entities. It attempts to remodel the financial structure of the debtors so as to enable the continuation of the business. This is referred to as a business turnaround or business recovery.

Unfortunately, bankruptcy is not uncommon. COVID, it is argued, had a significant impact on companies and the number of registered company insolvencies in February 2022 was 1,515:

- More than double the number registered in the same month in the previous year (685 in February 2021) and
- 13% higher than the number registered two years previously (pre-pandemic; 1,346 in February 2020).

There were some well-known names on the bankruptcy list. The Arcadia Group owned various major retail brands, including Topshop, Dorothy Perkins, Burton and Miss Selfridge. Unfortunately, the group went into administration on the 30th of November 2020 with 13,000 employees and 444 UK and 22 overseas stores. Topshop, Topman and Miss Selfridge have since been acquired by UK online fashion retailer ASOS, although they will only sell these brands online. Debenhams has been a familiar name but the 242-year-old department store chain announced the closing of its 124 stores at the end of 2020. The company went into insolvency in April 2020 and had been looking for a buyer since the summer.

The number of registered company insolvencies in February 2022 was 1,515:

- More than double the number registered in the same month in the previous year (685 in February 2021) and
- 13% higher than the number registered two years previously (pre-pandemic; 1,346 in February 2020).

In February 2022, there were 1,329 Creditors' Voluntary Liquidations (CVLs), more than double the number in February 2021 and 40% higher than in February 2020. Numbers for other types of company insolvencies, such as compulsory liquidations, remained lower than before the pandemic, although there were more than twice as many compulsory liquidations and almost double the number of administrations in February 2022 compared to February 2021. For individuals, 588 bankruptcies were registered, which was 36% lower than in February 2021 and 2% lower than in February 2020.

Statement of Comprehensive Income

The statement of comprehensive income recognises both realised and unrealised gains and losses that have increased or decreased the owners' equity in the business. The items that appear in a comprehensive income statement that were not reported in the traditional profit or loss account are such transactions as revaluations of non-current assets under IAS 16. Two other items are gains and losses from translating the financial statements of a foreign operation (IAS 21). The Effect of Changes in Foreign Exchange Rates and remeasurement of defined benefit plans (IAS 19 Employee Benefits) which we discuss after this section on comprehensive income. There has been considerable debate on the purpose of the statement of comprehensive income and its conceptual basis. Some argue that it is difficult to understand and provides little information of value to the users. Others claim that it has information value and preparers and users of financial data need time to become accustomed to it.

Defining profit or loss

The basic definition of profit or loss is the total income less expenses, excluding the components of other comprehensive income.

The above definition focuses on the calculation of profit or loss. This explains the mechanics of arriving at a figure of profit or loss but does not describe the nature of profit. Unfortunately, the terms profit and income tend to be used somewhat loosely in both IAS 1 and elsewhere. As the calculation of profit excludes other comprehensive income, the conclusion must be that profit does not tell the complete story or that investors require the information.

It is possible to calculate profit in two different ways. We can take our revenues and deduct the expenses, and the result will be a "profit" as defined above. This calculation is the accruals method and relies on conventions that have developed over many years. Our definitions and the identification of income and expenses determine what profit is.

An alternative method is to take the difference between how wealthy the entity is at the beginning of the financial period and how wealthy it is at the end of the financial period. The owners' equity can be used as the measure of wealth, assuming there have been no direct transactions with shareholders, such as payment of dividends during the financial period. If the owners' equity has declined over the period, there is a decrease in wealth. If the owners' equity has increased, there is an increase in wealth. This ignores any direct transfers to or from equity.

Profit, as we have measured it originally, tells part of the story, but it is argued that the statement of comprehensive income gives a fuller picture. It captures the gains and losses, both realised and unrealised, that increase or decrease the owners' equity. One example of a non-realised gain leading to a gain in equity is a revaluation of non-current assets. For example, an entity owns property that was purchased for £1 million. Due to the location of the property and a buoyant property market, the property has been revalued to £1.25 million. The entity is wealthier and using the accounting equation of assets − liabilities = capital, the shareholders are wealthier. If we have increased the assets by quarter of a million pounds, capital must have increased by the same amount. This can be considered good news for the shareholders but the gain has not been realised. The entity has not sold the property, and until it does, the gain will not be realised in the form of cash. The question arises as to what information should be given to shareholders and how it should be given.

The profit or loss account is essentially the output of the double entry system. Several critics have identified the deficiencies of the profit or loss from the users' view. The main weaknesses are as follows:

- It is transaction based. It only records profits that have been realised. An entity may own land or buildings that have increased in value. The impact of that increase is not recognised until the asset is sold and the gain realised.
- It is historical and does not reflect the impacts of inflation. Even over the period of 12 months, if inflation is high, the financial statements do not reflect this.
- It is not possible to compare the actual profit for the period with the predictions of managers. It is difficult to judge whether the entity has been as successful as managers anticipated.
- Depreciation is only an allocation on a fairly arbitrary basis of the original historic cost of an asset.
- The definition from IAS 1 emphasises that the profit or loss excludes comprehensive income, in other words, the income statement does not capture all transactions that may impact shareholder equity.
- It is not conceptually based and applies accounting conventions that sometimes do not have any conceptual basis.

Definitions of income

The definition of income is given in the Conceptual Framework which states that "income increases in economic benefits during the accounting period in the form of inflows or enhancements of assets or decreases of liabilities that result in increases in equity, other than those relating to contributions from equity participants".

Income encompasses both revenues and gains. Revenue arises in the course of ordinary activities of an entity and is referred to by a variety of different names including sales, fees, interest, dividends, royalties and rent. The term "gains" can refer to both realised and unrealised gains. An unrealised gain, for example, could be land owned by the company that has increased in value but has not been sold. Only realised gains are recognised in the profit or loss statement and they are usually shown separately to provide information that could be of interest to the user.

The Boards' argument for a statement of comprehensive income is that it adopts an asset/liability view (the accounting equation) rather than the revenue and expense (matching) perspective in measuring an entity's income. There are opposing views that contend that these two approaches are complementary and provide different information for different uses.

Despite the criticisms, the IASB introduced the Statement of Comprehensive Income.

Clean and dirty surpluses

Clean surplus accounting means that all changes in shareholder equity that do not result from transactions with shareholders (such as dividends, share repurchases or share offerings) are reflected in the income statement. Clean surplus allows investors to determine the companies that show the best financial performance. According to the clean surplus theory, accountants can determine the value of a company based solely on information found on balance sheets and income statements. A handful of factors, including net income, go into determining the value of a firm under clean surplus theory.

Dirty surplus accounting occurs when some items affect the shareholders' equity but do not appear in the traditional profit or loss account. In other words, the entity has become wealthier but the source of this increase is not identified. Two activities are foreign currency translation adjustments and certain pension liability adjustments. To adjust the profit or loss account to reflect a clean surplus, an investor can replace "net income" with "total comprehensive income".

It is argued that the users of financial statements should be concerned about dirty surplus items for several important reasons. First, by knowing how each dirty item is treated, it is possible to make any applicable changes to the bottom line to adjust for these dirty items. Second, if several dirty items are not included, in the income statement, this can distort the net income. Finally, only by being informed of dirty surplus items can users be fully aware of each item's specific effect on reported net income.

Others claim that too much emphasis is put on the importance of dirty surplus items. A rigorous study of four countries led the researchers to conclude that the results did not suggest that "dirty surplus flows are a consistent source of error in applications of accounting-based valuation models or that cross-country differences in dirty surplus accounting introduce significant problems in international application of those models.

Whatever the merits of the different opinions on dirty surplus items, we now have the comprehensive income statement. In the following section, we examine the requirements and, not surprisingly, the debate on the concept and value of comprehensive income continues.

Definition: Statement of comprehensive income

Total comprehensive income is the change in equity during a period resulting from transactions and other events, other than those changes resulting from transactions with owners in their capacity as owners. Total comprehensive income comprises all components of "profit or loss" and of "other comprehensive income". The standard requires that all non-owner changes in equity should be disclosed either in a single statement or in two statements. A single statement incorporates all items of income and expense. In other words, it is a statement of total comprehensive income.

With a two-statement presentation, we have the following:

- The first statement discloses income and expenses recognised in profit or loss.
- The second statement begins with the amount of profit or loss from the first statement. It then shows all items of income and expense that IFRSs require or permit to be recognised outside profit or loss. In other words, **other** comprehensive income.

The IASB preferred there would be one statement of comprehensive income, incorporating all the information given in the profit or loss account. The reasons it gave for this opinion were drawn from the Conceptual Framework. The Board argued that the Framework

- contains definitions of income and expenses that covered all items of non-owner changes in equity,
- does not define profit or loss and therefore does not clarify what the term expresses,
- does not provide criteria for distinguishing the characteristics of items that should be included in profit or loss from those items that should be excluded.

In its Basis for Conclusions, the Board argued that it was conceptually correct for an entity to present all non-owner changes in equity (i.e. all income and expenses recognised in a period) in a single statement. It argued that there are no clear principles or common characteristics to separate income and expenses into two statements. However, the Board accepted that there was a strong view that a separate profit or loss account should be retained. Accordingly, companies have the option.

To ensure that the financial statements provide all the necessary information, the Board requires that the other comprehensive income statement shows

- the profit or loss amount for the financial period,
- the line items of other comprehensive income for the period,
- a total of the comprehensive income for the period being the total of profit or loss and the other income for the period.

The following example is taken from Vodafone 2022 which provides an annual report of over 250 pages. We have chosen only sections of the text to emphasise the nature of the contents. The full financial statement is easily available on the company's website. The annual report has the following content in its finance section:

Reporting on our financial performance
Directors' statement of responsibility
Auditor's report

Consolidated financial statements and notes
Company financial statements and notes

On page 129 of Vodafone's 2022 Annual Report, there is a full Consolidated Income Statement followed by a Consolidated Statement of Comprehensive Income for the year ended 31 March 2022.

Although we have not been able to trace any literature on the subject, it would appear that many companies prefer to provide both a traditional Income Statement and a Statement of Comprehensive Income. We complete this section by providing explanations of comprehensive income and reclassifications.

Definition: Other comprehensive income

Other comprehensive income comprises items of income and expense (including reclassification adjustments) that are not recognised in profit or loss as required or permitted by other IFRSs.

The components of other comprehensive income include the following:

- changes in revaluation surplus on non-current and intangible assets,
- remeasurement of defined benefit plans,
- gains and losses from translating the financial statements of a foreign operation,
- gains and losses on remeasuring available-for-sale financial assets,
- the effective portion of gains and losses on a cash flow hedge.

The line items in the other comprehensive income statement are shown either

(a) net of tax-related effects or
(b) before related tax effects with one amount shown for the aggregate amount of income tax relating to those items.

If an entity selects alternative (b), the tax is allocated between the items that might be reclassified subsequently to the profit or loss section and those that will not be reclassified subsequently to the profit or loss section. The information disclosed must show separately the share of the other comprehensive income statements of associates and joint ventures accounted for using the equity method.

To assist the users' understanding, the financial statements should separately disclose every material expense. These can be included in the notes to the financial statements. The kind of material items that may require separate disclosure include the following:

- write-down of inventories to net realisable value,
- write-down of property, plant and equipment,
- disposals of investments,
- restructuring costs,
- discontinued operations,
- litigation settlements.

This is not an exhaustive list and other material expenses may need separate disclosure.

The other disclosure requirement that we discuss fully in the following section is reclassification. The standard requires the line items to be grouped into those that

- will not be reclassified subsequently to profit or loss and
- will be reclassified subsequently to profit or loss.

Definition: Reclassifications

Reclassification adjustments are amounts reclassified to profit or loss in the current period that were recognised in other comprehensive income in the current or previous periods.

Another term for reclassifications is recycling as the item moves from the other comprehensive income section to the profit or loss statement. Not all items of other comprehensive income can be recycled and the regulation states the following:

1. Reclassification adjustments are such items as the disposal of a foreign operation and when some hedged forecast cash flow affects profit or loss in relation to cash flow hedges.
2. There are no reclassification adjustments in revaluation surplus recognised in accordance with IAS 16 or IAS 38 or on remeasurements of

defined benefit plans recognised in accordance with IAS 19. These components are recognised in other comprehensive income and are not reclassified to profit or loss in subsequent periods.

Changes in revaluation surplus may be transferred to retained earnings in subsequent periods as the asset is used or when it is derecognised.

Other IFRSs specify whether and when amounts previously recognised in other comprehensive income can be reclassified to profit or loss. A reclassification adjustment is included with the related component of other comprehensive income in the period that the adjustment is reclassified to profit or loss.

These amounts may have been recognised in other comprehensive income as unrealised gains in the current or previous periods. The standard requires unrealised gains to be deducted from other comprehensive income in the period in which the realised gains are reclassified to profit or loss. This prevents their inclusion in total comprehensive income twice.

The debate on the nature and definition of profit has encouraged the IASB to require a statement of total comprehensive income. Their reasons for doing so have not received overwhelming agreement. Undoubtedly, there is confusion over the rationale for the contents of the statement and the mixture of realised and unrealised gains. Reclassifications are also likely to require considerable thought by both the preparers and the users. It is too early to assess the value of this statement to the user. As familiarity with the statement increases, doubts and uncertainties may be dispelled. It is also possible that the IASB will decide to revisit the requirements and produce a stronger conceptual basis.

IAS 21 The Effect of Changes in Foreign Exchange Rates

IAS 21 The Effect of Changes in Foreign Exchange Rates was issued long before the requirement for a Comprehensive Income Statement and it has been amended several times. The development of global business has resulted in many entities being involved in various forms of relationships with other entities in different countries. These may include transactions conducted with foreign buyers or sellers or participation in foreign operations and, in these circumstances, foreign currencies are involved. Entities require guidance to account for these currency transactions in a consistent manner.

The main requirements of IAS 21 are as follows:

- transactions in foreign currencies must be expressed in the entity's reporting currency,
- the financial statements of foreign operations must be translated into the entity's reporting currency.

IAS 21 has two objectives:

1. to set out how to include foreign currency transactions in an entity's financial statements,
2. to explain how to translate the financial statements of foreign operations into a presentation currency.

Functional currency

An entity's functional currency is the basis for determining whether the entity has any foreign exchange transactions. By identifying its functional currency, the entity is identifying the treatment of exchange gains and losses from the currency translation process and its reported results. If we are considering consolidated financial statements, each individual entity in the group, wherever it operates in the world, must prepare its financial statements in its functional currency. The two main indicators of a company's functional currency are as follows:

1. The one that mainly influences sales prices for goods and services. This is normally the currency in which sales prices for goods and services are denominated and settled. For example, the entity may operate in an active local sales market. It prices its products in the local currency and makes payments primarily in that local currency.
2. The currency of the country whose competitive forces and regulations mainly determine the sales prices of an entity's goods and services. The currency that mainly influences the costs of labour, materials, goods and services. If such costs are incurred and settled in the local currency, this will be the functional currency.

At the group level, various entities within a multinational group will often have different functional currencies which are identified at entity level for each group entity. Each group entity translates its results and financial position into the presentation currency of the reporting entity. An example would be where an Australian subsidiary prepares its accounts in Australian dollars which are the functional currency but the UK holding company would present its results in UK pounds which is the presentation currency for the financial reports.

In preparing group accounts, the financial statements of foreign subsidiaries are translated into the presentation currency. If the presentation currency differs from the functional currency, the financial statements are retranslated into the presentation currency. If the financial statements of the entity are not in the functional currency of a hyperinflationary economy, then they are translated into the presentation currency as follows:

- Assets and liabilities (including any goodwill arising on the acquisition and any fair value adjustment) are translated at the closing spot rate at the date of that balance sheet.
- Income and expenses for each statement of comprehensive income are translated at the spot rate at the date of the transactions (average rates are allowed if there is no great fluctuation in the exchange rates).
- All exchange differences are recognised in other comprehensive income.

Any goodwill and fair value adjustments are treated as assets and liabilities of the foreign entity and therefore retranslated at each balance sheet date at the closing spot rate.

Exchange differences on intra-group items are recognised in profit or loss unless they are a result of the retranslation of an entity's net investment in a foreign operation when it is classified as equity. In the financial statements that include the foreign operation and the reporting entity (e.g. consolidated financial statements when the foreign operation is a subsidiary), such exchange differences are recognised initially in other comprehensive income and reclassified from equity to profit or loss on disposal of the net investment.

Dividends paid in a foreign currency by a subsidiary to its parent firm may lead to exchange differences in the parent's financial statements. They are not eliminated on consolidation but recognised in profit or loss.

It is possible that an entity will dispose of a foreign operation. In these circumstances, the cumulative amount of the exchange differences recognised in other comprehensive income and accumulated in the separate components of equity is reclassified from equity to profit or loss (as a reclassification adjustment) when the gain or loss on disposal is recognised.

If there is a gain or loss on a non-monetary item, an entity recognises it in other comprehensive income. Any exchange component of that gain or loss of the entity is recognised in other comprehensive income. The alternative is where an entity recognises a gain or loss on a non-monetary item in the profit or loss account. It recognises any exchange component of that gain or loss in the profit or loss account.

IAS 19 Employee Benefits

When studying this standard, we are considering all forms of consideration given by an entity in exchange for services provided by its employees in a financial period. These include the following:

- short-term benefits fall due within 12 months of services being given e.g. wages, salaries, bonuses and non-monetary benefits,
- post-employment benefits e.g. pensions and continued private medical health care,
- other long-term benefits e.g. long-term disability benefits and paid sabbaticals,
- termination benefits i.e. when an employee leaves.

In this section, we are going to concentrate on short-term benefits, post-employment benefits and termination benefits. With all types of benefits, the general principle is that the cost of providing employee benefits should be recognised in the period where the employee earns the benefit, rather than when it is paid or payable.

Short-term employee benefits are regarded as those payable within 12 months after service is provided and should be recognised as an expense in the period that service is provided. This includes vacations and paid sick leave to other acceptable absences where the benefits are still payable.

Worked example

Short-term benefits

A company has 20 employees. They are all paid the same rate of £150 per day and are entitled to 10 days holiday on full pay. The expense to the company in its Income Statement for 2014 for the vacation pay is 20 × £1,500 = £30,000. One employee decides that she will take only 8 days holiday and the remaining 2 days she will take in 2015. The company agrees to this plan. The amount of £30,000 in the Income statement is correct but the company will not have paid the 2 days holiday to the employee as they have not yet been taken. The amount of 2 × £150 will be a current liability on the balance sheet.

The company should charge the benefit to the income statement. If the benefit remains unpaid at the end of the financial period, it would be treated as a current liability on the balance sheet. When it is finally paid, the amount of cash held by the company will decline by the amount of the payment and the liability will be removed from the balance sheet. This situation can be demonstrated in the following example:

Retirement benefits, also known as post-employment benefits, cause the greatest accounting policies. There are two types: the defined benefit plan and the defined benefit plan. For defined contribution plans, contributions are recognised as an expense in the period that the employee provides service. In many schemes, the employee and the employer both agree to contribute to the plan.

The amount paid into the defined contribution plan is fixed and the payments are invested to build up a "fund" for the particular employee. The amount of the contributions and the income that the investment has generated should be a substantial amount by the date the employee retires and can be used to provide regular pension payments.

The disadvantage of the defined contribution plan is that the amount of the final fund relies heavily on the success of the investments. If we have been through a very poor economic period, the fund will be much smaller than the employee hoped for and the pension will be correspondingly less. With the defined contribution plan, the risk lies with the employee: they may not receive the pension they anticipated. There is no risk to the employer and the only commitment is the agreed amount of contribution.

Defined benefit plans do not work on the basis of contributions but define the amount of pension a person will receive on retirement. This is usually calculated by using a formula that takes into account the employee's length of service and salary. For example, an employee may be in a scheme that pays one-sixtieth for each year of service multiplied by the employee's average salary for the last three years of their employment. An employee with 40 years service and an average annual salary of £120,000 will receive a pension of 40/60 × £120,000 = £80,000 each year.

From the employer's benefit, they will want to know the amount of contribution that they must make each year to pay for the final pension. Imagine that a company has an employee starting on 1 January 2010 and will retire in 2050. The company will have several questions it needs to answer so that it can calculate the annual contributions to the pension plan it must make between 2010 and 2050. Answers are needed to the following questions:

- Will the employee leave or die before they are due to retire?
- How many years of service will they actually have?
- What will their final salary be?
- What will be the investment return on the contributions made each year?
- How long will the employee live after retirement because the pension will have to be paid until the employee dies?

There are many other variations and possibilities that the company has to resolve and it is normal to rely on the expert judgement of actuaries when calculating the contribution payments. These are professional people who deal with probabilities and will be able to provide the required information.

The above is only a brief description and companies often have several types of pension schemes for different groups of employees. There are also hybrid plans that are part defined benefit and part defined contribution. Pension plans are really a task for the experts and accounting for them relies on their professional opinions. The main issue for companies is that with defined benefit plans, they have an obligation to make up any shortfall if there are insufficient funds to pay out the promised benefits. The risk lies with the employer and not the employee.

The amount recognised in the profit or loss (unless included in the cost of an asset under another Standard) in a period in respect of a defined benefit plan is made up of the following components:

- current service cost (the actuarial estimate of benefits earned by employee service in the period),
- interest cost (the increase in the present value of the obligation as a result of moving one period closer to settlement),
- expected return on plan assets* and on any reimbursement rights,
- actuarial gains and losses, to the extent recognised,
- past service cost, to the extent recognised,
- the effect of any plan curtailments or settlements,
- the effect of "asset ceiling".

Our discussion on pension plans has been concentrated on the accounting issues. The actual operation and regulation of pension plans for employees are conducted by companies and must comply with the laws of the countries in which they operate.

Chapter Review

In this chapter, we have explained, in depth, the requirements of IAS 7 Statement of Cash Flows. This is an important standard as the movement of cash is of interest to a company's shareholders. Although a company can look profitable, it can still fail because it has cash problems. A more complex standard is IAS 21 *The Effect of Changes in Foreign Exchange Rates*. This standard deals with complex accounting issues and has connections with some other standards. Increasingly, companies are becoming international and guidance on the correct procedures is given in this standard. Although the benefits employees receive would appear to be simple transactions, some companies have thousands of employees and there are many different benefits. This standard establishes procedures for companies to follow IAS 19 Employee Benefits.

CHAPTER 4 Cash and Income

Review Questions

1. The income statement of a company shows revenue of £11,000. The balance sheet shows that the accounts receivable have increased by £2,000. How much cash was received?
   a. £11,000
   b. £9,000
   c. £2,000
   d. £13,000
   e. £10,000

2. A company has purchased goods during the financial year for £120,000. The trades payable on the balance sheet have increased by £40,000. How much cash was paid out?
   a. £40,000
   b. £160,000
   c. £80,000
   d. £120,000
   e. £90,000

3. What are the three classifications identified in IAS 7 "Statement of Cash Flows"?

4. How does IAS 7 define short-term investments?

5. Which two methods does the standard allow for disclosing operating activities?

6. Why are the profit figures and cash amounts for a company usually different?

7. What are the two methods a company can use for disclosing operating activities?

8. Explain the two methods a company can use to disclose cash movements?

Chapter 5

Statement of Financial Position

Structure of Chapter 5

Section title	Main content
IAS 1 Structure and substance	The statement shows the assets at the end of the financial period "balanced" by the total liabilities and shareholders' capital.
IAS 16 Property, Plant and Equipment	Accounting for property, plant and equipment.
IAS 36 Impairment of assets	IAS 36 applies to both tangible and intangible non-current assets and explains that the carrying amount is determined by the depreciation.
The cash-generating unit	This is a group of assets that generates cash inflows mostly independent of the cash flows from other assets or groups of assets. The standard provides guidance for specific difficulties.
IAS 38 Intangible assets	This describes the intangible assets that can appear on a balance sheet and their accounting treatment.
Total equity	Overview of all the components of the statement of financial position.
Chapter Review	The above items identify those assets that are of value to the company.

The previous title of the statement of financial position was "balance sheet" and that term is frequently still used. Although the statements can be complex, the main purpose is to show the relationship between the assets, liabilities and capital of a business, and the "balance" is shown as follows:

Total of Fixed Assets + Current Assets = Total of Liabilities + Capital

We will be looking more closely at statements of financial position in this chapter but a note of caution. The decision of the IASB to rename the balance sheet to the statement of financial position is questionable. The term "financial position" may be interpreted by the reader to mean that the current value of the assets of the company is shown on the statement. That is not the case. The statement mainly captures what has happened in the past and is not necessarily an indication of what is the present financial position of the company.

For example, the statement of financial position may show the assets of the company, such as land, building and machinery. The figure for the land and buildings usually will be the amount that was paid originally. If the land was purchased some 20 years ago, you are looking at the amount paid at that time although one would suppose that its value has increased substantially. Even the current value of buildings is likely to be considerably higher than shown on the statement of financial position. Also, machinery will have been depreciated over the years, so the amount shown on the balance sheet will be lower than the original cost. However, this is unlikely to be its current value. Accountants usually refer to the amount as the Written-Down Value (WDV).

The balance sheet, despite the name change, remains as an output from the double-entry bookkeeping system. If you record every transaction using double-entry bookkeeping, it is inevitable that all the debit entries will add to the same amount as the credit entries.

A major part of the balance sheet is non-current assets. These are items held by the entity to generate future benefits. This can include tangible assets, such as property, equipment, machinery and vehicles, as well as intangible non-current assets, such as patents and goodwill. To contribute towards the balance, we have equity in the form of share capital and reserves and non-current liabilities including bonds. We will explain these amounts later in this chapter. At this stage, we take a brief look at the value of the assets held by some companies. The following note is from the annual report of GlaxoSmithKline plc for 2021. You will note that the statement states that the property, plant and equipment have a net book value of *£9,932 million.* This is not what it costs or what it is worth now on the open market. It is the initial cost less the depreciation which has been charged in past years. The word "value" could be misleading, but the identifier is **net book** value.

The total cost of our property, plant and equipment at 31 December 2021 was £20,778 million, with a net book value of £9,932 million. Of this, land and buildings represented £3,667 million, plant and equipment £4,558 million and assets in construction £1,707 million. In 2021, we invested £1,205 million in new property, plant and equipment. This was mainly related to a large number of projects for the renewal, improvement and expansion of facilities at various worldwide sites to support new product development and launches as well as to improve the efficiency of existing supply chains. Property is mainly held freehold. New investment is financed from our liquid resources. At 31 December 2021, we had contractual commitments for future capital expenditure of £616 million. We believe that our property and plant facilities are adequate for our current needs.

For many companies, when we are examining non-current assets, the amounts are substantial. However, the financial amounts shown on the Statement of Financial Position do not necessarily give any guide to the present value of non-current assets. There have been attempts to construct accounting regulations that would require companies to show the current values of non-current assets. These have failed and there are no indications that the issue will be re-examined.

IAS 1 Structure and Substance

The basic content and structure of a statement of financial position, previously known as the balance sheet, are very simple. It is the recognition of the total of all the assets and liabilities that a company has at the end of the financial period and the "equity" or "capital" which represents the shareholders' interest. The formula is Assets = Liabilities + Capital. As all the information comes from the current financial records that are based on the principles of the double-entry system of bookkeeping, it is easy to understand why the term balance sheet was originally used. For every business transaction, we record the transaction both as an asset and a liability. You purchase materials for £1,000 which is a debit to that account and there is a credit of the same amount to the cash account. Not surprisingly, at the year end, the total of the assets should equal the total of the liabilities, that is, they balance!

Although the term balance sheet is still frequently used, the correct term to use now is the statement of financial position. The information required by the standard is as follows:

a. property, plant and equipment,
b. investment property,
c. intangible assets,
d. financial assets,
e. investments accounted for using the equity method,
f. biological assets,
g. inventories,
h. trade and other receivables,
i. cash and cash equivalents,
j. the total assets classified as held for sale and assets included in disposal groups classified as held for sale,
k. trade and other payables,
l. provisions,
m. financial liabilities (excluding amounts shown under (k) and (l)),
n. liabilities and assets for current tax,
o. deferred tax liabilities and deferred tax assets,
p. liabilities included in disposal groups classified as held for sale,
q. non-controlling interests, presented within equity,
r. issued capital and reserves attributable to owners of the parent.

This is a somewhat bewildering array of items. Entities can also include additional line items, headings and subtotals when such presentation is relevant to an understanding of their financial position. The bad news for students is that most of these items have their own financial reporting standards. There is no particular format for the statement of financial position, and entities usually use a format with headings and subtotals based on the accounting equation or a variation. The very basic accounting equation is Assets = Capital + Liabilities and a simplified typical format for a statement of financial position is as follows:

Partial Statement of Financial Position as at ....

Assets	£	£
Non-current assets	50	
Current assets	30	
Total assets		80
Liabilities		
Current liabilities	20	
Non-current liabilities	25	
Total liabilities		45
Net assets		**35**

The above is a simple example and the purpose is to demonstrate the relationship between the values and this would not be the formal statement. In the following diagram, we take the example from Sainsbury's plc annual report 2022. We are only taking a small part of the statement of financial position for one year to demonstrate that assets minus liabilities equals equity. Note that the amounts shown in the following are in **£m**:

	2022	**2021**	**2020**
Non-current assets	20,162	18,089	20,351
Current assets	6,742	7147	7,582
Assets held for sale	8	24	4
Total assets	26,912	25,260	27,937
Net current liabilities	(3,118)	(4,658)	(4,464)
Non-current liabilities	(171)	(150)	(68)
Total liabilities	(18,489)	(18,559)	(20,146)
Net assets	8,423	6,701	7,791
Equity	8,423	6,701	7,791

We have extracted the above figures from a very lengthy annual report to demonstrate that even with very large amounts, the total assets £26,912 million less total liabilities £18,489 million equals the amount for equity £8,423 million. If you had any doubts that keeping accounting records and the accounting equation told us little about profit at the year end, the above example should encourage you to practice your double-entry bookkeeping!

IAS 16 Property, Plant and Equipment (PPE)

The objective of IAS 16 is to set out the accounting treatment for most types of PPE. Non-current assets should be recognised

- if it is probable that there will be future economic benefits and
- if the cost of the item can be measured reliably.

One particular feature of IAS 16 is the requirement for measurement to be originally at cost, but subsequently, the asset can be carried at either cost or a revalued amount. The revalued amount arises where a company considers the carrying amount of an asset shown in the balance sheet to be misleading. In practice, the great majority of entities use cost, but it is important to remember that revaluation of the non-current assets is an option.

Companies are usually very clear on their policies in respect of PPE and we show a small portion of the detailed information on the expected life of assets from the 2020/2021 annual report of Jaguar Land Rover Automotive plc.

Company example

Property, plant and equipment is stated at cost of acquisition or construction less accumulated depreciation and accumulated impairment, if any. Land is not depreciated. Cost includes purchase price, non-recoverable taxes and duties, labour cost and direct overheads for self-constructed assets and other direct costs incurred up to the date the asset is ready for its intended use. Interest cost incurred for constructed assets is capitalised up to the date the asset is ready for its intended use, based on borrowings incurred specifically for financing the asset or the weighted average rate of all other borrowings, if no specific borrowings have been incurred for the asset. Depreciation is charged on a straight-line basis over the estimated useful lives of the assets. Estimated useful lives of the assets are as follows:

Class of property, plant and equipment	**Estimated useful life (years)**
Buildings	20 to 40
Plant, equipment and leased assets	3 to 30
Vehicles	3 to 10
Computers	3 to 6
Fixtures and fittings	3 to 20

The above example is only a very small part of a comprehensive and useful annual report issued by the company. In the same annual report, it also shows its full statement of financial position and the total value in £ millions.

We now examine the requirements of IAS 16 Property, Plant and Equipment.

Measurement at cost

There are two categories of cost:

1. initial costs incurred to acquire or construct an item of property, plant and equipment to bring it to working condition for its intended use,
2. subsequent costs for additions to the original property, plant and equipment or to replace part of it.

Examples of cost for items of PPE are as follows:

- Land — purchase price, legal fees and preparation of site for intended use.
- Buildings — purchase price and costs incurred in putting the buildings in a condition for use.
- Plant and machinery — purchase price, transport and installation costs, testing costs.

Abnormal costs such as rectifying installation errors, design errors, wastage and idle capacity are not part of the original cost of the asset and they should be charged to the profit or loss account for the financial period in which they occurred.

Although the item of property, plant and equipment is ready for use, some subsequent costs related to the asset may be incurred. These subsequent costs should be charged to the profit or loss account. An entity cannot add the following to the carrying amount of the item:

- Initial operating losses, if any. For example, an entity may not be enjoying economic benefits until it achieves a certain level of production. The losses it initially makes cannot be capitalised.
- Costs incurred while waiting to bring the item into full use. For example, a hotel may be ready for opening but incurs security costs until the first guests arrive.
- Costs incurred in relocating or reorganising part or all of an entity's operations. For example, a factory may be reorganised to move some heavy machinery so that it fits better into the production flow. This cost cannot be added to the value of the machinery.
- Incidental operations that are not relevant to an item being in the location and condition for operations. For example, with the introduction of new machinery, a company may decide to move its storage facilities of raw materials. It cannot add this cost to the cost of the new machinery.

With some items, it is possible that when the activity has reached the end of its useful economic life, the entity will be obliged to dismantle and restore the site occupied to its original state. These expected future costs can be included in the original cost of the asset.

During the life of a non-current asset, it is possible that some parts need replacement. In this case, we are considering substantial replacements and not routine servicing and upkeep. For example, the heating system of a factory, the power trains for machinery and the interior fittings and equipment in buildings. In these cases, the entity recognises the full cost of the replacement as an addition to the carrying amount of the original non-current asset. It will depreciate the replacement part over its expected useful life. This may be different from other components of the asset.

Revaluation

IAS 16 permits the revaluation of non-current assets. This is a significant departure from the long-established measurement method of historical cost. The argument for introducing revaluations is that it provides more useful information to the users of financial statements. Whether a revaluation should take place is at the discretion of management. They decide whether to revalue, when to revalue and, with some restrictions, which assets to revalue.

One might suppose that where an asset has increased in value, an entity would be keen to demonstrate this. It would reveal financial strength, an ability to meet claims and, possibly, prevent a hostile takeover. However, relatively few entities use the option in IAS 16 to revalue some of their assets. There are reasons for this. First, by revaluing their assets, the ratio known *as return on assets* declines which is not the type of message to give to shareholders. The users might interpret this as a decline in company performance. Second, the revalued asset has to be depreciated over its useful economic life. The revaluation is likely to result in an increased depreciation charge in the statement of comprehensive income. This could have a negative effect on profits.

A further reason for entities not rushing to revalue assets is that the regulations are very strict as detailed in the following:

- Revaluations should be carried out regularly so that the carrying amount of an asset does not differ materially from its fair value at the balance sheet date.
- All assets in an entire class must be revalued and not a single item. A class of property, plant and equipment is a grouping of assets of a similar nature and use in an entity's operations. Examples are buildings, machinery, motor vehicles, furniture and fixtures. An entity must revalue all buildings and not only a few.
- Increases in revaluation value should be credited to equity under the heading of "revaluation surplus". If the increase is a reversal of a revaluation decrease of the same asset previously recognised as an expense, it should be recognised as income.
- Decreases as a result of a revaluation should be recognised as an expense to the extent it exceeds any amount previously credited to the revaluation surplus relating to the same asset.
- Disposal of revalued assets can lead to a revaluation surplus which may be either transferred directly to retained earnings or it may be left in equity under the heading "revaluation surplus".
- The revaluation model can only be used if the fair value of the item can be measured reliably.

The requirement to review revaluations regularly can occur annually or at least when there are indications that there have been changes in the prices in the market. Each class of assets must be revalued to prevent what is known as "cherry picking" i.e. the revaluation of only those particular assets in a class which have increased in value and excluding those in a class which have not increased in value.

Where fixed assets are revalued, this comes within the scope of IFRS 13 *Fair Value Measurements* both in terms of measurement and disclosure. Despite the work required to conduct a revaluation, some companies do so. They may use revaluations where there are borrowing constraints. By increasing the value of their assets, they appear richer and more able to secure a loan.

The revaluation of an asset impacts directly the accounting equation of Assets − Liabilities = Capital. Although there is no "profit" as the asset has not been sold, the increase is credited to comprehensive income. The increase appears on the balance sheet under equity with the heading "Revaluation surplus". The following example demonstrates this.

Revaluation example

Pitfall Co. owns land originally purchased for £150,000. The Board believes that a rival company intends to launch a hostile bid. To deter this action, it decides to use the regulations in IAS 16 that permit revaluations. The work is carried out and the revaluation figure is £180,000.

The accounting actions are as follows. The land is shown at the revalued amount of UK £180,000 on the balance sheet. There is a difference between the original cost and the revaluation amount of £30,000 which needs to be explained. This balance of £30,000 goes to the Statement of Comprehensive Income as a revaluation surplus. This example demonstrates that you must read financial statements and the notes that accompany them with care. The above example will result in the Statement of Comprehensive Income looking better by £30,000 and some readers of the financial statements may not be aware of the regulations on IAS 16.

Derecognition of assets

After the initial recognition and measurement of the asset, the final stage of derecognition comes. This occurs either at the end of the life of the asset, when it is disposed of, or when there are no expected future benefits to be gained from retaining the asset. Assets are derecognised by the removal of all or part of a previously recognised asset or liability from an entity's statement of financial position. The gain or loss from the sale or disposal of the asset is the difference between the net disposal proceeds, if any, and the carrying amount of the item. When the item is derecognised, the gain or loss arising from the derecognition goes to profit or loss. Although the company may sell the unwanted asset, gains on derecognition cannot be classified as revenue on the Income Statement.

Worked example: Gains and losses on derecognition

A company purchases equipment for £12,000. It considers it has a residual value of £2,000 and a useful economic life of 10 years. At the end of the 10 years, the company is able to sell the equipment for £2,800 but it incurs £300 costs in delivering it to the purchaser. The Production Manager suggests that the £2,800 be shown as revenue and the £300 as additional depreciation.

The accountant explains that **net** disposal proceeds of £500 must be shown on the profit or loss account as a gain on disposal. As the residual value of the asset is £2,000, the maximum gain could only be the difference between that amount and the selling price of £2,800. The standard states that the **net** disposal proceeds only can be shown as a gain. Thus, the £300 delivery costs must be deducted from the £800 to give the gain of £500. This transaction is not the method that is used to generate revenue and therefore cannot be included in that figure but must be shown separately.

IAS 36 Impairment of Assets

Impairment of an asset takes place if the carrying amount shown in the organisation's financial records is greater that the proceeds that would be received if the asset was retained in use or sold to an outside party. IAS 36 applies to both tangible and intangible non-current assets. For example, a company may have depreciated an asset over the years and the amount shown on the balance sheet is £18,000, that is, the "carrying amount". However, the company knows that the most it could obtain by selling the asset is £12,000 and even if it retains the asset, the most income it would generate from the "value in use" is £15,000. The value of the asset is impaired.

The above example is for one stand-alone asset but usually, there are several assets operating together to form the production unit and it is impossible to identify the fair value or value in use for any one item. In such circumstances, the calculation for impairment will be the cash-generating unit and not an individual item.

Indications of impairment

Entities must assess annually whether there has been an indication of impairment of all their assets. This could be a burden, but the keyword is "an indication of impairment". The process for ascertaining whether there has been impairment is in two stages. The first stage is assessing whether there are any indications of possible impairment. The indications can be external or internal and are as follows:

External indications

- an abnormal fall in the asset's market value,
- a significant change in the technological, market, legal or economic environment of the business in which the assets are used,
- an increase in market interest rates or market rates of return on investments likely to affect the discount rates in calculating the value in use of the assets,
- the carrying value of the net assets being more than its market capitalisation.

Internal indications

- evidence of obsolescence, that is, going out of date or physical damage,
- adverse changes in the use to which the asset is put,
- the asset's economic performance.

If there are no indications of impairment, no action is required, but, in addition to the indication assessment, there are certain assets where a full impairment assessment is required annually. The assets for the full test are as follows:

- intangible assets with indefinite lives. This is any intangible asset not being amortised over a set time,
- intangible assets not ready for use,
- goodwill arising through a business combination.

A company must go to the second stage of the impairment test for the above three classes of assets and do the same with those assets where there are indications of impairment.

Calculating impairment

The second stage involves calculating the recoverable amount of the asset and comparing it to its carrying amount in the balance sheet. The recoverable amount is the higher fair value less costs to sell and "value in use". The two terms "fair value" and "value in use" are defined in the standard as follows:

Definition: Fair value
Fair value is the price that would be received to sell an asset or paid to transfer a liability in an orderly transaction between market participants at the measurement date.

Definition: Value in use
This is the present value of the future cash flows expected to be derived from an asset or cash-generating unit. The two steps required to determine the value in use of an asset are as follows:

- Estimate the future cash flows anticipated over the remaining life of the asset. This is the cash flow forecast for the one asset. The company has to determine the cash inflows and cash outflows for which asset to find the cash surplus or deficit each year for its remaining years of use.
- The next stage is to calculate the present value of those cash surpluses and deficits. To do this, a discount rate is applied to those cash flows and the present value of those future cash amounts is calculated.

To calculate the possibility of impairment, the procedure to follow is given in the following:

1. Compare the recoverable amount to the carrying amount of the asset on the balance sheet.
2. If the carrying amount on the balance sheet is higher than the recoverable amount, the asset is impaired.
3. The amount of impairment is a charge to the profit or loss account and the carrying amount on the balance sheet is reduced.

Although the amount of work required to identify the various elements is significant, the principles are simple. The recoverable amount is either

- the estimated amount to be received if the asset is sold (fair value) or
- the discounted future cash flows if the asset is retained (value in use).

The business logic is that you would choose the highest fair value or value in use.

For many companies, a significant part of the assets they own is governed by IAS 16 which establishes the accounting treatment for most types of property, plant and equipment. These are intended to be used by the organisation for more than one financial period, and therefore they are non-current assets which should be recognised if the cost of the item can be measured reliably. One particular feature of the standard is the requirement for measurement to be originally at cost, but subsequently, the asset can be carried at either cost or a revalued amount.

With measurement at cost, there are two categories of cost:

1. initial costs that are incurred to acquire or construct an item of PPE and to bring it to working condition for its intended use,
2. subsequent costs for additions to the original PPE or to replace part of it. Service costs that improve the asset leading to additional economic benefits can be recognised but not normal servicing costs. For example, a major overhaul of a piece of machinery to obtain greater efficiency would lead to economic benefits. The cost of the major overhaul can be capitalised.

Examples of the total cost for acquired items of PPE are as follows:

- Land — Purchase price, legal fees and preparation of site for intended use.
- Buildings — Purchase price and costs incurred in putting the buildings in a condition for use.
- Plant and machinery — Purchase price, transport and installation costs, testing costs

There are some costs that cannot be added to the original cost of the item. Examples are rectifying installation errors, design errors, wastage and idle capacity, and these should be charged to the profit or loss account. Essentially, the standard requires a company to charge to the profit and loss account any damage it has caused through its operations.

During the life of a non-current asset, it is possible that some parts need replacement. In this case, we are considering substantial replacements and not routine servicing and upkeep. Examples of substantial replacements are the heating system of a factory, the power trains for machinery and the interior fittings and equipment in buildings. In these cases, the entity recognises the full cost of the replacement as an addition to the carrying amount of the original non-current asset. It will depreciate the replacement part over its expected useful life. This could be different from other components of the asset. The argument for introducing revaluations was that the statement of financial position would provide more valuable information to the users of financial statements. The concerns, both of the preparers and users of financial statements, were the amount of work that would be required and the reliability of the revaluation.

There is the possibility that where an asset has increased in value, an entity would be keen to demonstrate this. It would reveal its financial strength and an ability to meet claims and, possibly, prevent a hostile takeover. However, relatively, few entities use the option to revalue some of their assets. There are three possible reasons for this and these are as follows:

1. By revaluing their assets, the ratio known as return on assets declines, and users might interpret this as a decline in company performance.
2. The revalued asset has to be depreciated over its useful economic life. The revaluation is likely to result in an increased depreciation charge. This could have a negative effect on profits.

3. If an entity decides to revalue assets, it must comply with some very complex regulations that are detailed in the standard.

Where an asset has decreased in value, this is accounted for as an expense in the profit or loss account if there has been no previous revaluation upwards. Any subsequent revaluation downwards can be offset against any previous upwards increase in value of the same asset.

The other question is the estimate of the residual value of the asset at the end of its useful economic life. Once again, the entity decides the anticipated useful life of assets on an annual basis. An increase in the economic life has several implications for the user of the accounts. The first concern is how long the useful economic life is in reality. Second, the carrying amount in the balance sheet reduces at a slower rate annually as the asset is depreciated over a longer time. Third, the annual charge to the profit or loss account will be smaller, thus enhancing the profit. It is critical for the user to understand the following: What period an entity sets for the useful lives of assets, and how this is reassessed? If there is inflation, should this be accounted for in the residual value estimate?

Derecognition of assets

After the initial recognition and measurement of the asset, the final stage is derecognition. This occurs at the end of the life of the asset either when it is disposed of or when there are no expected future benefits. The gain or loss from the sale or disposal of the asset is the difference between the net disposal proceeds, if any, and the carrying amount of the item. When the item is derecognised, the gain or loss arising from the derecognition goes to the profit or loss account. Although the company may sell the unwanted asset, gains on derecognition cannot be classified as revenue on the income statement.

Impairment of an asset takes place if the carrying amount shown in the organisation's financial records is greater that the proceeds that would be received if the asset was retained in use or sold to an outside party. IAS 36 applies to both tangible and intangible non-current assets. For example, a company may have depreciated an asset over the years and the amount shown on the balance sheet is £18,000, that is, the "carrying amount". However, the company knows that the most it could obtain by selling the asset is £12,000, and even if it retains the asset, the most income it would generate from the "value in use" is £15,000. The value of the asset is impaired.

The above example is for one stand-alone asset, but usually, there are several assets operating together to form the production unit and it is impossible to identify the fair value or value in use for any one item. In such circumstances, the calculation for impairment will be the cash-generating unit and not an individual item.

The Cash-Generating Unit

A cash-generating unit is regarded as a group of assets that generates cash inflows mostly independent of the cash flows from other assets or groups of assets. Unfortunately, identifying a CGU can present problems in some industries. The standard provides several illustrative examples ranging from retail store chains to single product entities which provides helpful guidance for specific difficulties.

In most instances, the CGU will consist of tangible non-current assets, such as property, plant and equipment. The procedure for the CGU is the same as we have described above:

1. Calculate the fair value and value in use.
2. Compare them and the highest figure is the recoverable amount.
3. If this is lower than the carrying amount shown in the balance sheet, the asset is impaired. This impairment loss is an expense in the profit or loss account. This reduces the carrying amount on the balance sheet.

It is possible that the CGU will also consist of acquired goodwill. In this case, the fair value and the value in use are still calculated. If the recoverable amount of the CGU is higher than the carrying amount of the CGU as shown in the balance sheet, the unit and the goodwill allocated to the unit are not impaired and no action is required. However, if there is an impairment, the procedure is as follows:

1. Charge the entire impairment loss to the goodwill if it is sufficient. If the goodwill is insufficient to absorb the entire impairment loss, allocate the balance over the other CGU.
2. Assets in proportion to the carrying amount of each asset.

The cautious approach of the IASB to accounting for goodwill is apparent where, due to subsequent market improvement, the CGU is no longer impaired. In other words, the new carrying amount shown in the balance sheet is now less than the present recoverable amount. The standard allows the company to reverse the impairment but with two restrictions:

1. There can be no reversal of the impairment for goodwill. In other words, it cannot be placed back on the balance sheet.
2. The reversal on other assets is limited to their original carrying value. You cannot increase to the higher recoverable value.

The application of these rules is shown in following worked example:
The recoverable amount is £350,000.
Reversing impairment loss

	Pre-impairment £000	**Post-impairment £000**	**Reversal £000**	**Post-reversal £000**
Goodwill	60	—	—	—
Property	180	162	18	180
Machinery	120	108	12	120
	360	270	30	300

The new recoverable amount of the CGU is £350,000, but we have only increased the carrying amount in the balance sheet to £300,000. There is no reversal of goodwill and the other assets are reversed only to their pre-impairment value. A revaluation has not taken place to provide the users with up-to-date information.

The non-reversal of goodwill has been a controversial matter. The IASB's opinion was that an entity would need to calculate whether the subsequent increase in the recoverable amount of goodwill was attributable to the recovery of the acquired goodwill or an increase in the internally generated goodwill within the unit. Of course, there is no recognition of internally generated goodwill. The Board concluded that it was highly unlikely that such a calculation would be possible and, therefore, there is a prohibition for reversals of goodwill impairment losses.

The standard for impairment is now fully established, although the asset of goodwill is likely to continue to be debated.

IAS 38 Intangible Assets

IAS 38 *Intangible Assets* describes the intangible assets that can appear on a balance sheet and their accounting treatment. The definition of an intangible asset is an identifiable non-monetary asset without physical substance. Examples of intangible assets are brand rights and reputation, relationships and goodwill. One issue is the identification of such assets as the definition states that they have no "physical substance". Even where the intangible asset is identified, there are questions on the value of the asset. An intangible asset can lose value. Brand names are intangible assets and may generate sales for products, but what if there is an occurrence that impairs the brand name? We may buy certain food products or medications because the company has a good "reputation". A government investigation that casts doubt on the safety of the item could negatively affect sales.

Increasingly, entities have found that their most important assets for generating future benefits are not physical assets, such as buildings and machinery, but assets that have no physical substance. For example, in 2014, American Airlines paid £18.2 million for a pair of landing slots at Heathrow Airport, UK (*Sunday Times*, 22 June 2014). This gives the airline the right to take off and land at certain times. Other examples of intangible assets are as follows:

- broadcast rights,
- computer software,
- customer lists,
- drilling rights,
- franchise agreements,
- Internet domain names,
- licensing agreements,
- literary works,
- motion pictures and television programs,
- musical works,
- patented technology,
- service contracts,
- trademarks.

Other items not on the list can be a benefit to the entity. Possibly, the main one is "reputation". This may be due to highly trained employees, excellent products and a high degree of customer satisfaction.

The purpose of the standard is to set out the accounting requirements for intangible assets. These are defined as assets which are without physical substance and identifiable (either being separable or arising from contractual or other legal rights). Intangible assets must satisfy the criteria for any asset to be recognised which are that the future economic benefits must be expected and the asset can be measured reliably. The requirement of reliable measurement can prevent the recognition of some intangible assets. Reliable measurement means that the asset

- can be separated from the rest of the company,
- can be sold, licensed, rented or exchanged either individually or together with a related item.

The intangible asset can also be identifiable because it arises from contractual or legal rights even if those rights are not separable from the business.

An entity may generate an intangible asset itself or acquire it from another entity. Because of the necessity of reliable measurement, the standard has different requirements for acquired intangible assets and self-generated. Acquired intangible assets are measured by the price paid. The assumption is that the asset is acquired because there are anticipated future benefits. The regulations are more complex for self-generated intangible assets and we discuss these later in this chapter.

Acquired intangible assets

Recognition

The acquisition of the asset from another party can take place in three ways and this will determine the measurement criteria:

1. The intangible asset is acquired by payment to another party. As the transaction is between willing parties, the purchase price is the fair value.
2. The entity acquires an asset by exchanging another for it. As there is no "purchase price", the asset is measured at fair value as defined in IFRS 13. Fair value is the price that would be received to sell an asset or paid to transfer a liability in an orderly transaction between market

participants at the measurement date. This term is explained at greater length in IFRS 13 discussed in Chapter 9. Where it is not possible to ascertain the fair value, the asset is measured at the carrying amount of the asset given up.

3. The intangible asset is acquired in the course of taking over another business: a business combination. In these circumstances, recognition is at fair value.

Measurement

As with tangible assets, an entity has a choice of measurement methods. Disclosure on the balance sheet can be at either

- cost less any accumulated amortisation and impairment losses or
- a revalued amount (based on fair value) less any subsequent amortisation and any accumulated impairment losses. This method cannot be used at initial recognition.

Cost should be easy to identify from the transaction itself. The standard specifies those components of cost that can be recognised. There are certain items that cannot be included in the original cost and these are as follows:

- administration costs,
- costs of introducing new products or services,
- costs of conducting new business,
- costs incurred while waiting to use the asset,
- initial operating losses from operation.

Internally generated intangible assets

Recognition

Entities cannot recognise certain internally generated intangible assets, such as goodwill, brands and publishing titles. There are several products with well-known brand names, but these do not appear on their balance sheets. The reason is that they are internally generated and it is highly doubtful if their value can be measured reliably.

Although these particular intangibles should not be recognised if internally generated, they may meet the general recognition criteria if purchased from another company. This does lead to the somewhat bewildering position where the financial statements of some entities do not show their world-renowned brands on their balance sheet which therefore means that users of financial statements may not realise the value of these brands. If the brand had been acquired from another entity, it could be shown on the purchaser's balance sheet.

There is some scope in IAS 38 to recognise on the balance sheet development costs that have been incurred but not research costs. Expenditure on research must be charged to the Income Statement in the financial period in which it occurs and includes such costs as follows:

- the pursuit of new knowledge,
- the search for, or evaluation, and selection of applications of research,
- the search for such items as alternative materials, products and systems,
- the pursuit of possible alternatives for improved such items as materials, products and systems.

For the recognition of development costs on the balance sheet, it must be possible to separate them from the research phase. The expenditure for the development phase can only be capitalised if the following criteria are met:

- the technical feasibility of completing the asset so that it will be ready for sale or use,
- the intention to complete the asset and sell it or use it,
- the ability to use or sell the asset,
- that the asset will generate future economic benefits for the company,
- the availability of sufficient technical, financial and other resources to complete the development of the asset,
- the ability to be able to measure reliably the costs of development.

The transition from a research phase to a development phase may be difficult to identify or may not even occur. Many research projects are started but later abandoned as the results do not look promising. If the research is successful, the project will enter into a development phase. Usually, a business plan is required to prove that a project has entered into the development phase. The fact that the project is successful does not allow the company to go back and capitalise the research costs. They must be written off as they are incurred.

Measurement

There are varieties of possible methods for measuring an intangible asset. These approaches are as follows:

- It remains on the balance sheet unchanged until some event occurs which makes it no longer an asset. In other words, it is unable to generate future benefits.
- It can be depreciated, as with tangible assets, over its useful economic life.
- It can be depreciated over an arbitrary period of time established by the standard setters.

There are different opinions on which is the best method. Some argue that intangible assets rarely lose their value. They point to famous brand names that have been in existence for over 100 years as evidence. Others argue that nothing in this world has an indefinite life. The life may be unknown but nothing lasts forever.

In the absence of an international standard, countries adopted various approaches over the years. Accepting that nothing lasts forever, the method of depreciation over an arbitrary time has possibly been the most popular method for accounting for intangible assets. The term amortisation usually replaces the term depreciation.

Critics have argued that this was nonsense, as nobody knew the life of the intangible asset. If it was depreciated to zero, the company may still be generating sales from the asset, brand names being a good example. The user would have considerable difficulty in assessing a company where profits were being generated with no assets. After considerable debate, IAS 38 establishes an alternative approach that seems to be effective. There are two different situations specified:

1. Where intangible assets are similar to tangible assets. The process is the same as we discussed for tangible assets and companies can select the most appropriate method. As with tangible assets, the IASB does not allow a revenue-based method.

2. An intangible asset cannot have an infinite life only an indefinite one. If a company is unable to estimate the useful economic life, the standard requires testing of the asset for impairment annually. The requirements of IAS 36 Impairment of Assets apply.

Possibly, a good example of intangible assets is connected to the film industry. The following example shows an extract from Cineworld Group plc. The group is one of UK's leading cinema chains by Box Office revenues and provides a choice of how to watch a movie.

Non-current assets	**Dollars million**
Property, plant and equipment	2,039.5
Right-of-use assets	3,441.2
Goodwill	5,492.1
Other intangible assets	515.6

The above extract was taken from their annual report and the auditors were PricewaterhouseCoopers LLP Chartered Accountants and Statutory Auditors London. They state in their opinion the following:

We conducted our audit in accordance with International Standards on Auditing (UK) ("ISAs (UK)") and applicable law. Our responsibilities under ISAs (UK) are further described in the Auditors' responsibilities for the audit of the financial statements section of our report. We believe that the audit evidence we have obtained is sufficient and appropriate to provide a basis for our opinion. Independence We remained independent of the group in accordance with the ethical requirements that are relevant to our audit of the financial statements in the UK, which includes the FRC's Ethical Standard, as applicable to listed public interest entities, and we have fulfilled our other ethical responsibilities in accordance with these requirements.

Given the completeness of the company's annual report and the Auditor's statement, we could feel confident that we have an "accurate picture" of the company. However, whatever the diligence and ability of the company accountants and auditors, intangible assets do not last forever.

Some have such a long life that there is little concern, but some intangible assets gradually lose their financial power. With some intangibles that have a short life, you have to depreciate or amortise them. This can only be done if the intangible asset has a finite useful life and there are some intangibles that seem to last forever. Where companies amortise an intangible, they usually use the straight-line method. The calculation is as follows:

Amortisation Expense = (Initial Value − Residual Value)/Lifespan

To demonstrate how some companies tackle these issues, we show in the following two extracts from the annual report and accounts 2021 of Cineworld Group plc which we downloaded on the Internet. These give an extremely interesting and somewhat unusual insight into intangible assets that are accounted for by some companies:

> *Identifiable intangibles are those which can be sold separately or which arise from legal rights regardless of whether those rights are separable. Goodwill is stated at cost less any accumulated impairment losses. Goodwill is allocated to cash-generating units ("CGUs") and is not amortised but is tested annually for impairment. Other intangible assets that are acquired by the Group are stated at cost less accumulated amortisation and impairment losses. Distribution rights that are acquired by the Group are stated at cost less accumulated amortisation and impairment losses.*
>
> *Amortisation is charged to the Consolidated Statement of Profit or Loss on a straight-line basis over the estimated useful lives of intangible assets unless such lives are indefinite. Intangible assets with an indefinite useful life and goodwill are systematically tested for impairment at each Statement of Financial Position date. Other intangible assets are amortised from the date they are available for use. Distribution rights are amortised by film title from the date of release of the film, at 50% in the first year of release and 25% in each of the two subsequent years. The estimated useful lives are as follows: − Brands 10 years to indefinite life − Distribution rights 3 years − Other intangibles 4 to 10 year.*

Equity and non-current liabilities

The accounting equation compares assets with equity and non-current liabilities. The line items that fall under the heading of equity are share capital and reserves of various types. The examples of non-current liabilities are long-term borrowings, corporate income tax and provisions. One item that comes under non-current liabilities on most balance sheets is derivative financial instruments.

As with some other aspects of accounting, sometimes terminology can be fluid. This is particularly true in respect of both the words capital and equity that, sometimes, are used interchangeably. The word equity refers to the share capital and all reserves representing shareholders' total investment held by the entity. In other words, the assets minus all liabilities, both current and non-current. The term capital can refer to both the shareholders' investment and any long-term loans. You may see the term "share capital" meaning the shares purchased by the shareholders.

IAS 1 introduced a new financial statement in 2007 that relates to equity. The statement of changes in equity informs the users of financial statements of the factors that cause a change in the owners' equity over the accounting periods. This statement is of particular interest to shareholders wishing to assess the size of their financial interest in the entity.

Determining which items fall under the heading of equity is straightforward. When we consider liabilities, the division between current and non-current is less obvious than with assets. Some types of liability can fall into either category. IAS 1 differentiates by stating which liabilities are current. The basic points in identifying current liabilities are as follows:

1. The entity expects to settle the liability in its normal operating cycle. For example, your suppliers would expect payment promptly. In some industries, the normal operating cycle may exceed 12 months and may extend the recognition of current liabilities.
2. The entity holds the liability primarily for the purposes of trading.
3. The liability is due to be settled within 12 months after the reporting period. These liabilities are often related to large, long-term contracts. If the entity is able to defer payment of a liability later than the 12 months, that liability is non-current.

IAS 1 applies the default definition to identify non-current liabilities. If a liability does not meet the criteria as a current liability, it must be non-current. Fortunately, public limited companies are well aware of the detailed requirements of the standard and the classifications on their balance sheets are clear.

Equity

Using the word equity in its broadest sense to mean the "residual interest", the above definition follows the normal accounting equation, which applies because the value of the equity is on the balance sheet at its par value i.e. the face value of the shares. The balance sheet will balance. The balance sheet does not show the shares at their current market value. This needs to be emphasised as many of those investigating a company assume, wrongly, that the equity is shown at current market price. In some respects, the equity section on the balance sheet can be disappointing for most readers. You may find one that has unusual items, but most will be similar. Of course, the more familiar you are with the information normally published, the easier it is to spot the unusual ones.

As with all companies, the balance sheet provides summary information. You need to refer to the notes on the accounts to understand the separate elements. In this section, we will explain the most typical items coming under the heading of equity.

Definition — Share Capital: This is the amount that shareholders invest by purchasing shares from the issuing entity. The amount of share capital can increase if an entity issues new shares to the public in exchange for cash. Any price differences arising subsequently from price increases or decreases on the stock exchange are not reflected in the balance sheet.

Entities, generally, have two main types of shares: ordinary and preference. Ordinary shares are referred to as common stock in the US. The characteristics of the two types of shares are as follows:

Ordinary equity shares	Preference shares
Carry the main risk.	Usually, a fixed rate of dividend.
If there are no distributable profits, no dividend is paid.	Dividend is paid before any dividend to ordinary shareholders.
Holders of ordinary shares can vote at Annual General Meetings.	Preference shareholders have no voting powers.
Holders receive residual profit in the form of dividends after deduction of any fixed interest, preference dividend and tax.	Cumulative preference shares accrue the dividends if there are insufficient profits and pay them in a more successful year.

(*Continued*)

(*Continued*)

Ordinary equity shares	Preference shares
If entity stops trading, ordinary shareholders receive any net assets after creditors are paid.	Redeemable preference shares allow the entity to redeem the shares at a set future date and price.
Entities, usually, have a dividend policy that determines the share of profit paid to shareholders and the share of profit retained.	Convertible preference shares can be converted into ordinary shares at a set date and price.

You can come across shares that do not have all of these attributes. For example, there may be non-voting shares where the holders cannot vote at Annual General Meetings. Shares may be divided into type A shares and type B shares with differing rights and responsibilities. There can be a combination of the two types of shares in the form of convertible preferred shares. These allow the holder of the preference shares the option to convert them to ordinary shares at a particular date.

The terms of conversion for such shares specify the date when the conversion takes place and the conversion rate i.e. the number of ordinary shares exchanged for a specific number of convertible preference shares. The option to convert is normally that of the holder, although some entities may hold the right to compel a conversion.

Reserves

Definition: A part of the shareholders' equity excluding the amount of the basic share capital.

Reserves are an important part of equity. There are several types of reserves with their own conditions concerning their use. The following is a very small extract from the Annual Report and Accounts of 2012 pages for Whitbread PLC for the period 2020–2021. Each of the headings has a full explanation of the particular reserve:

Share premium reserve
Capital redemption reserve
Currency translation reserve
Treasury reserve

Merger reserve
Hedging reserve
Total other reserves

The reserves of an entity generally are of two types: distributable and non-distributable. The entity's own memorandum and articles can impose certain restrictions on the reserves that can be distributed to owners in the form of dividends. The main legal requirement is that retained earnings are distributable, but the following reserves are not.

Share premium reserve: This reserve arises when shares are issued at a price above their par value.

Capital redemption reserve: An entity can choose to buy back shares from its own shareholders. If it does, the entity must keep a reserve of similar value that cannot be paid to shareholders as dividends.

Merger reserve: This is a complex area. Merger relief, a provision of the Companies Act in the UK, permits entities to avoid creating a share premium account.

Retained earnings: Retained earnings are the accumulated net earnings not paid out as dividends, but kept by the entity. The entity may hold the earnings to reinvest them in assets that generate future profits or to decrease the amount of non-current liabilities, that is, pay back loans. A continuous growth in retained earnings can cause concerns. The shareholder is interested in whether the directors are using the reserves properly to improve the business. If not, an explanation is required from the directors on their intentions. Any future losses are deducted from the cumulative retained earnings. If this leads to a deficit, the term retained losses is used and there are some very unhappy shareholders.

Total Equity

The share capital amount added to the aggregation of all the reserves gives the shareholders equity. Non-controlling interests added give the total equity. The basic structure is as follows:

	£
Share capital	XX
Add Reserves	XX
Shareholders' equity	XX
Non-controlling interests	XX
Total Equity	XX

The total equity consists of the shareholders' equity i.e. the sum of the share capital and reserves, *plus,* the non-controlling interests that arise. The non-controlling interests are that part of the equity in a subsidiary that is not directly or indirectly attributable to a parent. For example, one entity may own 90% of the shares of another entity. The owners of the other 10% in that entity would have a non-controlling interest as they do not have sufficient power to influence decision-making.

Capital maintenance

Capital maintenance has two aspects: a legal one as included in the Companies Act 2006 and a conceptual one as discussed in the Conceptual Framework. We have already discussed some parts of the legal requirements. In this section, we expand on those. Our comments are concerned only with public limited companies.

The legal requirements for capital maintenance are to ensure that all creditors have some protection against shareholders withdrawing from the total shareholders' funds and leaving insufficient to pay creditors. The total shareholders' funds are the share capital, share premium and capital redemption reserve. To pay dividends to shareholders, first, an entity must have a distributable profit. Of course, a distribution of profits means paying out cash and an entity may wish to retain cash to maintain and expand the business and to pay creditors when the debt falls due. It is therefore unlikely to pay out all its distributable profit.

Bonds

A bond is a debt investment whereby an investor loans money to an entity. The funds are for a defined time. The entity must repay the loan at the end of the agreed period. There is a fixed interest rate on the bond. As with convertible shares, an entity may choose to issue convertible bonds. These give the holders the right to convert the bonds into ordinary shares. A convertible bond usually gives the holder a lower rate of interest than a non-convertible bond because there is the benefit of the holder having the right of conversion into shares. The lower rate of interest is of benefit to the entity, but the convertible bond is only attractive to holders if they consider that the entity is going to be profitable in the future.

One disadvantage of convertible bonds is that there will be a dilution for the existing ordinary shareholders. In other words, if the bondholders decide to convert to shares, there will be more shares on the market and more shareholders anticipating a portion of the profits. The impact of share dilution is explained when we discuss IAS 33 Earnings per Share in Chapter 10.

In the financial statements of some entities, you may see the term debenture. The debenture is a contract whereby the entity receives a loan for a specified period. It must pay a fixed interest on the debenture and that interest is chargeable against tax. As physical assets do not secure the debenture, the entity has to have a solid reputation for creditworthiness.

Derivative financial instruments

Definition: A derivative financial instrument is a contract where the value is derived from the performance of an underlying asset, index or interest rate. Derivative financial instruments include options, futures, forwards and swaps.

You are almost certain to find on the balance sheet of major entities a line item for derivative financial instruments. In our international economy, entities hold derivatives to minimise the risk of currency exchange rate fluctuations. Oil entities use them to hedge against or counteract the prospect of future price changes. Airlines use them to ensure favourable fuel prices. Manufacturers can avoid any sudden hikes in the cost of their inputs. The advantage of using derivatives is that the capital required upfront is minimal and the cost of transactions is low. Instead of having to buy and sell securities, derivatives mimic the performance of the underlying asset.

Entities normally take out insurance on their properties, vehicles and equipment to protect themselves from loss through fire, accidents and other calamities. Derivatives are also a way of guarding against loss. An entity's financial assets, for example, bonds, commodities and cash, change due to volatility in prices and interest rates. Derivatives offer protection.

From an accounting viewpoint, derivatives cause several problems. Namely, the question is how we value derivatives to place them on the balance sheet. There have been several years of discussion, but an acceptable solution seems to have been found. This required a complete overhaul of all the accounting standards that regulate financial instruments.

Provisions

Definition: A provision is a liability of uncertain timing or amount.

We examine derivatives more fully in Chapter 8 as standard IAS 37 regulates provisions. At this stage, we summarise the main points in the following:

- There must be a present obligation (legal or constructive).
- It must have arisen as a result of a past event.
- Payment is probable in order to settle the obligation.
- The amount can be estimated reliably.

The importance of provisions is such that they can affect both the profit and loss account and the balance sheet.

Conclusions

Non-current assets are relatively easy to understand as a company usually has a significant investment in property, plant and equipment and these are tangible. The regulations for accounting for these items are understandable and do not incur much variation. Even intangible assets can be discussed using familiar examples, such as brands.

For the student, there is a greater challenge in understanding equity and non-current liabilities because they are less easy to define simply and to give examples as with assets. Equity and non-current liabilities are, however, where the financing action is likely to be. The entity is using other people's money and there must be safeguards on the management of those funds. Capital maintenance is a key concept and the statement of equity provides information on the components leading to changes in equity.

Non-current liabilities can be difficult for the student because there is a range of such liabilities. Some have their own particular treatments and may be regulated by a specific accounting standard. In later chapters, we discuss the particular standards in detail.

Chapter Review

This chapter focuses on the accounting treatment for assets. Many companies have large amounts of finance invested in such items as property and machinery. IAS 1 sets out the approach to the subject and this is followed by specific standards for particular issues. For many companies, property, plant and equipment are major investments shown on the balance sheet and the correct accounting treatment is essential, and depreciation will be a large charge to the Income Statement. In conducting an analysis of financial statements, it should be borne in mind that amounts on the statement of financial position usually do not reflect current values. As far as property is concerned, if it was purchased several years ago, then the value shown on the balance sheet is likely to be far lower than the current value.

Possibly, the most difficult item to value on the balance sheet comes under the heading of Intangible Assets. The accounting standard setters have had several attempts to establish a standard that provides useful financial information but, in our opinion, have been unable to do so completely. However, intangible assets are increasingly playing an important part in some companies' financial activities. Some of these intangible assets may have a short life and others may significantly increase their value, if they were for sale in the open market. The question remains as to whether the present accounting regulations for intangible assets are providing the rigorous information that shareholders require.

CHAPTER 5 Statement of Financial Position

Review Questions

1. Which of the following assets does IAS 36 Impairment of Assets apply to?
   a. Current assets
   b. Assets held for sale
   c. Property plant and equipment
   d. Financial assets
2. Which of the following is NOT a specifically identifiable intangible asset?
   a. Patents
   b. Trademarks
   c. Goodwill
   d. Copyrights
3. What is the equation that is the basis of the Statement of Financial Position?
4. What are the two conditions that allow non-current assets to be recognised?
5. What are the two measures of cost under IAS 16 Property, Plant and Equipment?
6. Would a hotel that is ready for opening be able to capitalise security costs until the first guests arrive?
7. What is the definition of a cash-generating unit?
8. What is an intangible asset and what accounting action should be taken?

Chapter 6

Business Relationships

Structure of Chapter 6

Section title	Main content
UK Business	An explanation of the types of businesses in the UK. They are very similar to other countries with some differences.
IAS 28 Investments in associates and joint ventures	IAS 28 applies to all investments in associates with the following exceptions: Investments held by venture capital organisations or similar entities which are covered by IAS 39 which we explain in a later chapter.
IAS 27 Separate financial statements	This standard applies where an entity elects or is required to present separate financial statements accounting for investments in subsidiaries, joint ventures and associates.
IFRS 11 Joint arrangements	This standard applies to all parties that are part of a joint arrangement which may give rights to the assets, and obligations for the liabilities or the parties have rights to only the net assets.
IFRS 12 Disclosure of interest in other entities	The disclosures cover the nature of, and risks associated with, its interests in a subsidiary, a joint arrangement, an associate or an unconsolidated structured entity, and the effect on its financial position, financial performance and cash flows.

IAS 24 Related party disclosures	Companies must disclose any related party relationship as well as information on transactions and outstanding balances, as well as management personnel compensation.
Chapter Review	The review covers relationships with other companies that are financially important. This chapter identifies the types of relationships.

The business world can be complicated. You may purchase a product or receive a service from a company whose name is well known but that company may in turn be owned by another company. A "business" may be a totally separate entity, but it can also have financial connections with other businesses. You may regard it as a local "shop", but it is much more than that. For example, Tesco PLC is a British multinational grocery and general merchandise and is also the third-largest retailer in the world measured by gross revenues. In addition to being a "grocery store", it retails books, clothing, electronics, furniture, toys, petrol and software and also offers financial services, telecom and Internet services. It also has about 300,000 employees. When you have companies of that size and importance, identifying the financial information the company should disclose to shareholders and other interested parties raises complications.

In this chapter, we examine the different relationships that entities may have with each other that do not fall under the requirements of IFRS 3 Business Combinations and IFRS 10 Consolidated Accounts which we explain in the following chapter. There are several types of relationships and the five standards we discuss in this chapter have connections to each other. The business world and the relationships can be complicated and the standards issued address these issues.

The objectives of the standards are to identify the various types of business relationships that can exist and to establish the accounting regulations to address them. Both IAS 28 Investments in Associates and Joint Ventures and IFRS 11 Joint Arrangements concentrate on the types of relationships. IAS 27 Separate Financial Statements and IAS 12 Disclosure in Other Entities concentrate on the provision of information. We describe as a "mopping up" standard the final standard IAS 24 Related Party Disclosures. Essentially, if an entity is unable to define the relationship according to the requirements of IAS 28 *Investments in Associates and Joint Ventures*, the other entity becomes a related party. The standard explains the nature of related parties and the disclosures required.

UK Business

Before looking more closely at accounting standards in detail, it is valuable to explain the business structure in the UK. A Public Limited Company and its shares are traded on the stock exchange. It is the equivalent of a US publicly traded company that carries the term Inc. or corporation designation. The importance of PLCs to our way of living cannot be ignored. In addition to providing products and services, it has a major impact on employment and the environment in which we live. The main aspects of PLCs in the UK are as follows:

- PLC is a public limited company which can issue shares to the public.
- All of the companies listed on the London Stock Exchange are PLCs.
- Any retail investor may buy stock in a PLC.
- Unlike privately held companies, public companies must publish certain financial data and disclosures for the public at regular intervals.
- The financial statements must be audited.

The formal names of some familiar brands like Burberry and Shell include the suffix PLC. There are other types of businesses than PLCs in the UK and, as these do not need to comply with international accounting standards, it is useful to identify the types of business and their reporting responsibilities. Private companies can be owned by their founders, management or a group of private investors. Their shares are not quoted on the stock exchange and these companies do not follow international Financial Reporting Standards. However, after many years, the Financial Reporting Council in the UK decided that non-PLCs should provide certain financial information. Essentially, the FRC states that directors are required to prepare financial statements that give a true and fair view of the assets, liabilities and financial position of the company and its profit or loss (or income and expenditure) for the reporting period. The following accounting standards have been issued:

- FRS 100 Application of Financial Reporting Requirements,
- FRS 101 Reduced Reporting Requirements,
- FRS 102 The Financial Reporting Standard Applicable in the UK and the Republic of Ireland,
- 103 Insurance Contracts,
- FRS 104 Interim Financial Reporting,
- FRS 105 The Financial Reporting Standard applicable to the Micro-entities Regime.

Under UK company law, a private company (usually with the suffix "Ltd") may not offer its shares for sale to the public, although some large private companies issue their annual report and accounts which are available on the Internet. A company must deliver financial statements every year to Companies House. All companies must file annual accounts with Companies House, including dormant, that is, those not running a business and flat management companies which have few or no levels of middle management between staff and executives.

There are many very active private companies in the UK making a substantial contribution to the economy and the way we live. If we look at private companies with employees, there are about 1.5 million in the UK. One example is the William Hare Group which is family owned and has over 1,700 employees. The company has steel fabrication facilities at Bury, Wetherby, Scarborough, Wigan, Newport and Rotherham and in the United Arab Emirates. A Derby plant manufactures cold-formed steel components and engineered timber/hybrid structures. Another example is Virgin Atlantic Limited which is also a private company and in 2020, had over 7,000 employees. Of interest is the following report by Auditors which refers to FRS 101:

> *In our opinion the financial statements give a true and fair view of the state of the Group's and of the parent Company's affairs as at 31 December 2021 and of the Group's loss for the year then ended; the Group financial statements have been properly prepared in accordance with UK-adopted international accounting standards; the parent Company financial statements have been properly prepared in accordance with UK accounting standards, including FRS 101 Reduced*

Disclosure Framework; and the financial statements have been prepared in accordance with the requirements of the Companies Act 2006.

In addition to the companies, we also have many partnerships and sole traders in the UK. Owners of these construct financial statements for their own use. There are no regulations on the information they should contain, but the Inland Revenue will be very clear of the information it requires.

PLCs and the role of auditors

A very important aspect of preparing and issuing financial reports is the role of auditors. In the first year of a company, the directors will appoint auditors, but, in the following years, auditors are appointed by shareholders and are answerable to them. Remember, it is the shareholders who own the company. The main regulations apply to the appointment of auditors by public limited companies. Auditors are appointed at each annual general meeting. Their appointment usually holds until the close of the next annual general meeting. Usually, the same auditors will continue for each year unless the shareholders, for some reason, choose to vote for a change of auditors at the annual general meeting. There are several legal requirements on the role of the auditor, the main ones being the following:

- If, for some reason, there is a casual vacancy, the directors can appoint the auditors.
- If no auditor is appointed at the annual general meeting, the company can appoint an auditor until the next annual general meeting and fix the remuneration to be paid by the company for his services.
- The company must give notice in writing to an auditor of his appointment.
- Every company at a general meeting called for the purpose removes an auditor before the expiration of his term of office and appoints another auditor in his stead for the remainder of his term.
- The auditor must conduct an examination of the company and report the findings to the members at the Annual General meeting.
- If the auditor cannot give a favourable opinion, the reasons must be stated.
- The audit report is a lengthy document and we show in the following the main contents for Shell plc:

In our opinion, the financial statements of Shell plc (the Parent Company) and its subsidiaries (collectively, Shell or Group):

- *give a true and fair view of the state of Shell's and of the Parent Company's affairs as at December 31, 2021 and of Shell's income and the Parent Company's income for the year then ended;*
- *have been properly prepared in accordance with UK adopted international accounting standards and International Financial Reporting Standards (IFRS) as issued by the International Accounting Standards Board (IASB); and*
- *have been prepared in accordance with the requirements of the Companies Act 2006.*

Different relationships

In studying the detail of accounting standards, there is a temptation to assume that all possible eventualities have been addressed. This is not the case. Corporate relationships are complex and can be poorly described. It is not always easy for entities to decide which standard applies to a particular relationship with another business. It is also possible that particular relationships are not captured by a specific standard or are frequently changing. In 2002, the IASB commenced a comprehensive project to address inconsistencies in the existing regulations. The project reached the stage where, acting independently, the IASB split the project into two parts:

Part 1: Consolidation and Disclosure, resulting in IFRS 10 *Consolidated Financial Statements* and IFRS 12 *Disclosure of Interests in Other Entities* issued in 2011. We discuss this standard in the following chapter.

Part 2: Investment Entities, in 2012 produced *Investment Entities (Amendments to IFRS 10, IFRS 12 and IAS 27)* (effective 1 January 2014).

Concurrent with the issue of IFRS 10 and IFRS 12, the IASB also issued IFRS 11, *Joint Arrangements*, requiring a single method to account for interests in jointly controlled entities. Furthermore, the Board amended IAS 27 to retain guidance for separate financial statements and IAS 28

Investments in Associates and Joint Ventures, completing a new suite of consolidation standards. The introduction of new standards and the significant amendments to some existing standards changed the financial information being disclosed by companies. Before explaining the requirements of the standards, it is helpful to look at what companies are doing, and we show extracts from two major companies that comply with the relevant accounting standards.

Company examples

Accounting for the various relationships large companies enter into can cause headaches for companies and take up many pages of the notes in their annual report and accounts. We show in the following short extracts from two companies to demonstrate the complexities in practice.

AstraZeneca annual report and accounts 2021
Joint arrangements and associates. The Group has arrangements over which it has joint control and which qualify as joint operations or joint ventures under IFRS 11 'Joint Arrangements'. For joint operations, the Group recognizes its share of revenue that it earns from the joint operations and its share of expenses incurred. The Group also recognizes the assets associated with the joint operations that it controls and the liabilities it incurs under the joint arrangement. For joint ventures and associates, the Group recognizes its interest in the joint venture or associate as an investment and uses the equity method of accounting.

Unilever Annual Report and Accounts 2021
Joint ventures are undertakings in which the Group has an interest and which are jointly controlled by the Group and one or more other parties. Associates are undertakings where the Group has an investment in which it does not have control or joint control but can exercise significant influence. Interests in joint ventures and associates are accounted for using the equity method and are stated in the consolidated balance sheet at cost, adjusted for the movement in the Group's share of their net assets and liabilities. The Group's share of the profit or loss after tax of joint ventures and associates is included in the Group's consolidated profit before taxation. Where the Group's share of losses exceeds its interest in the equity accounted investee, the carrying amount of the investment is reduced to

zero and the recognition of further losses is discontinued, except to the extent that the Group has an obligation to make payments on behalf of the investee. Biological assets are measured at fair value less costs to sell with any changes recognized in the income statement.

These two examples demonstrate the complexity of accounting for business relationships. Essentially, relationships can be of many different types and it may be difficult to define the nature of the relationships. The standards we discuss in the following attempt to establish the accounting methods to be used for different types of relationships.

IAS 28 Investments in Associates and Joint Ventures

This standard, effective from 1 January 2009, has been revised several times with the latest being in 2017 by *Long-term Interests in Associates and Joint Ventures*. Investments in other businesses are common activities but raise accounting complexities. An investing company may have a significant influence on another entity that is not a subsidiary. In this case, the entity does not appear in the consolidated financial statements under the provisions of IFRS 3 and IFRS 10. We discuss these two standards in Chapter 7. It is important that the users of financial statements are aware of the nature and implications of this investment. IAS 28 applies to all entities that are investors with joint control of, or significant influence over, an investee. Investors must use the equity method to account for these investments.

The important points of the standard are that it

- only applies to investments in associates and joint ventures,
- requires the investor to show the investments in its balance sheet,
- provides definitions of associates and joint ventures,
- requires the investor to apply the equity method,
- does not contain disclosure requirements and these are in IFRS 12.

Joint ventures and associates

By definition, no single party can control a joint venture because of the term "joint". There must be two or more parties for a joint venture and a company must show the investments in its balance sheet. The standard distinguishes between joint operations and joint ventures.

- A **joint operation** is a joint arrangement whereby the parties have joint control of the arrangement (the joint operators) and they have rights to the assets, and obligations for the liabilities, of the arrangement.
- A **joint venture** is a joint arrangement whereby the parties have joint control of the arrangement and the joint venturers have rights to the net assets of the arrangement.

Both of the above types of arrangements fall under the general heading of joint arrangements, but IAS 28 *Investments in Associates and Joint Ventures* regulates only joint ventures. IFRS 11 *Joint Arrangements* applies to joint operations and we discuss this standard in a later section in this chapter. At this stage, we concentrate on accounting for joint ventures under IAS 28. It is more difficult to define an investment in an associate company than an investment in a joint venture. The definition states that an associate company is an entity over which the investor has significant influence. You can compare this to IFRS 3 which requires the acquiring entity to have control over the acquiree.

The key to understanding the importance of the two definitions is the meaning of the term significant influence. Unfortunately, this is not straightforward. The basic principle is the 20% rule as explained in the following section.

Significant influence

IAS 28 establishes the concept of significance influence and the criteria to establish significant influence. The standard setters decided that significant influence is where the investor has the power to participate in the financial and operating policy decisions of the investee but does not have control or joint control of those policies. Joint control is the contractually agreed sharing of control of an arrangement. This agreement exists only when decisions about the relevant activities require the unanimous consent of the parties sharing control. If the investing entity has significant influence, the entity in which the investment is made is an associate company.

The definition gives the breakpoint for significant influence by stating the level at which the investing entity is deemed to have significant influence. This normally arises where the investor has 20% or more of the voting power. Although the standard gives a breakpoint, the investor may be able to demonstrate that it does not have significant influence although its holding is above this level. Equally, an entity with a holding that is less than 20% may be able to prove that it does have significant influence.

In determining the 20% level, the existence and effect of potential voting rights that are currently exercisable or convertible, including potential voting rights held by other entities, are considered. In assessing whether potential voting rights contribute to significant influence, the entity examines all facts and circumstances that affect potential rights. For example, an investor may hold more than 20% of the voting rights but is unable to exercise significant influence because another investor holds the remaining voting rights. However, a substantial or majority ownership by another investor does not necessarily preclude an entity from having significant influence. The reverse situation can occur where the investor has less than 20% of the voting rights, but circumstances permit it to apply significant influence.

The standard provides the following examples of evidence that an entity does have significant influence:

- representation on the board of directors or equivalent governing body of the investee,
- participation in the policy-making process, including participation in decisions about dividends or other distributions,
- material transactions between the entity and the investee,
- interchange of managerial personnel,
- provision of essential technical information.

An entity loses significant influence over an investee when it loses the power to participate in the financial and operating policy decisions of that investee. The loss of significant influence can occur with or without a change in absolute or relative ownership levels.

Before we examine the method of accounting investing entities should use, we show in the following the policies on associates and joint ventures of Associated British Foods (Annual Report 2021):

> *"All the Group's joint arrangements are joint ventures, which are entities over whose activities the Group has joint control, typically established by contractual agreement and requiring the venturers' unanimous consent for strategic financial and operating decisions. Associates are those entities in which the Group has significant influence, being the power to participate in the financial and operating policy decisions of*

the entity, but which does not amount to control or joint control. Where the Group's share of losses exceeds its interest in a joint venture or associate, the carrying amount is reduced to zero and recognition of further losses is discontinued except to the extent that the Group has incurred legal or constructive obligations or made payments on behalf of an investee. Control, joint control and significant influence are generally assessed by reference to equity shareholdings and voting rights."

The company's statement of financial position lists its non-current assets as follows. The amounts are shown in millions of UK pounds:

Year	**2021**	**2020**
Intangible assets	1,581	1,629
Property, plant and equipment	5,286	5,651
Right-of-use assets	2,649	2,990
Investments in joint ventures	278	233
Investments in associates	60	56
Employee benefits assets	640	100
Income tax	23	—
Deferred tax assets	218	212
Other receivables	55	45

The above extract from the annual report demonstrates that the company has investments in joint ventures of £278,000,000 in 2021 and also investments in associates of £60,000,000. The annual report contains full information on these investments.

The equity method of accounting

This is a method of accounting where the investment is initially recognized at cost and adjusted thereafter for the post-acquisition change in the investor's share of the investee's net assets. The investor's profit or loss includes its share of the investee's profit or loss and the investor's other comprehensive income includes its share of the investee's other comprehensive income. Entities, with a significant influence or joint control over an investee, must use the equity method to account for its investment. The investing entity is not required to use the equity method if it is exempt from preparing consolidated financial statements or it meets all of the following conditions:

(a) It is a wholly owned subsidiary or is a partially owned subsidiary of another entity and its other owners, including those not otherwise entitled to vote, have been informed about, and do not object to, the entity not applying the equity method.
(b) Its debt or equity instruments are not traded in a public market (a domestic or foreign stock exchange or an over-the-counter market, including local and regional markets).
(c) It did not file, nor is it in the process of filing, its financial statements with a securities commission or other regulatory organization, for the purpose of issuing any class of instruments in a public market.
(d) The ultimate or any intermediate parent of the entity produces consolidated financial statements available for public use that comply with IFRSs.

The following explanation demonstrates the equity method in the following two distinct stages:

Stage 1: Initial recognition

An investor recognises at cost in the statement of financial position any investment in an associate or a joint venture. The investor uses the equity method from the date on which it becomes an associate or a joint venture. Any difference between the cost of the investment and the entity's share of the net fair value of the investee's identifiable assets is included in the carrying amount of the investment. There may be an excess of the entity's share of the net fair value of the investee's net assets over the cost of the investment. If so, this excess is included as income in the determination of the entity's share of the associate or joint venture's profit or loss. This is actioned in the period in which the investment is acquired.

Stage 2: Subsequent financial periods

The initial carrying amount is adjusted subsequently to recognise post-acquisition changes. The subsequent changes to the carrying amount can arise for several reasons. The investor will adjust the carrying amount to recognise the investor's share of the profit or loss of the investee. The investor recognises its share of the profit or loss of the investee in its own profit or loss. Distributions received from an investee reduce the carrying amount of the investment.

The investor may also find it necessary to adjust the carrying amount because of changes in the investor's proportionate interest in the investee arising from changes in the investee's other comprehensive income. Examples of these changes in the investee's comprehensive income are revaluations of property, plant and equipment and foreign currency translations. The investor recognises these changes in its statement of other comprehensive income.

An investor continues to use the equity method until the investment in the associate or joint venture ends. The reasons for this termination and the action the investor should take are as follows:

1. The investee becomes a subsidiary of the investor. The investor then accounts for the investment in accordance with IFRS 3 *Business Combinations* and IFRS 10 *Consolidated Financial Statements.*
2. The entity loses significant influence. In these circumstances, the investor treats the investment as a financial asset. The entity measures the retained interest at fair value, and the fair value of the retained interest is regarded as its fair value on initial recognition as a financial asset in accordance with IFRS 9 *Financial Instruments*. An investor may dispose of part of its interest in an investee. If so, the entity accounts in its profit or loss for any difference between (a) the fair value of any retained interest plus proceeds from the part disposal and (b) the carrying amount of the investment at the date the equity method was discontinued.

Other circumstances may occur that do not lead to the abandonment of the equity method:

1. An investment in an associate may change to an investment in a joint venture or an investment in a joint venture may change to an investment in an associate. The entity continues to use the equity method because the concepts of significant influence and joint control have only been exchanged. The investment remains and the underlying criterion of standard IAS 28 remains applicable.

2. An entity's ownership interest in an associate or a joint venture may be reduced, but the entity continues to have significant influence. In these circumstances, the entity continues to apply the equity method. There is no change in the way the entity accounts for investments, except for the reduction of its proportionate share of the investments' income.

Applying the equity method

Once the investing entity has decided to use the equity method, there are some issues to be resolved. We have separated these into procedural issues and technical issues. The procedural issues for applying the equity method are straightforward and we explain the following requirements:

Procedural issues

1. Unless it is unpractical to do so, the investing entity should ensure that the financial statements of the associate or joint venture share the same financial dates as itself. If it is not practical, the investing entity uses the most recent financial statements. The investor must adjust these statements for any significant transactions or events occurring between the accounting period ends. The reporting dates of the investor and associate should not differ by more than three months.
2. The accounting policies of the associate or joint venture should not differ from those of the investor. Where they do so, changes must be made to the policies so they comply with the investor's accounting policies.
3. The investing entity must account for an investment in an associate or a joint venture in its entity's separate financial statements (IAS 27 Separate Financial Statements).

Technical issues

These are more complex and we have arranged them in what we consider their order of complexity. We emphasise that not all investing entities will confront these problems.

1. If the investor is a non-investment entity and the investee is an investment entity, the investor can retain the fair value measurement used by the associate or joint venture to its interests in subsidiaries. In other words, the associate or joint venture is itself an investor with investments in subsidiaries. The main investing entity can retain the fair value measurement used by the investee.
2. The circumstance can arise where an investor's or joint venturer's share of losses of an associate or joint venture equals or exceeds its interest in the associate or joint venture. In these circumstances, the investor or joint venturer discontinues recognising its share of further losses. After the investor or joint venturer's interest reduces to zero, it recognises a liability only to the extent that it has incurred legal or constructive obligations or made payments on behalf of the associate. If the associate or joint venture subsequently reports profits, the investor or joint venturer resumes recognising its share of those profits only after its share of the profits equals the share of losses not recognised.
3. The final technical issue concerns transactions between the investor and the associate or joint venture. The standard refers to upstream and downstream transactions. Upstream transactions are from the associate to investor or joint venture to joint venturer. Downstream transactions are from the investor to associate or joint venturer to joint venture. Profits and losses resulting from transactions are eliminated to the extent of the investor's interest in the associate or joint venture. Unrealised losses are not eliminated to the extent that the transaction provides evidence of a reduction in the net realisable value or in the recoverable amount of the assets transferred.

As of 1 January 2016, an amendment entitled the *Sale or Contribution of Assets between an Investor and its Associate or Joint Venture* came into effect. This amendment is concerned only with gains or losses from downstream transactions. If such transactions involve assets that constitute a business between an entity and its associate or joint venture, the investor must recognise the assets in full in its financial statements. A downstream transaction is one that takes place between a parent entity and its subsidiary. The transaction is a flow of corporate activity from the parent to the subsidiary and it can be the sale of assets or securities or a debt transaction.

Application of other standards

We mentioned at the beginning of this chapter that investments in associates and joint ventures come under the requirements of other standards. From the investor's point of view, once it applies the equity method, IAS 39 Financial Instruments: Recognition and Measurement (see Chapter 9) regulates accounting for the investment. The investment entity must decide if it is necessary to recognise any additional impairment loss with respect to its net investment in the associate or joint venture.

If the investor decides that there is impairment, it calculates the amount by reference to IAS 36 Impairment of Assets (see Chapter 5). The entire carrying amount of the investment is tested for impairment as a single asset including any goodwill. The investor must assess the recoverable amount of an investment for each individual associate or joint venture. This does not apply if the associate or joint venture does not generate cash flows independently.

Any impairment loss is not allocated to any identifiable asset. This includes goodwill as this is an integral part of the carrying amount of the investment in the associate or joint venture. If there is a reversal of the impairment loss, it is recognised in accordance with IAS 36.

IAS 27 Separate Financial Statements

This standard became effective from January 1, 1990, and students may find the term in the title of "separate financial statements" confusing. The term means non-consolidated financial statements, in other words, where a number of companies that have the forms of relationship discussed in this chapter must still prepare their own financial statements. The standard applies to a parent or an investor in a joint venture or associate. In the case of an investor, the standard only applies where it accounts for its investments either at cost or in accordance with IAS 39 Financial Instruments: Recognition and Measurement or IFRS 9 Financial Instruments.

IAS 27 has the objective of setting the requirements to be applied in accounting for investments in subsidiaries, joint ventures and associates when an entity elects, or is required by local regulations, to present separate financial statements. The standard also outlines the accounting requirements for dividends. There are also some important disclosure requirements that we discuss at the end of this section. Before we explain separate financial statements, we distinguish the two types with the following definition.

Definition — Consolidated and separate financial statements

Consolidated financial statements are the financial statements of a group in which the assets, liabilities, equity, income, expenses and cash flows of the parent and its subsidiaries are presented as those of a single economic entity. Separate financial statements are the financial statements presented by a parent (i.e. an investor with control of a subsidiary), an investor with joint control of, or significant influence over, an investee, in which the investments are accounted for at cost or in accordance with IFRS 9 Financial Instruments.

In Chapter 7, we explain IFRS 10 Consolidated financial statements in depth and we identify the types of entities that must prepare consolidated accounts and those that must prepare separate accounts. The combination of IAS 27 and IFRS 10 results in the parent company with subsidiaries having to prepare consolidated financial statements for the group of companies and separate financial statements for itself. In this chapter, we focus on the part of IFRS 10 which contains the following important requirements:

1. The standard applies when an entity prepares separate financial statements that comply with International Financial Reporting Standards.
2. Financial statements in which the equity method is applied are not separate financial statements.
3. Similarly, the financial statements of an entity that does not have a subsidiary, associate or joint venturer's interest in a joint venture are not separate financial statements.
4. IFRS 10 excludes investment entities from its requirements and such entities prepare separate financial statements only under IAS 27.

The accounting method

An entity preparing separate financial statements has a choice of three methods under IAS 27 for measuring the investments.

1. At cost but if they are held for sale, the regulations in IFRS 5 Non-current Assets Held for Sale and Discontinued Operations apply (see Chapter 8). Investments carried at cost must be measured at the lower of their carrying amount and fair value less costs to sell.
2. In compliance with the requirements of IFRS 9 Financial Instruments. Some entities may not yet have adopted IFRS 9 and therefore must

comply with IAS 39. We discussed both these standards in a later chapter.

3. In compliance with the equity method in IAS 28 that we discussed earlier in this chapter.

There are some different requirements for investment entities. First, we provide the definition from IFRS 10 of an investment entity.

Definition — Investment entity

An entity that

(a) obtains funds from one or more investors for the purpose of providing those investor(s) with investment management services,
(b) commits to its investor(s) that its business purpose is to invest funds solely for returns from capital appreciation, investment income or both,
(c) measures and evaluates the performance of substantially all of its investments on a fair value basis.

The IASB introduced a consolidation exemption for investment entities that became effective for annual periods beginning on or after 1 January 2014. IFRS 10 requires a parent investment entity to measure its investment in a subsidiary at fair value through profit or loss. The investment entity must also account for its investment in a subsidiary in the same way in its separate financial statements.

It is possible for an investment entity that is a parent to cease being an investment entity but does not meet the above definition. In these circumstances, the entity has a choice. It can either account for an investment in a subsidiary at cost (based on fair value at the date of change or status) or in accordance with IFRS 9. There is the alternative where a parent entity becomes an investment entity. If so, it must account for any investment in accordance with IFRS 9 which we discuss in Chapter 9. The aim of the standard is to require accounting for a subsidiary at fair value through profit or loss.

The final situation in this section is where a parent reorganises the structure of its group by establishing a new entity as its parent. There are variations on this. There could be the establishment of an intermediate parent in addition to a new ultimate parent. Alternatively, the entity may not be a parent but establishes a new parent.

All of these reorganisations must comply with the accounting requirements of IAS 27 as long as the following criteria are met:

- the new parent obtains control of the original parent by issuing equity instruments in exchange for existing equity instruments of the original parent,
- the assets and liabilities of the new group and the original group are the same immediately before and after the reorganisation,
- the owners of the original parent before the reorganisation have the same absolute and relative interests in the net assets of the original group and the new group immediately before and after the reorganisation.

If the above criteria apply, then the new parent

- accounts for its investment in the original parent at cost and
- measures the carrying amount of its share of the equity items shown in the separate financial statements of the original parent at the date of the reorganisation.

A parent entity, under IFRS 10, may elect not to prepare consolidated financial statements but instead prepare separate financial statements. The standard contains a lengthy list of the disclosures required in the separate financial statements. For our discussions, the most relevant are as follows:

- the fact that the financial statements are separate financial statements,
- that the exemption from consolidation has been used,
- a description of the method used to account for the foregoing investments.

IFRS 11 Joint Arrangements

Joint arrangements can be difficult to identify and to determine how a company should account for the various business arrangements it may have entered into. In this section, we explain the requirements of IFRS 11, and in the following section, we explain the requirements of IFRS 12

Disclosure of interest in Other Entities. It is useful to understand the complexity of the various arrangements that companies may enter into. To demonstrate this, we show a very brief extract from the annual report of AstraZeneca:

> *Collaboration Revenue includes income from collaborative arrangements where either the Group has sold certain rights associated with those products, but retains a significant ongoing economic interest or has acquired a significant interest from a third party. Significant interest can include ongoing supply of finished goods, participation in sharing of profit arrangements or direct interest from sales of medicines. These arrangements may include development arrangements, commercialisation arrangements and collaborations. Income may take the form of upfront fees, milestones, profit sharing and royalties and includes sharing of profit arising from sales made as principal by a collaboration partner.*

With these complexities in arrangements, it can be difficult to determine which standards apply. In this section, we consider IFRS 11, and in the following section, we explain the requirements of IFRS 12.

In our explanation of IFRS 11, we focus on the requirements of the standard and not a discussion of the various arrangements that some companies enter into. IFRS 11 was effective from 1 January 2013 and there have been some subsequent amendments. Where there is joint control, IFRS 11 defines two types of joint arrangements. These are Joint Operations and Joint ventures. If the arrangement is defined as a joint operation, it falls under IFRS 11. We discuss the requirements of the standard in this section. If it is a joint venture, IAS 28 sets out the accounting requirements. IFRS 11 *Joint Arrangements* sets out the accounting requirements for entities that jointly control an arrangement. Joint control involves the contractually agreed sharing of control. Such arrangements can be either a joint venture or a joint operation. Arrangements subject to joint control are classified as either a joint venture (representing a share of net assets and equity accounted) or a joint operation (representing rights to assets and obligations for liabilities, accounted for accordingly). A joint arrangement is where the parties that have joint control of the arrangement have rights to the assets, and obligations for the liabilities, relating to the arrangement. A joint venture is where parties that have joint control of the arrangement have rights to the net assets of the arrangement.

The first stage in the application of IFRS 11 is to determine whether there is a joint arrangement. There are two determining factors:

1. A contractual arrangement binds the parties together.
2. The contractual arrangement gives two or more of those parties joint control of the arrangement.

The contract normally incorporates such issues as follows:

- the purpose, activity and duration of the joint arrangement,
- how the members of the Board of Directors, or equivalent governing body, of the joint arrangement are appointed,
- the decision-making process: the matters requiring decisions from the parties, the voting rights of the parties and the required level of support for those matters. In a joint arrangement, the decision-making process in the contractual arrangement establishes joint control of the arrangement,
- the capital or other contributions required of the parties,
- how the parties share assets, liabilities, revenues, expenses or profit or loss relating to the joint arrangement. The rights and obligations established by the contractual arrangement related to the assets, liabilities, revenue, expenses or profit or loss arising from the arrangement will determine how the arrangement is classified (as a joint operation or a joint venture).

Contractual arrangements need to be enforceable and will often, but not always, be in writing. Generally, the arrangements are in the form of a contract or documented discussions, such as minutes of meetings, between the parties. Where a separate vehicle is set up, the articles, charter or by-laws of that vehicle may set out some aspects of the contractual arrangement, for example, voting rights and percentage required to reach a decision. For there to be joint control, the parties should have agreed on a contract that shares control of the arrangement. The joint control exists only when decisions about the relevant activities require the unanimous consent of the parties sharing control. The key terms are decisions, relevant activities and unanimous consent:

- Decisions jointly made concern matters, such as the operating and capital arrangements. This includes budgets.

- Relevant activities are those activities that significantly affect the returns of the arrangement. Examples are the selling and purchasing of goods or services and researching and developing new products.
- Unanimous consent exists where any one of the parties concerned could block the decision.

Joint control does not mean that each party must have the same percentage share. Imagine that there are four parties. Three hold 30% share and the other party holds the remaining 10% share. If the contractual agreement states that a decision requires 70% of the votes, any combination of three of the four parties could pass the decision. Such an arrangement does not meet the requirements of IAS 11 unless the agreement specifies which parties are required to agree unanimously.

For example, the agreement may specify that parties 1, 2 and 4 must vote in favour for the arrangement to be considered joint. If party 4 is against the decision, the motion will not be passed. The requirement in IFRS 11 for unanimous consent means that any of the parties with joint control of the arrangement can prevent a decision and thus can prevent the other parties from making decisions without its consent.

The financial statements for joint operations

IFRS 11 sets out the requirements for the parties involved in joint operations and they must recognise their involvement in the joint operations in their own financial statements. The requirements are as follows:

Income statement

- the share of the revenue from the sale of the output by the joint operation,
- the share of the expenses, including the share of any expenses incurred jointly.

Statement of financial position

- the assets, including the share of any assets held jointly,
- the liabilities, including the share of any liabilities incurred jointly.

The initial investment in the joint operation is also shown on the balance sheet of the parties including the above items in their own financial statements; the parties must use the appropriate IFRSs unless they conflict with IFRS 11.

Disclosure

IFRS 11 does not specify any disclosure requirements and the requirements are in IFRS 12 *Disclosure of Interests in Other Entities.* The relevant requirements in IFRS 12 are as follows:

- where an entity has made significant judgements and assumptions in determining that it has joint control,
- if the joint arrangement has been structured through a separate vehicle, such as an incorporated entity, the significant judgements and assumptions made in determining whether the arrangement is a joint operation or a joint venture,
- the nature, extent and financial effects of its interests in joint arrangements, nature and effects of contractual relationships, and nature of, and changes in, risks associated with joint ventures.

IFRS 12 Disclosure of Interest in Other Entities

The objective of IFRS 12 is to require the disclosure of information that enables users of financial statements to evaluate:

- the nature of, and risks associated with, its interests in other entities,
- the effects of those interests on its financial position, financial performance and cash flows.

IFRS 12 does not refer to any particular accounting treatments for different economic transactions and events but confines itself solely to the disclosure of financial information in the form of investments in other companies. In doing this, a number of accounting standards are affected. The disclosures and the relevant standards are as follows:

- subsidiaries IFRS 3 and IFRS 10,
- joint operations IFRS 11,
- joint ventures IFRS 11,

- associates IAS 28,
- structured entities IFRS 12.

A structured entity is purposely constructed so that voting or similar rights are not the dominant factor in deciding who controls the entity. For example, any voting rights may refer only to routine administrative procedures. The entity has a narrow and well-defined objective and relevant activities are directed by means of contractual arrangements. Structured entities are such arrangements as securitisation vehicles, asset-backed financings and some investment funds. If compliance with IAS 12 does not give sufficient disclosure, an entity must disclose whatever additional information is necessary to provide the appropriate information to users. The following list summarises the main disclosure requirements in IAS 12:

Significant judgements and assumptions made in deciding

- that it controls another entity,
- that it has joint control of an arrangement or significant influence over another entity,
- the type of joint arrangement (i.e. joint operation or joint venture) when the arrangement has been structured through a separate vehicle.

Interests in subsidiaries to assist users of consolidated financial statements to

- understand the composition of the group,
- understand the interest that non-controlling interests have in the group's activities and cash flows,
- evaluate the nature and extent of significant restrictions on its ability to access or use assets, and settle liabilities, of the group,
- evaluate the nature of, and changes in, the risks associated with its interests in consolidated structured entities,
- evaluate the consequences of changes in its ownership interest in a subsidiary that do not result in a loss of control,
- evaluate the consequences of losing control of a subsidiary during the reporting period.

Interests in unconsolidated subsidiaries by investment entities disclosing

- the fact that the entity is an investment entity,
- information about significant judgements and assumptions it has made in determining that it is an investment entity,
- details of subsidiaries that have not been consolidated,
- details of the relationship and certain transactions between the investment entity and the subsidiary,
- information when an entity becomes, or ceases to be, an investment entity.

Interests in unconsolidated structured entities assisting users to

- understand the nature and extent of its interests in unconsolidated structured entities,
- evaluate the nature of, and changes in, the risks associated with its interests in unconsolidated structured entities.

IFRS 12 contains a fundamental weakness. It refers to disclosures to meet the needs of the users of corporate reports. It does not identify these users or suggest what their information needs may be. Shareholders in the company, those that have lent substantial sums to the company, employees and many other groups can be very interested in the financial status of the company.

IAS 24 Related Party Disclosures

The standards that we discussed in the previous chapter and in this chapter have identified and defined specific relationships. Business relationships can be very complex and for the user of financial statements, these relationships can be extremely important as they may influence the activities and financial performance of an entity.

To some extent, IAS 24 is a "mopping up" standard that attempts to ensure that all business relationships are covered. It states that its objective is to ensure that an entity's financial statements contain the disclosures necessary to draw attention to the possibility that its financial position and profit or loss may have been affected by the existence of related parties and by transactions and outstanding balances with such parties. The standard defines a related party as a person or entity that is related to the reporting entity. It has an exhaustive list of those persons and entities that may be related to the reporting entity. It also has a much smaller list of those who are deemed not to be related. A related party transaction is a transfer of resources, services or obligations between related parties, regardless of whether a price is charged.

An entity must disclose the name of its parent and, if different, the ultimate controlling party. If neither the entity's parent nor the ultimate controlling party produces financial statements available for public use, the name of the next most senior parent that does so must also be disclosed. These disclosures are required even if no transactions have taken place in the financial period.

On a more general basis, where transactions have taken place with related parties excluding subsidiaries, the entity must disclose the nature of the related party relationship as well as information about the transactions. This standard requires disclosures separately for each category of related parties. The information must show

- the amount of the transactions,
- the amount of outstanding balances, including terms and conditions and guarantees,
- provisions for doubtful debts related to the amount of outstanding balances,
- expense recognised during the period in respect of bad or doubtful debts due from related parties.

We illustrate the information provided by companies with the following brief extract from the annual report and accounts of Kingfisher plc. This is an international home improvement company with approximately 1,490 stores, supported by a team of over 80,000 colleagues. It operates in eight countries across Europe under retail banners, including B&Q, Castorama, Brico Dépôt, Screwfix, TradePoint and Koçta. We have shown only a few extracts from its annual report to illustrate the related parties' relationships.

Kingfisher plc
During the year, the Group carried out a number of transactions with related parties in the normal course of business and on an arm's length basis. The names of the related parties, the nature of these transactions and their total value are shown below:

Income Receivable Transactions with Koçtaş Yapi Marketleri Ticaret A.S. in which the Group holds a 50% interest Commission and other income Transactions with Crealfi S.A. in which the Group holds a 49% interest Services are usually negotiated with related parties on a cost-plus basis. Goods are sold or bought on the basis of the price lists in force with non-related parties.

Complex relationships

The relationships between companies can become complex and existing standards do not cover every eventuality. Large companies frequently make agreements with other companies for different types of business relationships. But there are circumstances where companies have to make specific disclosures of financial information. These corporate relationships involve not only strategic and management decisions but are also subject to legal, tax and financial accounting requirements. The standards now in issue have resolved many of the problems but accountants still have to make estimates and judgements depending on the nature of the relationships. If it is evident that one company has acquired another, there are still the following issues to be resolved:

- whether there is an acquisition or has one company only purchased assets,
- the date when the relationship occurred,
- identifying the fair values of assets and liabilities,
- identifying intangible assets if there are any.

There is also the issue of measuring the actual cost of the acquisition as this may involve shares when there is no active market to value them.

Chapter Review

Corporate relationships arise in different types of industries and for various reasons. The relationships can be complex and not confined to institutions in only one country. The IASB and the IFRS have issued standards intended to capture the essence of these relationships and to establish the accounting regulations. One key issue for entities is to determine the nature of the relationship that exists. The choices are as follows:

- IAS 28 Investments in Associates and Joint Ventures. The standard distinguishes between joint operations and joint ventures and describes the concept of significant influence. The standard only regulates associates and joint ventures and requires the application of the equity method of accounting.
- IFRS 11 Joint arrangements establish the accounting requirements for entities that jointly control an arrangement. Joint control involves the contractually agreed sharing of control. Such arrangements can be either a joint venture or a joint operation.
- IAS 24 Related Party disclosures define related parties and the disclosures an entity should make.

Our discussions above and our examples demonstrate that the task is difficult, for both the standard setters and the entities that must comply with the regulations. If a company has an arrangement, regardless of what the contractual agreement states, a charismatic person on the board of directors may well control or significantly influence decisions. Although the standards have addressed the essence of relationships, we would argue that it is impossible to regulate specifically every type of relationship. There are times when entities must examine their activities and determine themselves how best to account for them. If this is the route they take, it must be explained to the users of the financial statements.

CHAPTER 6 Business Relationships

Review Questions

1. Which one of the following does not apply to a public limited company?
   a. It is unable to issue shares to the public.
   b. It must publish specific financial data and disclose this to the public.
   c. The financial statements should be audited.
   d. It can list its shares on the London Stock Exchange.
2. Which one of the following is not an aspect of IAS 28 Investments in Associates and Joint Ventures?
   a. It requires the investor to show the investments in its balance sheet.
   b. It provides definitions of associates and joint ventures.
   c. It requires the investor to apply the equity method.
   d. It does not contain disclosure requirements.
3. If an auditor, for any reason, cannot be appointed at the Annual General Meeting, what action should the company take?
4. What is the equity method of accounting?
5. What does the term separate financial statements mean?
6. What are the two types of joint arrangements?
7. Which standards identify the types of relationships?
8. Who appoints the auditors of a company?

Chapter 7

Combining Businesses

Structure of Chapter 7

Section title	Main content
IFRS 3 Business combinations	This standard sets out the principles and requirements for the acquirer in a business combination. Essentially, the cost is the total amount of consideration paid from which part is allocated to the acquired assets and liabilities on the basis of their fair values with any balance being recognised as goodwill. If it is a "bargain purchase", it is recognised in profit or loss.
IFRS 10 Consolidated and separate financial statements	Where an entity controls a number of separate entities, it must prepare consolidated financial statements as set out in IFRS 10.
Chapter Review	It is essential that business relationships are disclosed. The standards set out the regulations and the accounting for business relationships.

In this chapter, we consider two standards concerned with accounting for business relationships. The first is IFRS 3 concerned with the process of a business combination, one major example being Marks and Spencer Group plc which is a major British multinational retailer with headquarters in London, England. The group specialises in selling clothing, beauty, home products and food products. It has over 75,000 employees and has subsidiaries in a number of countries.

The second standard, IFRS 10, is applicable where an entity has control of several other entities and must prepare consolidated financial statements. These statements show the assets, liabilities, equity, income, expenses and cash flows of a parent and its subsidiaries as those of a single economic entity. You may come across the wording "holding company" and this is a separate parent company created to own a controlling interest in a subsidiary company or companies. A holding company doesn't necessarily trade itself; its main purpose is to form a corporate group and there are usually advantages in such a configuration.

IFRS 3 Business Combinations

This standard was first issued in 2004 and there have been several revisions over the years. The standard seeks to enhance the relevance, reliability and comparability of information provided about business combinations (e.g. acquisitions and mergers) and their effects. It sets out the principles for the recognition and measurement of acquired assets and liabilities, the determination of goodwill and the necessary disclosures. The standard concentrates on explaining the acquisition method that entities must follow for all business combinations. The application method requires the following:

1. identifying the acquirer,
2. determining the acquisition date,
3. recognising and measuring the identifiable assets acquired, the liabilities assumed and any non-controlling interest in the acquiree,
4. recognising and measuring goodwill or a gain from a bargain purchase.

The IFRS Foundation published a research document in 2015 entitled Post-implication Review (PIR). This document describes how the IFRS Foundation conducts a review. First, the IFRS Foundation identified certain issues and then conducted a public consultation. The IFRS Foundation assessed the comments it received and referred to other sources of information, such as academic research. From these sources, the IFRS Foundation gave an indication of the actions it contemplates taking. In this chapter, we refer to the PIR to clarify certain parts of the standard and to illustrate where entities are identifying problems.

In our explanations, for simplicity, we assume that one single entity is acquiring another single entity. This rarely happens in practice with major companies. These can be very active in the disposal and acquisition of several businesses in a financial year. We give in the following some picture of the levels of activity for 2015 when the IFRS Foundation conducted its research:

- There were 93 successful domestic and cross-border M&A transactions involving UK companies reported in quarter 2 (April to June) 2015, compared with 118 in quarter 1 (January to March) 2015.
- In quarter 2 (April to June) 2015, there were 46 completed domestic acquisitions (UK companies acquiring other UK companies). This is similar to the level of domestic M&A activity reported in quarter 1 (January to March) 2015 (43 transactions).
- In quarter 2 (April to June) 2015, there were 21 completed inward acquisitions of UK companies made by foreign companies, the lowest number since quarter 1 (January to March) 2013, when 19 transactions were reported.
- The number of mergers and acquisitions made abroad by UK companies (outward M&A) fell to 26 in quarter 2 (April to June) 2015, from 48 in quarter 1 (January to March) 2015.
  (Office for National Statistics 2015)

Identifying the acquirer and the acquiree

The standard applies to the acquisition or merger of one business by another to form a business combination. We need to know what the terms business and business combination mean and the standard provides the following definitions:

Business: An integrated set of activities and assets that is capable of being conducted and managed for the purpose of providing a return in the form of dividends, lower costs or other economic benefits directly to investors or other owners, members or participants.

Business combination: A transaction or other event in which an acquirer obtains control of one or more businesses. Transactions sometimes referred to as "true mergers" or "mergers of equals" are also business combinations.

The PIR research (quoted above) revealed that respondents considered that the definition of a business is broad and there is insufficient guidance in distinguishing between an acquired set of assets and the acquisition of an entire business. This is because the structure of large businesses is usually complex and the inter-entity transactions can be accordingly difficult to identify.

In discussing corporate acquisition, we may be referring to either "asset purchases" in which the buyer buys specific business assets from a selling entity or "equity purchases" in which the buyer purchases equity interests in a target entity from one or more shareholders willing to relinquish their ownership. For example, one entity may purchase several assets from another entity. It would show these on the balance sheet as assets. However, the entity must comply with the requirements of IFRS 3 if the acquisition falls within the broad definition of a business. The distinction between a set of assets and a business can also be very important as the acquisition of a business may result in the purchase of goodwill whereas the acquisition of an asset does not. We explain the issue of goodwill later in this chapter.

The IFRS agrees that defining a business is extremely difficult in industries, such as real estate, extractive industries, pharmaceutical, technology and shipping. Their response is to encourage research to ascertain whether it is possible to improve the definition of a business and the related application guidance.

Applying the standard

The standard does not apply to the following:

- the accounting for the formation of a joint venture in the financial statements of the joint venture itself (refer to IFRS 11 discussed in the following chapter),
- the acquisition of an asset or group of assets that is not a business, although general guidance is provided on how to account for such transactions,

- combinations of entities or businesses under common control,
- acquisitions by an investment entity of a subsidiary that is required to be measured at fair value through profit or loss.

The standard identifies a business as where there are activities being conducted to convert inputs into outputs. There are processes, employees and plans to produce outputs, and there is the prospect of customers willing to purchase the output. Where one business acquires another business on an agreed date either by offering shares or cash or a combination of both, the acquirer must apply the acquisition method to the transaction. The acquirer (parent) gains control of the acquiree (subsidiary). This may be either a 100% acquisition where the parent holds all the equity in the subsidiary or where the acquirer holds only part of the equity but has gained control. In a partial ownership, there will be other owners called non-controlling interests, previously known as minority interests. The concept of control is important but IFRS 3 does not explain the term. To understand the concept of control, we must refer to IFRS 10. The details are complex and explain them later in this chapter.

The basic principle in a business combination is that there will always be an acquirer and an acquiree and it is possible to identify the acquirer. You will see references in business newspapers from time to time about the "merger" of two companies. From an accounting perspective, this is more likely than not an acquisition. The standard requires the application of the acquisition method for all business combinations, both acquisitions and mergers. The standard provides the following definitions of the terms that are used:

Acquisition date: The date on which the acquirer obtains control of the acquiree.

Acquirer: The entity that obtains control of the acquiree.

Acquiree: The business or businesses that the acquirer obtains control of in a business combination.

The above definitions assume that it is always possible to identify the acquirer and the main indicator will be whether the acquirer has obtained control of the other entity. Where control is not easy to demonstrate, the standard offers guidance to determine which entity is the acquirer in different circumstances:

1. The acquiring entity is usually the one that transfers cash or other assets where this is the agreed method.
2. The acquiring entity is usually the largest entity measured by assets, revenue or profit.
3. The acquiring entity is usually the one that issues equity interests where this is the agreed method. The following factors may influence the conclusion:
   - relative voting rights in the combined entity after the business combination,
   - the existence of any large minority interest if no other owner or group of owners has a significant voting interest,
   - the composition of the governing body or management of the combined entity,
   - the terms on which equity interests are exchanged.
4. Where there are multiple entities involved in the business combination, the entity initiating the combination and the relative sizes of the combining entities are important.

Cost of the acquisition

The general principle is that the cost of a business combination is the total of the fair values of the consideration given by the acquirer plus any directly attributable costs of the business combination. The acquirer should charge expenses, such as fees of lawyers and accountants acting as advisers, to the Income Statement. These costs are not part of the consideration.

IFRS 13 Fair Value Measurement regulates the determination of fair value and we discussed this standard in Chapter 9. We can regard fair value as the price an entity would receive on selling an asset or pay to transfer a liability. The transaction should be orderly and between market participants at the measurement date. Although IFRS 13 applies to various transactions, in this chapter, we discuss its application and the issues involved specifically concerning business combinations.

As far as the payment is concerned, the consideration paid may be as follows:

- cash or other assets transferred to the acquiree,
- liabilities assumed by the acquirer, for example, taking on the liability for a bank loan of the acquiree,
- the issue of equity instruments, such as ordinary shares.

There are instances where only a provisional fair value is possible at the acquisition date. If there are adjustments arising within 12 months of the acquisition date, they can be set back to the acquisition date and the goodwill recalculated.

Provisional fair value (Worked example)

An entity may have made an acquisition of 100% of another entity on 1 January 2014 for the sum of £650,000. A provisional fair value of the net assets at that time was £500,000. The goodwill would be £150,000 at that stage. On 1 July, a final fair value is set at £620,000 so the goodwill is recalculated to £120,000. These would be the amounts reported in the parent's financial statements at the year end. If there were any further adjustments to the fair value after the year end, these are recognised in profit or loss.

There are business combinations where the acquirer and acquiree agree that, if some future specific events occur, the acquiree is entitled to further payment. One possibility is the acquirer has the right to the return of previously transferred consideration if specified conditions occur. The agreement for further payments by the acquirer to the acquiree or for the acquirer to have previously made payment returned introduces the term contingent consideration. This term means that the potential payment is dependent on certain agreed occurring.

With an acquisition, the acquirer usually believes that the acquired business will continue to make profits in the future and even increase those profits. In some businesses, for example, in the advertising industry, the value of the business acquired is mostly the creative abilities of the employees and the loyalty of the clients of the business. The acquirer does not want to lose these benefits and may insert a clause in the agreement that specifies the targeted future profits for the next 3–6 years. If these are achieved, or surpassed, the acquirer agrees to pay further consideration. These agreements can be complex and for both the acquirer and acquiree involve financial and management decisions. The advantage of contingent consideration agreements is that the acquirer has some reassurances on the future success of the business but any future payment they make is contingent on that success. For the previous owners, they have the possibility of receiving a much higher consideration in total than if they had settled for one amount at the time of the acquisition.

The standard requires the acquirer to recognise, at the date of acquisition, the fair value of the contingent consideration as part of the consideration for the acquiree. The application of this definition to contingent consideration is not easy and may result in problems for some entities.

Worked example — Contingent consideration

InterAD plc acquires completely the business of EuroAd. The acquisition agreement states that there is a contingent consideration to be paid of 100,000 shares in two years' time. This is based on EuroAD achieving certain levels of profit. Both parties agree that these are achievable. At the acquisition date, the published share price of InterAD plc quoted shares is £1.00 per share. The problem is the measurement of the contingent consideration in number of shares instead of a specific financial sum. In making the agreement, InterAD has to predict the share price at the end of the period to know the full amount of the payment. A specified payment amount in financial terms is easier to manage and presents less risk. However, EuroAd may be bargaining to receive the shares in the belief that the share price will increase in two years' time.

We return to the topic of contingent consideration later in this chapter. At this stage, we discuss what the acquirer obtains for its money. At the acquisition date, the acquirer must recognise the acquiree's assets, liabilities and contingent liabilities at their fair value if they meet the following criteria:

- Assets other than intangible assets should be recognised where it is probable that the associated future economic benefits generated by the use of the assets will flow to the acquirer and their fair value can be measured reliably.
- Liabilities, other than contingent liabilities, should be recognised where it is probable that an outflow of economic benefits will be required to settle the obligation and their fair value can be measured reliably.
- Intangible asset or contingent liability should be at fair value where they can be measured reliably. Recognition can only occur where they meet the definition of an intangible asset complying with IAS 38 *Intangible assets* and their fair value is capable of being measured reliably.

Not surprisingly, respondents to the IFRS's call for feedback stated that they confronted several difficulties in the concept of fair value in acquisitions as well as practical difficulties. Although agreeing that fair value measurement provided useful information to investors, the respondents identified the following concerns:

- It does not facilitate the comparison of trends between companies that grow organically and those that grow through acquisitions.
- Upward revaluations of acquired inventory to fair value reduce profitability in the first period following the acquisition. In other words, the inventory is measured by the acquired entity at the price it was originally purchased and this may have increased by the acquisition date.
- Measuring the fair value of contingent consideration is highly judgemental and difficult to validate. In the pharmaceutical industry, the research and development period of a drug can take more than 10 years and it is common for acquisition agreements to have multiple success-based contingent consideration payments linked to stages of successful completion
- The fair value of contingent liabilities is difficult to measure as it depends on a number of assumptions and because of a general lack of guidance. We discussed contingent liabilities in Chapter 8 — IAS 37 Provisions, contingent liabilities and contingent assets.

Intangible assets and goodwill

Intangible assets are not physical in nature — you cannot touch them as with tangible assets, such as buildings and machinery. Examples of intangible assets are brand names and intellectual property, such as patents, trademarks and copyrights. A company may have legal rights to ownership of such items but they are not items that you can physically touch and hold. One intangible asset which causes significant accounting problems is goodwill. This is usually defined as the value of the business that exceeds its assets minus the liabilities. It occurs when one company acquires another company for a price greater than its net asset. The situation arises frequently where a company has developed its own intangible assets such as a brand name or a customer's list. Under IAS 38, the acquiree cannot recognise these on its balance sheet as it generated these intangible assets internally and did not purchase them from another company in a takeover.

You will appreciate that accounting for intangible assets, particularly goodwill, causes many different points of view. We have a standard

IAS 38 which addresses these issues but not everyone would agree with the requirements of the standard. The Application Guidance of IFRS 13, which we discuss in Chapter 9, provides some clarification and we summarise the main points in the following:

There must be separate recognition of identifiable intangible assets and goodwill. The intangible asset is identifiable if it meets either the separability criterion or the contractual legal criterion. Separability criterion is where the acquired intangible asset can be separated or divided from the acquiree. It can be sold, transferred, licensed, rented or exchanged, either individually or together with a related contract, identifiable asset or liability. The contractual-legal criteria are satisfied where the intangible asset is identifiable even if the asset is not transferable or separable from the acquiree or from other rights and obligations.

The Guidance gives examples of the contractual legal criterion. One example is where the acquiree owns and operates a nuclear power plant under licence. The licence cannot be sold or transferred separately from the power plant. An acquirer can recognise the fair value of the licence and the operating plant as a single asset for financial reporting purposes if the useful lives of these assets are similar. A separate calculation is made for any goodwill.

Having gone through the exercise of determining the fair value of the identifiable net assets (assets — liabilities), including intangible assets, the acquirer is likely to find that the amount it is paying is higher than the fair value of the net assets it is acquiring. The critical factor in the calculation is that only identifiable assets are included. The acquiring company is, in all probability, acquiring the reputation of the business, loyal customers, procedures and processes that are established. These characteristics all contribute to the future economic benefits the acquirer hopes to enjoy but cannot identify them specifically and individually. The acquirer will group them together under the general description of "Goodwill". The acquirer will usually pay more than the value of the tangible assets and intangible assets added together. The reason for this is that it wishes to acquire an operating and a profitable business or one with the promise to be so. It is not just acquiring assets but all those other ingredients that make up that business. These are such things as reputation of the business, experience and knowledge of workforce, contacts with suppliers, customer base and established systems and procedures. All of these ingredients fall under the heading of goodwill. Goodwill is therefore an integrated part of the business that cannot be separated from it.

In Chapter 5, we explained the standard IAS 38 Intangible assets. Those regulations require an intangible asset to be identifiable to distinguish them from goodwill. Intangible assets can be rights under licensing agreements for items such as motion picture films, video recordings, plays, manuscripts, patents and copyrights. The IFRS Foundation in its response recognises the problems raised by identifying intangible assets and goodwill. It recommends research to explore whether particular intangible assets are part of goodwill. It also considers additional guidance on the recognition and measurement of different types of intangible assets. Until there is that guidance, entities must comply with the existing requirements. When one entity acquires another, it will expect to pay for all the tangible non-current assets, such as property, plant and equipment. It will also expect to pay for the identifiable intangible assets that it acquires.

If it is so difficult to identify and classify the ingredients of goodwill, the question arises as to how one places a value on goodwill at the acquisition of another business. The standard requires that the acquirer recognises goodwill at the acquisition date. The acquirer arrives at the amount of the goodwill by the following:

1. Calculating and aggregating the consideration transferred and the amount of any non-controlling interests. In a business combination achieved in stages, the acquisition-date fair value of the acquirer's previously held equity interest in the acquiree.
2. Deducting from the aggregate amount in 1, the net of the acquisition-date amounts of the identifiable assets acquired and the liabilities assumed.

As Step 1 calculates the consideration, the deduction of Step 2 means that the resulting balance is goodwill.

The payment made for the acquisition allows the calculation of the value of goodwill, even though it is only a balancing figure. Given the ephemeral nature of goodwill, understandably IAS 36 requires the annual testing of goodwill from a business for impairment.

In Chapter 5, we reviewed IAS 36 Impairment of Assets. In that chapter, we explained that where there is an impairment of a cash-generating unit, the entity must write off any goodwill immediately. The standard does not permit the reinstatement of goodwill in the financial statements even if the impairment no longer applies. The standard assumes that, as the acquirer has paid more than the value of the net assets, the excess must have value. The acquirer must recognise goodwill on acquisition. However, an entity may make an acquisition for various reasons and may be willing to pay more than net assets. It is possible that an acquirer seeks to make the purchase not with the expectation of future benefits but for strategic reasons. For example, a small start-up business may have developed a new technology that would pose a threat to the acquirer's present business. One solution may be to acquire control of the start-up through acquisition. The payment would be high but the question is whether the excess amount is goodwill or due to the strategic decision to control or even prevent the new technology. Another example could be a competitor attempting to move into a new business or marketing area through acquisitions. The acquirer may purchase a business to block the competitor.

Negative goodwill or bargain purchases

To some extent, in the situation where one company purchases another for an amount greater than the tangible assets, the calculation of goodwill can be understood. A difficult situation arises where an acquiring entity may make a bargain purchase where the cost of acquiring the entity is less than the fair value of the identifiable net assets acquired. In these circumstances, there is a "negative" goodwill and the acquirer has made a gain that it will record in the Income Statement. However, prior to the recognition of a gain from a bargain purchase, the entity must reassess the identification and measurement of the following:

- the identifiable assets acquired and liabilities assumed,
- the non-controlling interest in the acquiree, if any,
- a business combination achieved in stages, the acquirer's previously held equity interest in the acquiree.

The required accounting treatment of intangible assets and goodwill does not meet with the satisfaction of everyone. Although the IFRS PIR found some agreed with the impairment approach to goodwill, there were several criticisms and proposed changes. The main points raised are as follows:

(a) Over time, internally generated goodwill will replace acquired goodwill.

(b) Estimating the useful life of goodwill is possible and is no more difficult than estimating the useful life of other intangible assets.
(c) Goodwill has been paid for and so, eventually, it should affect profit or loss.
(d) Amortising goodwill would decrease volatility in profit or loss when compared to an impairment model.
(e) Amortising goodwill would reduce pressure on the identification of intangible assets because both goodwill and intangible assets would be amortised.

The response from the IFRS Foundation, although recognising the issues, is not favourably disposed to a combined amortisation and impairment approach. It argues that there is evidence demonstrating that the impairment model is operating effectively. However, the Foundation accepts that there can be improvements to the impairment test and recommends further research. Any future changes would likely be directed at IAS 36 and not IFRS 3.

Non-controlling interest

A non-controlling interest is that part of the equity in a subsidiary that is not attributable, directly or indirectly, to a parent. The control of the subsidiary rests with the holder of the greatest share of the equity: the parent. Where another party holds a minor part of the equity, this is a non-controlling interest. We discuss more fully non-controlling interests when we examine IFRS 10 later in this chapter. At this stage, we can assume that with the acquisition, the acquirer owns all the equity in the acquiree, or owns sufficient equity to control the acquiree. The acquirer is the parent and the acquiree is a subsidiary.

It is possible that the acquirer does not own all the equity and others own a minority proportion. These are termed non-controlling interests. IFRS 3 allows the acquirer a choice in the accounting policy it uses to measure the non-controlling interest. The acquirer can make this choice on a transaction-by-transaction basis. The acquirer can measure the non-controlling interest of one of the following:

1. Fair value at the acquisition date (sometimes referred to as the full goodwill method). If the acquiree's shares are quoted on an active market, this price can be used as long as the acquirer's and NCI's fair

value per share does not differ. If there is no quoted share price, the acquirer must resort to other valuation methods.

2. The NCI's proportionate share of the acquiree's net assets. The net assets, as explained earlier in this chapter, are tangible assets plus intangible assets minus liabilities.

There are three possible situations with an acquisition:

1. The acquirer has 100% ownership of the acquiree.
2. The acquirer does not have full control and there are non-controlling interests. The acquiree opts to use the fair value of the acquiree at the acquisition date.
3. The acquirer does not have full control and there are non-controlling interests. The acquirer opts to use the NCI's proportionate share of the acquiree's net asset.

IFRS 3 provides additional guidance on the acquisition method. This provides assistance to entities where circumstances in the acquisition have some differences from the normal transaction. Two of the examples provided are of a stepped transaction and another is where there is no transfer of consideration.

Stepped transaction

An acquirer may already hold equity but subsequently gains control of an acquiree immediately before the acquisition date. The standard refers to this as a business combination achieved in stages or as a step acquisition. The acquirer owned equity previously but then acquires more equity to give control. The stage of obtaining control requires remeasurement of previous investments (equity interests). The acquirer remeasures its previously held equity interest in the acquiree at its acquisition-date fair value and recognises any resulting gain/loss in profit or loss.

Non-transfer of consideration

There are two situations that can arise. It could be that the acquirer and acquiree agree to combine their businesses with no consideration being transferred. The agreement for the combination is solely by contract.

Another situation would be the acquiree repurchasing a number of its own shares. In doing so, it allows an existing investor to hold a sufficient proportion of equity to gain control. The standard requires the application of the acquisition method in both these circumstances.

IFRS 3 sets out the requirements for accounting for goodwill. It would be fair to argue that not everybody is in agreement with the regulations. One obvious dispute is that acquired goodwill can be shown on the balance sheet of the acquiree but internally generated goodwill can never be recognised on the balance sheet. However, goodwill is not amortised, although it is subject to impairment testing at least annually as per IAS 36 requirements which we discussed in Chapter 5.

IFRS 10 Consolidated and Separate Financial Statements

Defining terms

The objective of IFRS 10 is to establish principles for the presentation and preparation of consolidated financial statements when an entity controls one or more other entities. The standard has a single consolidation model, based on control, applicable to all entities regardless of the nature of the investee. It is important to note that IFRS 10 has no disclosure requirements. These are contained in IFRS 12. The definition of consolidated financial statements is as follows:

The financial statements of a group in which the assets, liabilities, equity, income, expenses and cash flows of the parent and its subsidiaries are presented as those of a single economic entity.

Although most people have some understanding of the term subsidiary companies, we believe it is useful to give it some explanation. A group of companies can consist of a large number of subsidiaries. The IASB considered that the requirements in IFRS 10 will lead to more appropriate consolidation; that is, entities will consolidate investees only when they control them but, at the same time, will consolidate all investees that they control.

Reading the requirements of the accounting standard can somewhat obscure the challenge that companies can face when producing a consolidated financial statement. Before explaining the requirements of the standard, it is helpful to realise the potential difficulties confronting the accountant in achieving "consolidation" and we show in the following the Comprehensive Statements for Rio Tinto. They issue a lengthy and comprehensive financial report. The amount of information given for its financial statements takes up nearly 150 pages. A daunting task for the accountants!

Key principles

(a) requires a parent entity (an entity that controls one or more other entities) to present consolidated financial statements,
(b) defines the principle of control and establishes control as the basis for consolidation,
(c) establishes how to apply the principle of control to identify whether an investor controls an investee and therefore must consolidate the investee,
(d) explains the accounting requirements for the preparation of consolidated financial statements,
(e) defines an investment entity and sets out an exception to consolidating particular subsidiaries of an investment entity.

The concepts of control and power are the basis of the regulatory requirements. These two concepts are linked. Consolidated financial statements are only required where the investee (the parent) has control and power over the investee. The notions of control and power are central to the standard and the definitions are as follows:

Definition — Control and power

An investor controls an investee when the investor is exposed, or has rights, to variable returns from its involvement with the investee and has the ability to affect those returns through its power over the investee.

An investor has a right to variable returns from the investee when the investor's returns may fluctuate because of the investee's performance. The returns could include dividends and remuneration. There are also other forms of returns not available to other interest holders. Examples are scarce products, cost reductions, synergies, economies of scale and proprietary knowledge.

Control should be assessed on a continuous basis. Significant judgement may be required to determine whether an investor has control over an investee. The investor must consider the following factors — the purpose and design of the investee:

(a) the relevant activities and making decisions on those activities. Relevant activities are activities of the investee that significantly affect the investee's returns,
(b) whether the rights of the investor give it the current ability to direct the relevant activities,
(c) whether the investor is exposed, or has rights, to variable returns from its involvement with the investee,
(d) whether the investor has the ability to use its power over the investee to affect the amount of the investor's returns.

An investor must have the ability to use its power to affect its returns from the investee. By having the ability to direct relevant activities, the investor has that power. In some cases, identifying the investor's power may be straightforward. For example, through voting rights granted by equity instruments. In other cases, the assessment may be complex, such as when power results from contractual arrangements, such as the rights to appoint key personnel or decision-making rights. When the investor contains control of the investee, consolidated accounts must be prepared. It is possible that the investor does not hold all the equity and other parties hold a minor part. These are non-controlling interests.

Where the parent entity loses control of a subsidiary, it must carry out the following actions:

- derecognition of the subsidiary's assets and liabilities from the consolidated statement of financial position,
- recognition of any investments retained in the former subsidiary,
- recognition of the gain or loss associated with the loss of control.

Consolidation

Following an acquisition, the parent entity will have to bring all the separate financial statements of the individual subsidiaries together to prepare consolidated financial statements. Formerly, IAS 27 provided guidance, but IFRS 10 Appendix B has replaced it. The requirements themselves are straightforward, but we have supplied some worked examples to demonstrate their application.

The first stage of consolidation is to determine the assets, liabilities, income, expenses and cash flows of the parent and combine these with like items of the subsidiaries. The next stage is to eliminate the carrying amount of the parent's investment in each subsidiary and the parent's portion of equity in each subsidiary. This may give rise to an amount for goodwill. IFRS 3 sets out the accounting regulations in these circumstances.

The final stage is the most complex. In all probability, the entities in the group will have conducted some transactions among themselves. As these transactions have not been conducted with outside entities, the group has made neither a profit nor a loss. Profits or losses that individual entities recognised at the time of the transaction must be eliminated in full. We provide some examples of such transactions in the following:

Non-current asset transfers

One group entity may have transferred non-current assets, such as machinery, to another group entity at a price higher than the written-down amount in its own accounts. This transaction may have given rise to a profit. Using the single entity concept, the consolidated accounts should show the non-current asset in the consolidated group accounts at the amount as if the transfer had not been made. In other words, you must remove the profit element, as a profit cannot be made between two members of the group of companies. This removal of the profit element will also involve an adjustment to depreciation.

Worked Example — Inter group profits

On 1 January, a subsidiary sells equipment that had cost £20,000 to its parent for £25,000. The parent depreciates equipment at 10% each year. For the group accounts at the year end, both the profit of £5,000 and the additional depreciation of £500 (£2,500−£2,000) must be eliminated.

Intercompany balances

Members of a group usually trade with each other. One subsidiary may show accounts receivable in the set of financial statements. This amount is due from another subsidiary. The other subsidiary will have an equal account payable in its own financial statements. For the individual entities, that is correct, but it is misleading to show the group owing cash to and from itself. On consolidation, the intercompany amounts are cancelled.

Unrealised profit

A member of a group may hold inventory at year end purchased from another member at market price. The group member that bought the goods will record the inventory at the cost to itself, but this is not the actual cost to the group. The group entity making the sale will show a profit in its accounts — but the group has not made a profit. For the consolidated accounts, the inventory in the balance sheet and the closing inventory in the income statement are reduced to the cost without the “internal” profit.

Worked example — Inventory adjustments

At the year end, the parent has £250,000 of inventory that it purchased from its wholly owned subsidiary. The cost to the subsidiary of manufacturing these goods was £220,000 and it correctly shows in its own accounts a profit of £30,000. For the group accounts, the “profit” on the inventory must be eliminated by showing the inventory in the balance sheet and the income statement at its cost of £220,000.

We will explain some of these transactions further by looking at a simple example of a consolidated balance sheet with one wholly owned subsidiary. The holding entity is the trading entity and the wholly owned subsidiary manufactures the goods. To illustrate the transactions more clearly, we use tables instead of the usual balance sheet format.

Worked example — Muggles Manufacturing and Northern Trading

The consolidated balance sheet

Northern Trading has a fully owned subsidiary: Muggles Manufacturing. All of the output of Muggles is sold to Northern Trading. Following are the balance sheets, in table format, of Northern and Muggles on 31 December 2020:

	Northern	**Muggles**
	£000	£000
Tangible assets	350	450
Investment in sulphur (shares at cost)	400	
Inventories	160	120
Accounts receivable	80	90
Cash at bank	10	—
Total assets	**1000**	**660**
Equity	700	400
Retained earnings	150	200
Accounts payable	150	60
Total equity and liabilities	**1000**	**660**

Note: Northern has £50,000 in its accounts receivable that is due from Muggles. This amount is shown in Muggles' accounts payable.

The approach to this problem is to draw up the consolidated financial statements by adding the two balance sheets together. We cancel items that appear as assets in one statement of financial position and as a liability in the other Statement of financial position.

In this example, there are two such items. The first is the shares held by Northern in Muggles. This amount appears as an asset in Northern's balance sheet. This Muggles equity of £400,000.

The second item is the accounts receivable of £50,000 in Northern's statement of financial position matched by the accounts payable of Muggles. The accounts receivables for the two entities total £170,000. We deduct the intercompany debt of £50,000 to give a total accounts receivable of £120,000. Similarly, we add the two accounts payable together to give a total of £210,000 and deduct the £50,000 for the consolidated total of £160,000.

Consolidated statement of financial position on 31 December 2020

	£000	£000
Non-current assets		800
Current assets		
Inventories	280	
Accounts receivable	120	
Cash	10	410
Total assets		**1,210**
Equity		700
Retained earnings		350
Accounts payable		160
Total equity and liabilities		**1,210**

In the above example, the subsidiary is wholly owned. We will take the same figures but assume that Northern owns 80% of Muggles' shares that it bought at cost. We need to make the following adjustments to draw up the consolidated balance sheet:

1. The adjustment is made for the minority interests. We adjust for Northern's ownership of the shares, that is, 80%. We repeat the above example but we reduce Northern's investment to £320,000 (80% of £400,000)
2. We have increased Northern's inventory by £80,000 to compensate for the decrease in Northern's investment. We have made this

mathematical adjustment so that we retain consistency and comparability between the two examples as far as all the other items are concerned.

3. We will assume, once again, that £50,000 in Northern's accounts receivable is due from sulphur and shown in that entity's accounts payable.

	Northern	**Muggles**
	£000	£000
Tangible assets	350	450
Investment in sulphur (80% shares at cost)	320	
Inventories	240	120
Accounts receivable	80	90
Cash at bank	10	—
Total assets	**1000**	**660**
Equity	700	400
Retained earnings	150	200
Accounts payable	150	60
Total equity and liabilities	**1000**	**660**

Before we construct the consolidated statement, we will calculate the non-controlling interest. The non-controlling interest is 20% of Muggles capital (£80,000) and 20% (£40,000) of the retained earnings. The total for non-controlling interests is therefore £120,000, and in the following statement, we show it after retained earnings:

Consolidated statement of financial position on 31 December 2020 (80% owned subsidiary)

	£000	**£000**
Non-current assets		800
Current assets		
Inventories		360
Accounts receivable		120
Cash	10	490
Total assets		1,290

(*Continued*)

	£000	**£000**
Equity		700
Retained earnings (150,000 = 80% of £200,000)	310	1,010
Non-controlling interests		120
Accounts payable		160
Total equity and liabilities		**1,290**

The consolidated income statement

Our final topic in this section on consolidated accounts is the Income Statement. We will use the example of Northern, the parent, having an 80% investment in Muggles. You may have realised at this point that of the consolidated profit, 80% will belong to Northern and 20% will belong to the non-controlling interests.

	Northern	**Muggles**	**Adjustment**	**Consolidated**
	£000	£000	£000	£000
Sales	150	76	(12)	214
Cost of sales	60	40		
Gross profit	90	36	(4)	122
Admin expenses	30	6		36
Profit before taxation	60	30		86
Tax	20	10		30
Profit after taxation	40	20		56
Non-controlling interest				4

Notes:

1. The sales figure is reduced by £12,000, the amount of the sales that Muggles made to Northern.
2. Gross profit must be reduced by £4,000 being the amount that Muggles would have taken in its own Income Statement.

   The cost of sales figure can be calculated by deducting the consolidated gross profit from the consolidated sales.
3. The non-controlling interest share of the profit is calculated at 20% of Muggles profit after tax because it is in that entity the shares are held.

Note that we have calculated the tax on an arbitrary basis to demonstrate this example and not according to the requirements of IAS 12 that we discussed in Chapter 15.

The only complication we will include is that Muggles made £12,000 in sales to Northern during the year. These goods had been purchased from an outside supplier for £8,000. You will remember from our earlier discussions in this chapter that a group cannot make a profit by member companies trading with one another. We will assume taxation is 50%.

Investment entities

An investment entity obtains funds from one or more investors and provides investment management services to them. The investment entity has the business purpose of investing funds solely for returns from capital appreciation, investment income or both. The entity will measure and evaluate the performance of substantially all of the investments on a fair value basis. IFRS 10 requires a qualifying investment entity to account for investments in controlled entities, associates and joint ventures at fair value through profit or loss. This does not apply if the investee is a subsidiary that provides investment-related services or engages in investment-related activities with investees. In this instance, the investment entity has to prepare consolidated financial statements.

IFRS 10 also requires a parent to determine whether it is an investment entity. To do this, the entity must comply with three essential tests.

- It obtains funds from one or more investors to provide those investors with investment management services.
- Its declared business purpose is to invest for returns solely from capital appreciation and/or investment income.
- It measures and evaluates the performance of substantially all investments on a fair value basis.

The parent is an investment entity that should have one or more of the following characteristics:

- It has more than one investment.
- It has more than one investor.
- It has investors that are not related parties of the investee.
- It has ownership interests in the form of equity or similar interests.

Accounting issues

Business relationships are complex and they are numerous. Large entities frequently make agreements for different types of business relationships with others. These corporate activities not only involve strategic and managerial decisions but also are subject to legal, tax and accounting requirements. The standards now in issue have resolved many of the difficulties for business combinations. There remain many areas where accountants must make substantial estimates and judgements. We have explained the requirements of IFRS 3 and IFRS 10, but we highlight the main practical issues. These are separated into the time of acquisition and the preparation of consolidated financial statements.

The acquisition

- whether one business has acquired another or merely purchased assets,
- the date on which the acquisition is made and the identifying the acquirer,
- identifying and placing a fair value on the assets acquired and the liabilities so that the deduction of net assets from the acquisition price correctly identifies goodwill,
- identifying separate intangible assets so that they are not subsumed into goodwill,
- measuring the consideration given by the acquirer for the acquiree. Consideration may include shares where there is no active market to price them. There may also be contingent consideration.

Preparation of consolidated financial statements

- deciding any adjustments that should be made if the parent and subsidiary have different year ends,
- identifying asset classification of the subsidiaries' assets at the group level,
- deciding which items should be disclosed separately in the corporate financial statements and those items that can be aggregated as they are immaterial at the group level,
- amalgamating financial information measured in different currencies.

IFRS 3 applies to both acquisitions and mergers. Our explanations have focussed on acquisitions without comment on any particular difficulties that may arise with a "true merger". Fortunately, the announcement made by Dow and Dupont in December 2015 that they would merge is an excellent and unusual example of a merger.

The case is well documented in the press, but we list in the following some aspects as an illustration of the ingredients in a merger. We would emphasise that both are US companies and IFRS 3 and IFRS 10 do not apply.

- The two companies have a combined workforce of more than 110,000.
- Under the terms of the merger, Dow shareholders will receive a fixed exchange ratio of one share of DowDuPont for each Dow share, and DuPont shareholders will receive a fixed exchange ratio of 1.282 shares in DowDuPont for each DuPont share. Dow and DuPont shareholders will own about 50%, respectively, of the combined company.
- The two companies will first form DowDuPont and then separate into three independent publicly traded companies focused on agriculture, material science and speciality products.
- The merger should cut annual expenses by $3 billion.

Given the size of the companies, the amounts involved and the proposal to change the two companies into three publicly traded companies, this is a huge undertaking. If you reread the steps that have to be taken to account for an acquisition or merger, you will realise both the practical complexities the companies face and the difficulties in standard setters in establishing regulations.

Chapter Review

Business relationships are extensive and vary in structure and operation. Although there were several accounting standards addressing different forms of organisational relationships, there were inconsistencies and situations where the regulations did not "fit". As part of the convergence project with the FASB, in 2002, the IASB commenced a comprehensive project to address inconsistencies in the existing regulations. The project has produced two standards, IFRS 3 and IFRS 10, both concerned with mergers and acquisitions and consolidated financial statements. We have focussed on these two standards in this chapter. In the following chapter, we examine other forms of business relationships that do not comprise a business combination.

IFRS 3 covers the principles on the recognition and measurement of acquired assets and liabilities, the determination of goodwill and the necessary disclosures. The emphasis is on the application of the acquisition method. Entities must use this for all business combinations. There are four stages:

(1) identifying the acquirer,
(2) determining the acquisition date,
(3) recognising and measuring the identifiable assets acquired, the liabilities assumed and any non-controlling interest in the acquiree,
(4) recognising and measuring goodwill or a gain from a bargain purchase.

IFRS 11 explains the principles for the presentation and preparation of consolidated financial statements when an entity controls one or more other entities. The standard has a single consolidation model, based on control, applicable to all entities regardless of the nature of the investee. The standard contains no disclosure requirements. We discuss in the following chapter, the requirements for the disclosure contained in IFRS 12.

The standards have emerged from a network of former standards and attempt to bring clarity to a complex subject. Although the standards have contributed significantly to accounting for business combinations, problems remain. The nature of these problems has been published in a research document (IFRS 2015). The public consultation revealed several concerns and the IFRS responded with the steps it intended to take. The document emphasises that more research is required to provide solutions to some of the issues. This could mean subsequent amendments to IFRS 3. However, our final summary of the issues suggests that accounting for business combinations will always be a complex topic.

CHAPTER 7 Combining Businesses

Review Questions

1. What is regarded as the cost of a business combination?
   a. The fair value of the consideration plus attributable expenses
   b. Cash transferred to the acquiree
   c. The equal share of future profits
   d. The issue of equity instruments, such as ordinary shares
2. Which one of the following is not defined as an intangible asset in IAS38?
   a. Brand names
   b. Intellectual property
   c. Patents
   d. Strong management
3. What is the definition of the term "business combination"?
4. What is the basic principle where a business combination has taken place?
5. How is the term "goodwill" defined?
6. What is the principle of a business combination?
7. What is a non-controlling interest?
8. To what business arrangements do IFRS 3 Business Combinations apply?

Chapter 8

Contextual Disclosures

Structure of Chapter 8

Section title	Main content
IAS 8 Accounting policies, changes in accounting estimates and errors	A lengthy standard but very important in determining the content of the financial statements.
IAS 37 Provisions, contingent liabilities and contingent assets	This standard requires companies to disclose the methods they apply in the way that they account for future uncertainties.
IFRS 4 Insurance Contracts	A difficult standard to apply, and after much debate, it was replaced by IFRS 17 which we discuss in Chapter 9.
IFRS 5 Non-current assets held for sale and discontinued operations.	These assets are not profit generators and it is useful for investors to know their value.
IFRS 8 Operating segments	Larger companies may have several identifiable operating segments with various levels of profitability.
Chapter Review	An explanation of various corporate activities and their accounting treatment in the financial statements.

Some standards do not address a specific financial transaction or items but are more general in their coverage. The standards that we discuss in this chapter are useful to investors as they help provide a context in which to place the organisation's activities. They also ensure that users receive information that other standards may not include. In this chapter, we deal with four standards that help frame the context in which users can better understand financial statements. From a technical perspective, none of these standards is complicated but does ensure that useful information is available to investors.

IAS 8 *Accounting Policies, Changes in Accounting Estimates and Errors* is the key to understanding the financial statements of an entity. The standard covers three aspects: policies, estimates and errors. The disclosure of accounting policies assists users in understanding how an entity executes its transactions, events and conditions. An entity's financial statements include many pages explaining the entity's policies used in constructing their financial statements. In preparing their financial statements, entities must make some estimates because not all the information will be available at that time. The entity must therefore make estimates based on the most recent information it has. In earlier chapters, we discussed depreciation and the need for management to determine the useful economic life of an asset and its future scrap value. As the years pass, management may revise its estimates. The standard explains the procedure for making changes in the financial statements. A change in an estimate will impact an entity's expected future benefits and obligations, and therefore it must adjust its financial statements to provide this information.

In addition to policies and estimates, IAS 8 also addresses prior period errors. It is possible that there was a mistake in past financial statements, but the entity has only now realised it. Errors can be due to such occurrences, such as computer malfunctions, fraud and mistakes in applying accounting policies. These errors are not changes in accounting policies or in accounting estimates. The entity, unknowingly at the time, published information that was misleading and the entity now has the information to correct the error. The error may be so minor as to have no effect on the financial statements and no special actions need to be taken. Where the error is material, the entity must correct it retrospectively as the previous financial disclosures were incorrect. The standard explains the procedure.

The second standard we discuss, IAS 37 *Provisions, contingent liabilities and contingent assets*, has the objective of preventing accounting abuses. At one time, entities had considerable latitude in making provisions for future events that might impact their profits. It is reasonable for entities to make a provision for some future occurrence they anticipates. However, they should not use these provisions as a method for managing earnings or misdirecting shareholders although it may be tempting for them to do so. The standard therefore requires that there is a future obligation arising from a past event, payment is probable and a reliable estimate can be made of the amount. Although an entity may wish to make a provision, the circumstances may not satisfy the above criteria. In particular, there may be a level of uncertainty. The standard sets out the treatment of these uncertainties under the topics of contingent liabilities and contingent assets.

The final two standards are important in ensuring investors are fully informed but narrower in their scope. IFRS 5 deals with non-current assets held for sale. IFRS 8 requires the disclosure of operating segments and this is highly relevant with some larger companies.

IAS 8 Accounting Policies, Changes in Accounting Estimates and Errors

A company's accounting policies are important to the users of financial statements as they determine the financial information which is disclosed. IAS 8 sets out the criteria for selecting and applying accounting policies, and accounting for changes in accounting policies. It requires the disclosure of these policies, the judgements used in applying them, and assumptions and other sources of estimation uncertainty.

The purpose of disclosing the accounting policies is to assist users in better understanding the treatment of transactions, other events and conditions the company has taken and incorporated in the financial report. The following arguments support the disclosure of accounting policies:

- The users of the financial statements would expect the entity to disclose certain policies because of the nature of its operations.
- A policy may be significant in the present financial period because of the nature of the entity's operations even if amounts for current and prior periods are not material.

- An entity has selected a particular policy from alternatives allowed in IFRSs.

Accounting policy disclosures of companies applying IFRS often fill many pages in the financial statements, as companies usually disclose more than only the significant accounting policies. There has been discussion and experiments by companies in determining the most effective way to make the disclosures. The Financial Reporting Council Lab has conducted research into the possible needs of users. It concluded that investors apply their knowledge and experience to determine which accounting policies are significant for an entity's specific business and transactions. However, the FRC Report identified several attributes policies should have and we summarise these in the following:

- *Material transaction classes and amounts*: While not every material balance indicates a significant policy, the policy on revenue is considered always significant. Investors are particularly interested in policies that are important or unique to the business' operations.
- *Accounting policy choices*: While the number of explicit choices of accounting policy allowed in IFRS is decreasing, where a choice is allowed, that policy should be considered significant unless it is clearly immaterial.
- *Judgement and/or estimation*: Accounting policies that require significant levels of estimation and/or judgement in their application are significant. Investors want insight into the sensitivity of balances and earnings amounts stemming from elements of estimation and judgement.

Investors in the FRC study wanted accounting policy disclosure to be entity-specific and they should enable a user to understand:

- the relevance of the policy to the entity and its business transactions,
- where the entity has made a policy choice and why that choice is most appropriate for the business,
- how the entity applies its policies,
- the impact of judgement and estimation required in the application,
- consequences for the reported amounts.

IAS 8 provides examples of different formats and placings of information on the accounting policies of the entity under the three main headings which we discuss in the following.

Selecting and applying accounting policies

An entity should follow the requirements of standards or interpretations in selecting and applying its accounting policies and introducing any subsequent changes. Where the regulations do not address specific issues, the management must use its own judgement in setting its policy by referring to the following sources:

- any other IASB Standard or Interpretation dealing with relevant matters,
- definitions, recognition criteria and measurement concepts for assets and liabilities, income and expenses contained in the IASB's Framework for the Preparation and Presentation of Financial Statements,
- recent pronouncements by other standard-setting bodies that do not conflict with IFRSs and Framework.

Although an entity should be consistent in applying its policies, there are two circumstances where it can make a change:

- The issue by the IASB of a standard or interpretation that requires companies to make the change. In this case, the new standard will provide transitional arrangements to assist the entity in introducing the change.
- The entity is of the opinion that a change is required to improve the reliability and relevancy of information in the financial statements.

In the second case, the entity must apply the change retrospectively to all periods presented in the financial statements as if the new accounting policy has always been applied. In other words, the financial statements of the current period and each prior period presented are adjusted so that it appears as if the new accounting policy had always been the one used.

Retrospective application can create a substantial amount of work for an entity. The standard setters recognize this, and an entity need not make retrospective application where it is impracticable and the entity has made every reasonable effort to do so. There is some potential for scope in judgement where terms such as "impractical" and "reasonable effort" are used. The standard aims to ensure that entities do not overstretch the notion of impracticability and requires that entities meet the following criteria:

- The effects of the retrospective application cannot be determined or requires assumptions about what would have been management's intent at that time.
- Significant estimates of amounts are required and it is impossible to distinguish objectively information about those estimates that provides evidence of circumstances that existed on the dates at which those amounts are to be recognised, measured and disclosed, and would have been available when the financial statements for that prior period were authorised for issue from other information.

The ability of management to change accounting policies is severely restricted and should not be confused with accounting estimates that we discuss in the following section.

Accounting estimates

The standard emphasises that changes in accounting estimates are not corrections of errors but estimates resulting from new information or new developments. The estimates involve the carrying amount on the balance sheet of an asset or a liability or the amount of the periodic consumption of an asset, in other words, the asset's expected life. At the year end, when an entity is preparing its financial statements, not all the information that is required will be available. The entity must therefore make estimates. Examples of activities where estimates may be required are in the following list:

- Doubtful debts: This is the amount customers owe, but the entity believes it may not be able to collect for various reasons. An estimate must be made on the amount which is not collectable.
- Depreciation: Companies have to estimate both the useful economic life of the asset and the future scrap value of the asset. These estimates may change for many reasons. Machinery and equipment may last longer than anticipated, possibly because there has not been significant usage.
- Inventory obsolescence.
- The carrying value of assets which may be subject to impairment.

Understandably, as time progresses, entities receive new information and this may cause them to change their estimates. The standard explains how these changes are actioned in the financial statements. A change in an estimate affects the expected future benefits and obligations of the entity. The entity, therefore, must adjust the carrying amount in the financial statements. There is no need to change the financial statements for previous years as the entity issued these based on the best information available at that time. When there is a change in estimates, an entity should change the financial statements in the present period and in future periods if appropriate. We show two hypothetical examples in the following of appropriate changes in accounting estimates.

Worked example

Change in Doubtful Debts Estimate

Because the economic environment is rapidly declining, an entity decides that it should increase the amount for doubtful debts from 2% to 3% of the accounts receivable. This is a change in the accounting estimate of the amount that it expects to recover from account receivables. There is no need to revise precious financial statements as they were constructed on the best information at that time i.e. when the economy was heathier.

Note that many entities will refer to a provision for doubtful debts. This can be misleading as doubtful debts are NOT a provision as defined under IAS 37 that we discuss in the following section.

An entity should not apply any change in accounting estimates retrospectively. The entity has received new information currently that persuades it to change its estimates of future events and transactions.

Prior period errors

Prior period errors are omissions from, and misstatements in, the entity's financial statements for one or more prior periods arising from a failure to use, or misuse, of reliable information. They arise where there was a mistake in past financial statements, but the entity has only now realised it. Examples of prior period errors are as follows:

- mathematical errors,
- fraud,
- mistakes in applying accounting policies
- misinterpretations or failure to observe facts.

Worked example

Change of asset life estimate

A company purchases machinery on 1 January 2019 for £100,000. The company considers that the machinery has a useful life of 10 years and no residual value. The annual depreciation charge using the straight-line method is as follows:

$$\text{Annual depreciation charge} = \frac{£100{,}000}{10\,\text{years}} = £10{,}000$$

Three years later, on 31 December 2021, the carrying amount of the machinery is £70,000.

On 1 January 2022, the company decides that the remaining useful life of the machinery is only 5 years and not 7 years. The annual depreciation charge from 1 January 2022 and for the following years will be as follows:

$$\text{Annual depreciation charge} = \frac{£70{,}000}{5\,\text{years}} = £14{,}000$$

Such errors are not changes in accounting policies or changes in accounting estimates. The entity has made a mistake in its financial statements. Errors will frequently be so insignificant that they have no impact on the financial statements. In this case, the error can be corrected through net profit or loss for the current period. To determine whether an error is insignificant, an entity has to apply the concept of materiality. This can be difficult to determine. The standard explains that an error is material if it could influence the economic decisions of users. It adds that materiality depends on the size and nature of the omission or misstatement judged in the surrounding circumstances. These requirements leave it to the entity to determine materiality and whether users will make different economic decisions. This is a difficult task and you may consider that the accounting requirements are not rigorous.

Where the error is material, the entity must correct it retrospectively. There are two possibilities:

- restating the comparative amounts for the prior periods in which the error occurred,
- where the error occurred before the earliest prior period presented, restating the opening balances of assets, liabilities and equity for that period.

For example, if a prior period error has occurred, the entity must adjust the financial statements for when they occurred and not the present financial statements. Thus, an entity preparing its financial statements for 2021 may find a previous error in the 2020 financial statements. The correction should not be made in the 2021 financial statements but in the year when the error took place. To do otherwise would make the 2020 financial statements incorrect.

Prior period errors are fundamental in nature. An entity should recognize them only if it is clear that they should not have issued the original financial statements because of these errors. The error could have arisen due to a fault in an accounting estimate. However, it was the best estimate that the entity could make at that time with the information available. In this situation, the error is a change in accounting estimates.

As with accounting policies, the standard permits companies not to make the changes if it were impracticable but various disclosures are required.

IAS 37 Provisions, Contingent Liabilities and Contingent Assets

This standard presents no conceptual issues but is messy to study as it covers three related topics that require specific explanations of terms and examples. IAS 37 attempts to regulate the way that companies account for future uncertainties. It deals with three related topics: provisions, contingent liabilities and contingent assets and the definitions of these are:

Provision: A liability of uncertain timing or amount.

Contingent assets: Due to past events and confirmed by the occurrence or non-occurrence of uncertain future events outside the entity's control.

Contingent liability: There is significant uncertainty with a number of aspects regarding a liability.

Before we explain the requirements of the standards, it is helpful to illustrate the amount of information a company provides in relation to the financial statements. In the following, we show an extract from the annual report of Diageo plc for 2022. The annual report is over 200 pages in length and, as can be seen from the following extract, sets out its accounting policies in detail:

Details of critical estimates and judgements which the Directors consider could have a significant impact upon the financial statements are set out in the related notes as follows:

- *Exceptional items — management judgement whether exceptional or not — page 156.*
- *Taxation — management judgement of whether a provision is required and management estimate of amount of corporate tax payable or receivable, the recoverability of deferred tax assets and expectation on manner of recovery of deferred taxes — pages 160 and 192.*
- *Brands, goodwill and other intangibles — management judgement of the assets to be recognised and synergies resulting from an acquisition. Management judgement and estimate are required in determining future cash flows and appropriate applicable assumptions to support the intangible asset value — page 166.*
- *Post employment benefits — management judgement in determining whether a surplus can be recovered and management estimate in determining the assumptions in calculating the liabilities of the funds — page 172.*
- *Contingent liabilities and legal proceedings — management judgement in assessing the likelihood of whether a liability will arise and an estimate to quantify the possible range of any settlement and significant unprovided tax matters where maximum exposure is provided for each — page 191.*

Provisions

Some people refer to "provision for depreciation" and "provision for doubtful debts". Neither of these items is provision under IAS 37. They are accounting estimates and IAS 8 set out the requirements for accounting estimates. We discuss that standard in the previous section. In this section, we discuss provisions, contingent liabilities and contingent assets; IAS 37 regulates these three areas. The standard was introduced to prevent dubious accounting practices that were being exploited by some entities. The objective of the entity was to manage the amount of profits reported. If an entity had a very profitable year, it would reduce the profit by creating a provision: a type of fund to deal with future uncertainties. If in future years profits declined for some reason, the entity would use these provisions to boost its profits. As far as the users of the financial statements were concerned, the entity was reporting a steady profit every year. The true picture may have been that the entity had moved from high profits to low profits but was hiding this by the use of provisions.

It is very important under the standard that companies do not make provisions for something they consider may happen in the future. For example, businesses cannot make provisions for future operating losses. The abuse of provisions was well known. Some types of provisions were known as "Big bath provisions" or "Cookie jar provisions" because entities were using them to sweeten their profits and clean up any financial messes they did not like. The result was that the financial statements for any particular financial period could mislead users. The standard introduces the criteria that an entity must fulfil to make a provision. Essentially, a provision is a liability of uncertain timing or amount. There are four key criteria for determining if the entity can make a provision:

1. Present obligation arises from a past event.
2. Payment is probable.
3. The amount can be estimated reliably.
4. There is a present obligation.

Present obligation

The requirement of a "present obligation", in other words, a liability, is very important. The standard defines two types of obligations: legal and constructive. A legal obligation is possibly the easiest to identify and could be

- a contractual entered into by the parties,
- due to legislation,
- a result of some other operation of law.

Looking first at the present legal obligation, an entity may be embroiled in a court case where there is some uncertainty about whether the entity has a present obligation. In other words, whether it is likely to win or lose the case. In such an event, the entity would seek legal advice as to the likely outcome. If the advice is that the entity is probably going to lose the case, the entity makes a provision for the estimated amount of damages. When we are considering court cases for international companies, the time span can be many years and the levels of uncertainty are complex.

Constructive obligation

In addition to the obligation being present, there must also be a constructive obligation. This is an obligation arising from an entity's own practices or policies in that it has led others to believe that it will act in a certain way. This includes those circumstances where past practice leads third parties to assume that the entity will settle the obligation. For example, a retailer may have a favourable return policy on goods purchased by customers. A constructive obligation is established.

Payment is probable

The payment will involve an outflow of economic resources and it is more likely than not that the entity will have to make this payment. This is a challenging judgement the management has to make. Probable is explained by the phrase "more likely than not," but this could be construed in several ways, particularly where the issues are complex.

Amount can be estimated reliably

Reliably does not mean exactly. If you refer to the definition, it states that a provision is uncertain in amount. The amount recognised as a provision should be the best estimate of the expenditure required to settle the present obligation at the balance sheet date. A business should assess the risks and uncertainties that may operate in reaching its best estimate. If there are any material future cash flows, the entity should discount these to present values. If the entity considers that it can estimate the amount reliably, this could be an indication that payment is probable.

Examples of provisions include warranty obligations, a retailer's policy on refunds to customers, obligation to clean up contaminated land and restructuring and onerous contracts.

The regulations on the requirement to make a provision are unambiguous and the following hypothetical example demonstrates the position:

Worked example

"Hometown plc operates in the UK where there is legislation compelling to clean up environmental damage it may cause. In the month of December 2020, the company causes environmental damage and estimates that it will cost approximately £750,000 to remedy. It intends to carry out this work in June 2021. Its year-end is the 31st December.

Hometown should make a provision of £750,000 in its financial statements for the year ended 31 December 2020."

There are occasions where an entity might consider making a provision, but the situation does not meet the requirement of the standard. Essentially, there is no present obligation because of a past event. The most common examples are where the entity is confronting a future problem or opportunity and is making the decision in the current financial year but will not take action in the following year. Another example is where an entity may be aware that a competitor is launching a new product next year that will affect its own sales. It decides to launch its own version of the product next year with a massive advertising campaign. However, the entity cannot make a provision this year for the campaign it plans for next year.

The standard refers specifically to some events that do not meet the conditions of the standard but where an entity can make a provision. The first we discuss is where some form of entity restructuring is taking place. The second is where there are onerous contracts.

Companies include in their annual reports the position that they have taken with provisions and we show an example from the 2021 annual report and accounts of the Compass Group:

"Provisions are recognised when the Group has a present obligation as a result of a past event and it is probable that the Group will be required to settle that obligation. Provisions are measured at the directors' best estimate of the cost of settling these liabilities and are discounted to present value where the effect is material. Restructuring provisions are recognised if a detailed restructuring plan is in place, a valid expectation that the plan will be implemented has been created in those

impacted by it and there is a reliable estimate of the costs involved. Restructuring provisions only include the direct costs of the restructuring and exclude future operating costs. A provision for onerous contracts is recognised when the expected benefits to be derived by the Group from a contract are lower than the unavoidable cost of meeting its obligations under the contract."

Corporate restructuring

It is not unusual for entities to decide that they need to make some form of organizational restructuring. This could be the closure of parts of the business or some form of amalgamations or reorganisation. The entity may have determined in the present financial year the action it will take but has decided not to implement them until the following year. As this is a future and not a past event, it does not meet the main requirements of the standard. However, if the entity complies with the criteria laid down in the standard for restructuring it may make a provision. The events recognised in the standard as entity restructuring are as follows:

- sale or termination of a line of business,
- the closure of a business location in a country or region or the relocation of business activities from one country,
- changes in management structure, for example, eliminating a layer of management,
- fundamental reorganizations that have a material effect on the nature and focus of the business operations.

Where the above events are going to occur, the restructuring may be identified as a constructive obligation. The standard defines this as an obligation arising from an entity's own practices or policies in that it has led others to believe that the entity will act in a certain way. To demonstrate there is a constructive obligation, the entity must fulfil two criteria. There must be a detailed formal plan that the entity communicates to those affected by the restructuring. The main contents of a formal plan are shown in the following:

Outline of a formal restructuring plan

- the business or part of a business concerned,
- the principal locations affected,

- the location, function and approximate number of employees who will be compensated for terminating their services,
- suppliers and customers who will be affected,
- the expenditure that will be undertaken,
- the date the plan will be implemented.

The critical element in the plan is the communication with those likely to be most affected: the employees who will lose their jobs. It is normal for an entity to make a public announcement and discuss the details of the plan with those affected. Frequently, the trade unions will be closely involved if there are any in the organisation. We demonstrate the importance of the timing in the two following scenarios.

Worked examples — Provisions for restructuring

Scenario 1
A company makes up its annual financial statements on 30 April. The Board approves on 20 March 2022 to close permanently one of its factories on 31 July that year. The Board is unable to communicate its decision to any of those affected before 30 April. In these circumstances, no provision for the costs to be incurred in 2022 can be made in the financial statements.

Scenario 2
The details are similar to Scenario 1 but by 12 April, the company has informed the affected employees at a meeting and has written to all its suppliers and customers. In this case, a provision can be made in its financial statements for the year ended 30 April 2022 for the costs it can reliably estimate that it will incur.

Onerous contracts

During the course of business, an entity will enter into many contracts. Some will have terms that allow them to cancel the contract without incurring any financial penalties. There are others containing terms that compel the entity to pay some form of damages on cancellation of the contract. This falls under the concept of onerous contracts and the entity is able to make a provision.

An example of an onerous contract is a non-cancellable lease. An entity may enter into a non-cancellable lease to occupy office premises.

With two years of the lease remaining, the entity decides to move to another location. The lease is non-cancellable so the entity still has to make the lease payments for the office it is vacating until the end of the contract. The accepted accounting method is to make a provision for the outstanding amounts that the lessee still has to pay to the lessee under the lease agreement.

Reversing provisions

An entity may have made a provision that complies fully with the standard. For example, there may be a planned restructuring and all the various parties affected have been informed. However, circumstances may have changed and the restructuring will not take place. As the provision is no longer required, the entity should reverse the provision by a credit to the profit or loss account.

The standard requires entities to make an annual review of provisions. If the provisions are no longer required, they should be reversed. The entity cannot use a provision it made for one eventuality that did not occur for another eventuality that was not predicted.

Contingent liabilities

Definition

A contingent liability is where there is significant uncertainty with a number of aspects regarding the liability.

The key term in the above definition is “significant uncertainty” and this can take one of two forms:

1. There is a possible obligation, arising from past events, but more information is required to determine whether it is a present obligation. Note that the term “present obligation” refers to provisions that we discussed above.
2. There is a present obligation but it is uncertain whether it will be settled or it cannot be measured reliably.

The standard requires contingent liabilities to be disclosed in the Notes in the Annual Report and Accounts whereas provisions appear as a charge in the profit or loss account.

There is a relationship between provisions and contingent liabilities. Differentiating between the two is a matter of the level of certainty and this may take a considerable time to determine. For example, an entity may recognize a particular event as a contingent liability. However, as time passes, the nature of the event changes. It may change to such an extent that the entity can define it as a provision.

A contingent liability

It is more likely than not that no present obligation exists; the entity discloses a contingent liability in the notes to the accounts.

A provision

It is probable (more likely than not) that an outflow of resources embodying economic benefits will be required to settle the obligation. A charge will be made to the profit or loss account.

Where the possibility of an outflow of resources embodying economic benefits is remote, no disclosures are required. The following example illustrates the "certainty" relationship between a contingent liability and a provision.

Worked example — Contingent liability to provision

Endcap plc is being sued for damages by one of its major customers who commences legal action in 2020. When preparing the year end 2020 financial statements the directors opinion was that the likelihood of any payments being made to the claimant was ***remote****. In accordance with IAS 37 they did not adjust their financial statements or make any disclosures.*

In 2021 the court case was still proceeding. The company's lawyers informed the directors that they considered that it was ***possible*** *the customer would win the case. The directors therefore disclosed a contingent liability in its financial statements for 2021.*

In 2022 the lawyers advised Endcap that it was ***probable*** *that the customer would win the case and their best estimate is that the damages would be £2.5 million. Accordingly, the directors would make a provision in its financial statements for that amount.*

You will find that most disclosures on contingent liabilities refer to court cases. As these cases can take many years to resolve, an entity may disclose a court case as a contingent liability. As the case proceeds and it becomes probable that the entity will lose the case, it will make a provision based on the best estimate of the costs it will suffer.

Contingent assets

A contingent asset is a possible asset that arises from past events and whose existence will be confirmed only by the occurrence or non-occurrence of one or more uncertain future events not wholly within the control of the entity.

The above definition, taken from the standard, is not easy to follow. Fortunately, contingent assets do not appear frequently in Annual Reports. When they do appear, they are usually related to court cases. An example is a legal claim that an entity is pursuing but is uncertain it will be successful. Contingent assets should not be recognised in the financial statements themselves but are disclosed when an inflow of economic benefits is probable.

In a court case, an entity is dependent on legal advice. If this states that it is probable that the entity will win the case, it should disclose a contingent asset in the Notes to the accounts. If the legal advice states that it is virtually certain that the entity will win the case, it is no longer regarded as "contingent" and would appear in the balance sheet as an asset. If it is only possible that the entity will win, then nothing will appear in the Annual Report regarding the matter.

IAS 37 Provisions, Contingent assets and Contingent liabilities is a standard that causes some difficulties for entities in its application. The concepts of probable, possible and remote are matters of judgement and opinions may differ. Additionally, we are dealing with uncertainties, and our ability in predicting future events and measuring them in monetary terms is not foolproof.

IFRS 4 Insurance Contracts

This is not a subject that one would rush to read but very important to a company entering into insurance contracts. The purpose of the standard was to differentiate "insurance risk" from "financial risk". It applies to insurance contracts that an entity issues and defines an insurance contract as a contract under which one party (the insurer) accepts significant insurance risk from another party (the policyholder) by agreeing to compensate the policyholder if a specified uncertain future event (the insured event) adversely affects the policyholder. Insurers are exempted from applying the Conceptual Framework and some accounting standards. A replacement standard, IFRS 17, has been issued and becomes effective on January 1, 2023. The argument in favour of the replacement standard is that it removes some of the problems in the old standard and applies more consistent principles to be applied. It is too early to assess the application of the new standards.

IFRS 5 Non-current Assets Held for Sale and Discontinued Operations

The objective of the standard is to require disclosure of discontinued operations so that the user of financial statements can evaluate their effects on the entire entity. If the users are analysing the financial statements, they are interested in the profit the assets can generate. If the entity is in the process of trying to sell some of the assets, the users will find this information helpful.

The entity should disclose the following:

1. the net cash flows, classified as operating, investing and financing, attributable to a discontinued operation for the current and comparative period on the face of the statement cash flows or in the notes,
2. a single amount on the statement of comprehensive income that shows the total
   (a) after-tax profit or loss from discontinued operations and
   (b) the after-tax gain or loss recognised on the remeasurement to fair value less costs to sell or on disposal.

The entity should also disclose on the face of the income statement or in the notes the revenue, expenses, pre-tax profit or loss and the related income tax expense of the discontinued operation.

IFRS 5 is a straightforward standard, although it contains several definitions that need attention in their application. The classification, presentation and measurement requirements of IFRS 5 also apply to a non-current asset (or disposal group) that is classified as held for distribution to owners. The key definition is for a discontinued operation.

Definition: Discontinued operations

A component of an entity that either has been disposed of or is classified as held for sale and both represents a separate line of business or geographical area of operations and is part of a single coordinated plan to dispose of a separate major line of business.

The "component" is easily identifiable. It is part of an entity where the operations and cash flows can be clearly distinguished, operationally and for financial reporting purposes, from the rest of the entity. They are cash-generating units or a group of cash-generating units while being held for use.

The discontinued operation may be a single non-current asset or a group of non-current assets. The standard defines a group of non-current assets as follows:

- a group of assets to be disposed of, by sale or otherwise,
- together as a group in a single transaction,
- liabilities directly associated and transferred with those assets.

At the end of the financial year, the entity either has disposed of the component or intends to. The reasons for the disposal could be many. It may be strategic if the entity is shifting the focus of its operations, political if the component is in a region that the entity does not regard as favourable or simply that the entity believes it can obtain more by disposal than continuing to operate the component.

At the end of the financial year, the entity will be in one of the following positions:

Discontinued operations accounting treatments

Held for sale

The asset must be ready for immediate sale in its present condition and a sale must be highly probable.

Sold

Disposed of during the financial year and transaction shown in financial statements.

Non-current assets held for sale

An asset is held for sale when an entity does not intend to use it for its ongoing business. The entity will make this decision by comparing the asset's carrying amount to the proceeds from a sale transaction and through continuing use. If the proceeds from the sales transaction are higher than both the carrying amount and the amount from continuing use, the entity may decide to sell. This is the immediate business rationale, although other factors may be taken into account.

Once certain criteria have been met, a non-current asset (or disposal group) will be classified as held-for-sale.

The criteria required for an entity to determine whether an asset or disposal group is held for sale are as follows:

1. The asset is available for immediate sale in its present condition. The terms of the sale should be usual for sales of such assets (or disposal groups).
2. The sale must be highly probable. To be highly probable, we have the following:

    (a) Management must be committed to a plan to sell the asset (or disposal group).
    (b) There must be an active programme to locate a buyer and complete the plan.
    (c) The asset (or disposal group) must be actively marketed for sale at a reasonable price.
    (d) The sale should be expected to be completed within one year from the date of classification unless events or circumstances beyond the entity's control delay it.
    (e) It is unlikely that significant changes to the plan will be made or that the plan will be withdrawn.

All of these criteria must be met for the asset to be classified as held for sale. For example, if it is evident that what the entity believes reasonable price is too high to attract buyers, the management may decide not to continue with the plan. They may decide to keep using the asset itself and it will remain on the balance sheet similar to other assets. If an entity is unable to sell a disposal group and decides to abandon the disposal group, the entity will classify it as a discontinued operation.

Criteria for classification as a held-for-sale asset must be met at the end of the reporting period. The key to this requirement is timing. The asset may not meet the criteria until after the end of the reporting period. However, some weeks later, before the authorisation of the financial statements, the asset may meet the criteria. This does not allow the asset to be classified as held for sale. The asset must meet the criteria before the end of the financial period.

Once an entity has determined that a non-current asset or disposal group is held for sale, the calculation method of measurement is based on the lower of its carrying amount and the fair value less costs to sell. Costs to sell are the incremental costs that the entity will incur because of the disposal of the assets. Examples may include costs to advertise the assets, costs to transport the assets and costs to uninstall the assets from their present location. Any depreciation on the asset should cease.

Any difference between the carrying value and the fair value less costs to sell is recognised in the income statement as an impairment loss. This is an exception to IAS 36 *Impairment of Assets,* as this requires the carrying amount to be compared to the recoverable amount. By applying this exception under IFRS 5, the entity recognises immediately any anticipated losses from the sale of the assets as soon as the decision to sell the assets has taken place.

An entity may reverse the classification held for sale of a non-current asset or disposal group. If so, the entity will measure the asset or disposal group at the lower of

- its carrying amount before the held-for-sale classification, adjusted for any depreciation that would have been charged if the asset had not been held for sale and
- its recoverable amount at the date of the decision not to sell.

This regulation means that an entity cannot write up an asset past its original carrying value prior to the decision to sell the asset or disposal group. An example will clarify some of these requirements.

Topends plc

Topends plc has a year end on 31 December 2021. It holds a non-current asset it wishes to sell with a carrying amount of £100,000. It was classified as held-for-sale in September 2021. Its fair value less costs to sell at that time was considered to be £70,000. In the statement of financial position, the asset is recorded at £70,000 on a separate line item from ordinary assets held for use. Therefore, an impairment loss is required of £30,000 in profit or loss to record the asset at its new value of £70,000. Impairment losses are recorded as part of income from continuing operations in profit or loss unless the specific criteria for discontinued operations are also met.

If the company decided not to sell the asset, the measurement of £70,000 would be reversed to the lower of its carrying amount when it was classified as held-for-sale less any subsequent depreciation and its recoverable amount at the date of the decision not to sell.

IFRS 8 Operating Segments

Definition: Operating segment

A component of an entity

- that engages in business activities that may earn revenue and incur expenses,
- whose operating results are regularly reviewed by the chief operating decision maker. The term "chief operating decision maker" is not as such defined in IFRS8 as it refers to a function rather than a title. In some entities, the function could be fulfilled by a group of directors rather than an individual,
- for which discrete financial information is available.

An entity may arrange its business activities over a number of segments. These can be very different in character and may be in different geographical locations. This division into segments assists management control and planning. IFRS 8's core principle is that an entity should disclose information to enable users of its financial statements to evaluate the nature and financial effects of the types of business activities in which it engages and the economic environments in which it operates. The standard applies to the financial statements of any entity:

- whose debt or equity instruments are traded in a public market or
- is seeking to issue any class of instruments in a public market.

Other entities that choose to disclose segment information should make the disclosures in line with IFRS 8 if they describe such disclosures as "segment information".

The standard does not offer specifications of a segment but the chief operating decision maker determines segmental activities using the standard as the basis. The standard states that "chief operating decision maker" identifies a function, not necessarily a manager with a specific title. That function is to allocate resources to and assess the performance of the operating segments of an entity.

Some commentators have criticised the "management approach" as leaving segment identification too much to the discretion of the entity and therefore hindering comparability between financial statements of different entities. Some have queried the entities' level of discretion when they apply the management approach using the chief operating decision maker. The following example demonstrates the method used.

Identification of reportable segments

Not every part of an entity is necessarily an operating segment. IFRS 8 quotes the example of a corporate headquarters that may earn no incidental revenues and so would not be an operating segment. Once an entity has identified an operating segment, it must report segment information if the segment meets any of the following quantitative thresholds:

- its reported revenue (external and inter-segment) is 10% or more of the combined revenue, internal and external, of all operating segments,
- its reported profit or loss is 10% or more of the greater, in absolute amount, of (i) the combined profit of all operating segments that did not report a loss and (ii) the combined loss of all operating segments that reported a loss or
- its assets are 10% or more of the combined assets of all operating segments.

IFRS 8 states that if the total external turnover reported by the operating segments identified by the size criteria is less than 75% of total entity revenue, then additional segments need to be reported until the 75% level is reached. There may be a number of segments with similar economic characteristics. In this instance, the entity can aggregate them into a single operating segment for the purposes of the size criteria.

An entity must report consistently both current period and comparative segment information. The situation can arise where the entity reports a segment in the current period but did not report it in the previous period. Where this occurs, the entity must provide equivalent comparative information unless it would be prohibitively costly to obtain. Entities do have discretion to report information regarding segments that do not meet the size criteria. Entities can report on such segments where, in the opinion of management, information about the segment would be useful to users of the financial statements.

Disclosures by reportable operating segments

IFRS 8 provides a framework on which to base the reported disclosures. Entities should report

- general information on such matters on the method entities have used to identify the reportable segments and the segments' types of products or services from which it generates its revenue.
- a measure of profit or loss and total assets for each reportable segment. Both should be based on the information provided to the chief operating decision maker.
- if the chief operating decision maker is regularly provided with information on liabilities, these liabilities should also be reported on a segment basis.

The required disclosures for profit or loss and assets where the amounts are included in the measure of profit or loss and total assets are as follows:

- revenues: internal and external,
- interest revenues and interest expense. These must not be netted off unless the majority of a segment's revenues are from interest and the chief operating decision maker assesses the performance of the segment based on net interest revenue,

- depreciation and amortisation,
- material items of income and expense disclosed separately,
- share of profit after tax of, and carrying value of investment in, entities accounted for under the equity method,
- material non-cash items other than depreciation and amortization,
- the amount of additions to non-current assets other than financial instruments, deferred tax assets, post-employment benefit assets and rights arising under insurance contracts.

The measurement basis for each item separately reported should be the one used in the information provided to the chief operating decision maker. The internal reporting system may use more than one measure of an operating segment's profit or loss, or assets or liabilities. In such circumstances, the measure used in the segment report should be the one that management believes is most consistent with those used to measure the corresponding amounts in the entity's financial statements.

Entities are required to provide a number of reconciliations:

- the total of the reportable segments' revenues to the entity's revenue,
- the total of the reportable segments' profit or loss to the entity's profit or loss,
- the total of the reportable segments' assets to the entity's assets,
- where separately identified, the total of the reportable segments' liabilities to the entity's liabilities,
- the total of the reportable segments' amounts for every other material item disclosed to the corresponding amount for the entity.

Entity-wide disclosures

Unless otherwise provided in the segment report, IFRS 8 requires entities to provide information about their revenue on a geographical and "class of business" basis. Entities also need to provide information on non-current assets on a geographical basis but not on a "class of business" basis. If revenues from a single external customer amount to 10% or more of the total revenue of the entity, then the entity needs to disclose that fact plus the following:

- the total revenue from each customer (although the name is not needed),
- the segment or segment reporting the revenues.

The "entity-wide disclosures" are required even where the entity has only a single operating segment and therefore does not effectively segment report. If the standard leads to a lower level of disclosures, there is the question of whether the replacement standard meets the needs of users. Although the standard only becomes applicable in certain circumstances, segmental reporting is considered a valuable disclosure. The question arises whether IFRS 8 is sufficiently robust or whether the standard setters need to revisit it.

Chapter Review

In this chapter, we have concentrated on the disclosures of financial information as required by the International Accounting Standards Board. Many companies not only comply fully with the requirements of the accounting standards but go much further in their provision of information in their annual report. We show in the following two extracts from the Annual Report of Rentokil Initial plc.2021:

> *We have made a good start on our journey to net zero by 2040. Vehicle migration to ultra-low emissions fleet is underway with 177 vehicles, and renewable energy contracts have been introduced for our properties around the world, with Italy our first country operation to use 100% renewable electricity. Approximately 750,000 fluorescent tubes have been removed from the waste stream by using LED lamps in our Lumnia LED fly units and we have also saved 10 tonnes of plastic by changes in our packaging.*
>
> *Below is an overview of our approach to environmental matters, colleagues, social matters, human rights, and anti-corruption and anti-bribery. You can find further details throughout this Responsible Business section on pages 49 to 72. You will find details of our business model on pages 28 and 29, and our principal risks are on pages 74 to 79. Our key policies are published on our website at rentokil-initial.com/responsible-delivery.*

One might argue that, given the nature of their services which are pest control and hygiene, their statement of interests and disclosures of certain items is understandable. However, the annual report displays a strong commitment to environmental issues and we would recommend students view their website.

Rio Tinto Group which is an Anglo-Australian multinational company with over 46,000 employees is the world's second-largest metals and mining corporation. It makes the following statement in its annual reports:

> *This year, we re-examined our approach to the UN Sustainable Development Goals (SDGs) — in conjunction with our purpose, business and sustainability strategies and risks — to better understand how we can work alongside governments, civil society and others to pursue meaningful impact on development. We decided to focus on the two goals — SDG 12 (responsible consumption and production) and SDG 8 (decent work and economic growth) — that we feel are most relevant to operating our business responsibly. SDG 12 relates to how we — as a custodian of natural and mineral resources — mine, process and produce materials and contribute to ethical global supply chains, including trusted lifecycle assessments. This SDG builds on our existing health, safety, environment and community performance standards and our membership of responsible production and product stewardship programmes, including the Aluminium Stewardship Initiative, Copper Mark, the International Council on Mining and Metal's Performance Expectations, the Responsible Jewellery Council and the Mining Association of Canada's Towards Sustainable Mining. SDG 8 speaks directly to our values and priorities, including our commitments to creating a safe and inclusive working environment, as well as promoting education and training partnerships that support social and economic development, including by helping to develop skills for the future. We are committed to supporting underrepresented groups; in particular, we seek to ensure Traditional Owners and Indigenous peoples have a stronger voice in the decisions that affect their lands. In our business, efforts to further these two 'lead' goals are naturally supplemented by efforts to further several other 'supporting' goals. These are also strongly aligned with our sustainable development and business drivers — climate action, water, gender diversity, health and wellbeing, reduced inequalities, innovation and quality education, and environment. SDG 17 (partnerships for goals) reflects our approach to sustainability and is fundamental to the way we run our business. We work purposefully with technology partners, local suppliers, governments, community groups, industry leaders and NGOs at all stages of the mining lifecycle to deliver real benefits to all our stakeholders.*

The above two examples were selected to illustrate the approach of some companies, and we accept that not all companies have a similar approach to ESG issues. However, the two examples above demonstrate a dedicated approach to environmental issues by some companies.

IAS 8 *Accounting Policies, Changes in Accounting Estimates, and Errors* and IAS 37 *Provisions, Contingent liabilities and contingent assets* are key standards. They ensure that the user of financial statements can assess the context in which the financial statements are constructed. Students will find that they are also popular with examiners. The nature of the accounting policies that an entity decides to adopt determines the information in the financial statements. It is argued that too many entities merely repeat the wording of various standards without demonstrating the effect on their activities.

IAS 37 is future orientated as it gives users of financial reports information on what might happen, but one must accept the uncertainty and complexity of the business world.

The two standards in this chapter attempt to illustrate the components that make up an entity. Users are interested if an entity is divesting any of its activities, and IFRS 5 *Non-current assets held for sale and discontinued operations* requires appropriate disclosures. The rigour of IFRS 8 *Operating segments* has been questioned. One would assume that users are interested in such information, but some argue that the standard does not provide the detail that is required.

CHAPTER 8 Contextual Disclosures

Review Questions

1. A contingent liability
   a. must be shown on the balance sheet.
   b. is the same as a provision.
   c. should be made when there is a possibility of future losses.
   d. should be shown in the notes to the accounts.
2. If a company identifies a non-current asset for sale the asset must
   a. be ready for immediate sale in its present condition
   b. the decision to identify the asset must be made after the end of the financial period
   c. depreciation of the asset should continue until it is sold
   d. a company can write-up an asset past its original carrying value prior to the decision to sell
3. Why does IAS 8 require the disclosure of accounting policies?
4. What is the difference between changes in accounting estimates and corrections of errors?
5. What is a contingent liability?
6. What is the key term to define the components of an entity as an operating segment?
7. What is the definition of a provision?
8. Can a business make a provision for expected future operating losses?

Chapter 9

Financial Instruments

Structure of Chapter 9

Section title	Main content
The 2007/2008 crisis	Explains the impact of the crisis on accounting for financial instruments.
The Financial Environment	Describes the various ways companies use to obtain finance to support their activities.
IAS 32 Financial Instruments: Presentation	Explains financial assets, financial liabilities, equity and derivatives.
IAS 39 Financial Instruments: Recognition and Measurement	A difficult standard but essential for correct financial reporting.
IFRS 7 Financial Instruments: Disclosures	Require disclosures regarding financial instruments to their importance.
IFRS 9 Financial Instruments	Explains the accounting treatment for financial instruments.
IFRS 13 Fair Value Measurement	This applies where another standard requires fair value measurement.
Chapter Review	Financial instruments contain complexities in their requirements and this chapter explains the relevant standards.

The number of standards that set out the requirements for accounting for financial instruments is several. The structure and complexity of accounting for financial instruments are conveyed in the definition of financial instruments in IAS 32 which defines it as any contract that gives rise to a financial asset of one entity and a financial liability or equity instrument of another entity. We will look more closely at the above definition as we work through this chapter. The main points to note are that there must be a contract and this will give one party to the contract a financial asset and the other party a financial liability.

The above simple definition does not reflect the complexity of accounting for financial instruments or does it hint at the corporate practices that have evolved over the years and the several financial crises that occurred. This chapter is an introduction to the subject of financial instruments. The catalyst in bringing us to the present regulations was the global financial crisis 2007/2008, and we start this chapter by explaining the impact of the crisis. we discuss the financial environment, the use of financial instruments and the different types of financial instruments. The standards we discuss are as follows:

- IAS 32 Financial instruments presentation,
- IAS 39 recognition and measurement,
- IFRS 7 Disclosures,
- IFRS 9 Financial instruments,
- IFRS 13 Fair value measurement.

The 2007/2008 Crisis

A crisis frequently commences with a single, spectacular event. Most commentators would identify the collapse of Lehman Brothers as that event. The company has reported record revenue and earnings for 2007. In September 2008, it became the largest company in US history to file for bankruptcy. The day that Lehman Brothers Holdings Inc. (LBHI) filed for bankruptcy, its affiliates had over 930,000 derivative contracts outstanding. It was claimed that the fate of these contracts illustrates the challenges facing those who work with derivatives. The failure of Lehman was part of the global financial crisis of 2007–2008. This caused considerable panic. Understandably, people wanted to know the cause of the crisis and accounting for financial instruments became the focus. The reasons offered for financial instruments being the culprit fell into two main camps.

There were those who argued that speculators and investment houses used complex financial instruments inappropriately. Others, particularly the banks, argued that it was not the financial instruments that were to blame but the way that they had to be accounted for, in other words, the accounting regulations. The accounting standards were criticised because of the requirement for fair value accounting instead of historical cost. There are two main methods for fair value accounting. Marking "to market" is the valuation of financial assets at the price found for identical assets being traded.

The defenders of fair value accounting argued that the method was not the cause of the crisis. They claimed that fair value only revealed the effects of poor decisions by the banks. Whatever the merits of this argument, the accounting focus on financial instruments had started early in 2006 as part of the project to converge all international and US accounting standards. The FASB and the IASB declared their intentions to work together to improve and converge financial reporting standards by issuing a Memorandum of Understanding (MoU), *A Roadmap for Convergence between IFRSs and US GAAP — 2006–2008*. As part of the MoU, the Boards worked jointly on a research project to reduce the complexity of the accounting for financial instruments.

The 2007/2008 crisis may have accelerated their efforts, but, as with all efforts to develop a new or revised standard, progress was slow. Considerable pressure and lobbying took place and the Boards were strongly encouraged to speed their deliberations. The Boards were aware of the need for short-term responses to the worldwide credit crisis and emphasised their commitment to developing common solutions aimed at providing greater transparency and reducing complexity in the accounting of financial instruments.

The Boards' work resulted in the IASB's issuance of the March 2008 Discussion Paper, *Reducing Complexity in Reporting Financial Instruments*, which the FASB also published for comment by its constituents. Focusing on the measurement of financial instruments and hedge accounting, the Discussion Paper identified several possible approaches for improving and simplifying accounting for financial instruments.

The Financial Instruments Project made very slow progress, despite the many meetings and documents issued. It would appear that the FASB and the IASB could not agree on which approach they should adopt. In 2014, we reached the stage where the FASB had decided its own approach and the IASB had issued its own standards. Whatever happened behind the scenes, the FASB has gone its own way and, at the international level, we now have a constellation of standards. Before we examine the individual standards in detail, we list in the following the main requirements of each standard:

- IAS 32 Financial Instruments Presentation requires the presentation for financial instruments as liabilities or equity and offsetting financial assets and liabilities. It defines financial assets and liabilities IAS 39 and IFRS 7 need to be read together.
- IAS 39 Recognition and Measurement addresses derivatives and hedging and links to IAS 32 and IFRS 7.
- IFRS 9 Financial Instruments provides relevant and useful information so that users can assess amounts, timing and uncertainty of entity's future cash flows.
- IFRS 13 Fair Value Measurements applies when another IFRS requires or permits fair value measurement or disclosures about fair value measurement.

The Financial Environment

Obtaining finance

Entities need finance to operate. They may raise finance internally by their own activities or externally by transactions in various financial markets. External financial markets are either short term or long term. Short-term financial markets, usually less than a year, are often called money markets. Long-term financial markets are capital markets and include the equity market, the debt market that includes borrowing from other firms and the bank market.

Multinational companies that used to raise equity capital solely from sources within their own country now look to other countries for potential shareholders by listing their shares on a foreign exchange. Companies engage in cross-border financing for a variety of reasons. Financial reasons include the fact that an entity might be able to obtain cheaper financing outside its own borders, lowering its overall cost of capital.

In addition, it might find be convenient to obtain external financing in countries where it has significant operations.

Non-financial reasons to engage in cross-border financing include the objective to be a world-class enterprise maintaining financial relationships in many countries. An entity might wish to broaden its shareholder base to include citizens and other institutions from many countries in addition to its home base. An entity also could find it politically expedient to maintain financial relationships inside a particular country. The relationship could lead to additional business contacts both inside and outside a foreign government or favourable recognition by the national government. In any case, cross-border financial activity is increasingly compatible with the cross-border movement of goods and services. You may go abroad for your holidays, and purchase or sell goods and services from other countries. International finance is a normal business activity.

However, the problem of borrowing and lending substantial amounts in foreign countries can result in exposure to risks of various types. This can range from political instability to economic fluctuations. From a financial instrument perspective, there are two main risks:

- The interest rate risk: The fair values or cash flows of interest-sensitive assets or liabilities will change if interest rates increase or decrease.
- The exchange rate risk: The risk that changes in foreign currency exchange rates will negatively affect the profitability of their international operations.

Entities can use derivatives to offset the risks that these market forces will negatively affect fair values or cash flows.

Companies and investors face all types of risk, both nationally and internationally. There are those risks that are associated with the conduct of the business itself and the manufacturing, trading and retailing operations. Other types of risk arise because of the financial transactions that take place in the normal course of business. It is impossible to eliminate risk completely but entities can attempt to reduce it by hedging the risk. Hedging is reducing risk by taking action now to reduce the possibility of future losses, usually with the possibility of not enjoying any future gains.

An example of hedging is as follows: an entity decides that it must purchase supplies of materials in three months' time. The materials, such as agricultural crops, may not be ready to purchase immediately, or the entity may not wish to hold the materials for three months. There is a risk that the price of materials will increase before the end of the three months. The entity can enter into an agreement (contract) **now** to purchase the goods in three months' time but at the current price. The entity avoids the risk of the prices increasing in three months' time when it requires the materials. However, it also loses the opportunity to make a gain if the price decreases in three months' time. To avoid the potential loss if there is a significant increase in price, an entity can hedge this risk.

IAS 32 Financial Instruments: Presentation

IAS 32 establishes principles for presenting financial instruments as liabilities or equity and for offsetting financial assets and financial liabilities. The stance that it adopts for the classification is that of the issuer of the financial instruments. The standard links with IFRS 9 that deals with the recognition of financial assets and financial liabilities and with IFRS 7 that deals with the disclosure of financial instruments. The standard uses the term "entity" to include individuals, partnerships, incorporated bodies, trusts and government agencies. It does contain a long list of circumstances where the regulations do not apply. This is usually because other standards regulate certain entities and types of financial instruments.

The main aim of IAS 32 is to ensure that, on initial recognition, the entity correctly classifies a financial instrument as a financial liability, a financial asset or an equity instrument. Classification of financial assets usually presents no problems. The major difficulty addressed by the standard is determining whether the instrument is an equity instrument or a financial liability.

To be classified as an equity instrument, there are two conditions:

1. The instrument must not include an obligation to deliver cash or another financial asset to another entity or to make a potentially unfavourable exchange of financial assets or liabilities with another entity.
2. If the instrument can be settled by the issuer's own equity, it must either be a non-derivative that does not require the issuer to deliver a variable number of its own equity instruments or a derivative that can only be settled by the issuer exchanging a fixed amount of cash or another financial asset for a fixed number of its own equity instruments.

There are two instruments that cause particular problems: puttable instruments and compound instruments.

Puttable instruments

Puttable instruments come in two different forms that either

1. give the holders the right to put the financial instrument back to the issuer for cash or another financial asset or
2. automatically put back the instrument to the issuer on the occurrence of an uncertain future event or the death or retirement of the holder of the puttable instrument.

For example, an entity such as a partnership may require any new owners to subscribe capital into the business. When a partner leaves or retires from the partnership, the capital that he or she initially paid is repayable at fair value. Under the standard, the partners' capital meets the definition of a puttable instrument.

Puttable instruments can be considered as a financial liability or an equity instrument. To meet the second classification, the instrument must contain certain features detailed in the standard. We summarise these as follows:

(a) If an entity is liquidated, the holder of the puttable instrument is entitled to a pro rata share of the entity's net assets.
(b) It must be in the class of instruments that is subordinate to all other classes of instruments. This subordinate class of instruments must have identical features.
(c) The only condition the contract must have is the obligation for the purchaser to purchase or redeem the asset for cash or another financial asset.
(d) The total cash flows from the instrument are based on the profit or loss and changes in the recognised net assets or changes in the fair value of recognised and unrecognised net assets.

Compound financial instruments

An entity may issue a compound financial instrument that has both liability and equity components. In such cases, the entity must classify the components separately. Examples of compound financial instruments are convertible bonds. These usually require the issuer to deliver cash or another financial asset (a liability) but also grant the holder the right to convert the bond into a fixed number of ordinary shares (the equity).

To be classified as compound financial instruments, the main requirements in the standard are as follows:

- They are non-derivative instruments that possess both equity and liability characteristics.
- The equity and liability components must be separated on initial recognition. This is a process sometimes referred to as "split accounting". This involves first calculating the fair value of the liability component. The equity component is then determined by deducting the fair value of the financial liability from the fair value of the compound financial instrument as a whole.
- The split and the amount of the liability and equity components are determined on initial recognition and not altered subsequently.

Many convertible bonds are classified as compound instruments and split accounting can be used:

(a) The first stage is to calculate the carrying amount of the liability component. The method involves calculating the net present value of the discounted cash flows of interest and principal without including the possibility of exercise of the conversion option.
(b) The carrying amount of the equity instrument represented by the conversion option is then determined by deducting the fair value of the financial liability calculated in (a) from the fair value of the compound financial instrument as a whole.

For the above method to be applied, the bond must satisfy a "fixed for fixed" test. For example, with a convertible denominated in a foreign currency, the conversion component may fail the fixed for fixed test. This is because the fixed amount of foreign currency is not considered to represent a fixed amount of cash. The solution is to scrutinise the terms of each financial instrument to determine whether separate equity and liability components exist.

The standard, under certain conditions, permits the offsetting of financial assets and liabilities. This is a process where the holder of financial assets and financial liabilities can set the amount of one against the other and only show the net amount on the statement of financial position. An entity can only make this type of transaction where it has a current legally enforceable right to set off recognised amounts and intends either to settle on a net basis or to realise the asset and liability at the same time.

IAS 39 Financial Instruments: Recognition and Measurement

A financial instrument whose characteristics and value depend upon the characteristics and value of an underlier, typically a commodity, bond, equity, currency. These items come under the general heading of "derivatives" with the following characteristics:

1. The value of the derivative changes in response to changes in a specified interest rate, financial instrument price, commodity price, foreign exchange rate, index of prices or rates, credit rating or credit index or other variables.
2. It requires no initial investment or an initial investment less than required for other types of contracts expected to have a similar response to changes in market factors.
3. It is settled at a future date.

Entities understandably wish to reduce risk in their transactions to minimise the possibility of not being paid with sales on credit. They have the risk that they are party to a contract to purchase goods at a certain price in the future but the market price falls. A common risk many entities grapple with is the change in foreign exchange rates. Entities can use derivatives for risk management by hedging (i.e. to "hedge"). This technique provides offsetting compensation in case of an undesired event. In this case, it is a type of insurance. Like insurance, derivatives are a way of guarding against loss. Instead of insuring plant and equipment, an entity is limiting the exposure to risk of financial assets to volatility in prices and interest rates.

Derivatives are also used for speculation (i.e. making a financial "bet"). The use of derivatives for speculation offers entities and investors a risky opportunity to increase profit. As we saw in the example of Diageo plc, few companies would embrace this strategy. However, stakeholders in the entity may not properly understand the risk even when an entity makes it clear that the purpose of using derivatives is a speculative one. The four main types of derivatives we discuss in this section are forward contracts, futures contracts, options and swaps.

Forward contract: A forward contract is an agreement to buy or sell an asset at a certain future time for a certain price. These are the simplest form of derivative and are traded in the over-the-counter market. One of the parties in a forward contract agrees to buy the underlying asset on a future specified date for a certain specified price. The other party agrees to sell the asset on the agreed date for the agreed price. The price at which the parties agree to transact in the future is the delivery price. No money changes hands at the time the parties enter into a forward contract.

Futures contract: A futures contract is very similar to a forward contract. The main difference is that futures contracts are traded on an exchange that sets rules for trading. This simplifies the process and helps the market achieve higher liquidity. Futures contracts are traded on a variety of commodities, including live cattle, sugar, wool, lumber, copper, gold, tin and aluminium. They are also used on a wide array of financial assets, including stock indices, currencies, and Treasury bonds.

Options: In contrast to forwards and futures, options give the owner the right, but not the obligation, to transact. As there is only the right, the cost of the option is much less than the complete transaction. The owner of the option will only transact if it is profitable to do so. The price at which the parties transact in the future is the strike price. When the transaction takes place, the owner of the option exercises the option. There are two types of options. A call option can give the holder the option to buy shares at a predetermined price. For example, an investor has the option to buy 5,000 shares in Exton Company at £25 per share. If the share price on the open market rises from £25 to £28 per share, it is worthwhile for the investor to exercise the option and purchase the shares at the agreed price of £25. A profit has been made. If the share does not increase above £25, the investor does not exercise the option and makes a small loss on the cost of the derivative. A put option gives the holder to sell the shares at a preset price. If the investor believes the shares will decline in price, he will enter into an agreement to sell the shares at a preset price. If the share price falls, then the holder will exercise the put option. The general rule is a call option increases in value when the underlying asset increases in value. A put option increases in value when the underlying asset decreases in value.

Swaps: A swap is simply an agreement between two parties to exchange cash flows in the future. The agreement defines the dates when they will exchange the cash flows and the calculation of the amounts. Swaps typically lead to cash flow exchanges on several future dates. There are interest rate swaps. The parties agree to exchange a floating-rate loan for a fixed-rate loan by paying a fixed amount in return for a variable amount. Similarly, currency swaps can be used to transform borrowings in one currency to borrowings in another currency, by agreeing to make a payment in one currency in return for a payment in another currency. An entity holds a bond with a fixed interest rate of 5%. It predicts that interest rates generally will increase in the future. If interest rates go up, a 5% return is not attractive and the bond will consequently lose value. Management can enter into an interest rate swap arrangement in which they pay a fixed interest payment in exchange for a payment based on a variable interest rate.

Embedded derivatives: These are sometimes referred to as hybrid instruments as they have characteristics of both debt and equity. For example, a convertible bond we examine at length in our explanation of IAS 32 is a hybrid instrument as it is both a debt security with an option to convert the bond to shares, which is the embedded derivative. The accounting treatment for such hybrid securities is to separate the value of the debt security and the embedded derivative. The entity then accounts for the embedded derivative in the same way as all other forms of derivatives.

Examples of the type of financial instruments that remain in the scope of IAS 39 are as follows:

- cash,
- demand and time deposits,

- commercial paper,
- accounts, notes, and loans receivable and payable,
- debt and equity securities. These are financial instruments from the perspectives of both the holder and the issuer. This category includes investments in subsidiaries, associates and joint ventures,
- asset-backed securities such as collateralised mortgage obligations, repurchase agreements and securitised packages of receivables,
- derivatives, including options, rights, warrants, futures contracts, forward contracts and swaps.

The purpose of IAS is clearly established in its statement of scope that requires the regulations to be applied by all entities to all financial instruments within the scope of IFRS 9 Financial Instruments if and to the extent that

1. IFRS 9 permits the application of the hedge accounting requirements of IAS 39,
2. the financial instruments are part of a hedging relationship that qualifies for hedge accounting in accordance with this Standard.

The standard defines the various terms connected to the process of hedging. These are as follows:

Firm commitment: A binding agreement for the exchange of a specified quantity of resources at a specified price on a specified future date or dates.

Forecast transaction: An uncommitted but anticipated future transaction.

Hedging instrument: A designated derivative (applies to foreign exchange hedges only) or a designated non-derivative financial asset or non-derivative financial liability whose fair value or cash flows are expected to offset changes in the fair value of a designated hedged item.

Hedged item: An asset, liability, firm commitment, highly probable forecast transaction or net investment in a foreign operation that (a) exposes the entity to risk in changes of fair value or future cash flows and (b) is designated as being hedged.

Hedged effectiveness: The degree to which changes in fair value or cash flows of the hedged item that are attributable to a hedged risk are offset by changes in the fair value or cash flows of the hedging instrument.

Although we have used some of these terms earlier in this chapter, the above list is slightly overpowering. The actual meaning of the terms becomes clear as we draw from the requirements of the standard to demonstrate their application.

Hedge accounting

Hedging is a technically complex transaction and new developments occur from time to time. Entities are attempting to reduce their exposure to financial risk and several different methods are used. Establishing the accounting for these hedging transactions has proved difficult for the standard setters. The main regulations are that there are three types of hedging relationships and these are as follows:

1. Fair value hedge: This is a hedge relating to a recognised financial asset, liability or firm commitment where there is the risk of changes in fair value.
2. Cash flow hedge: This is a hedge where there is the risk of variability in cash flow that is associated with a recognised asset or liability.
3. The hedge of net investment in a foreign operation which is discussed in IAS 21 The Effects of Changes in Foreign Exchange Rates (Chapter 4).

Accounting for fair value hedges

1. Any gain or loss from remeasuring the hedging instrument at fair value is recognised in profit or loss.
2. Any gain or loss on the hedged item attributable to the hedged risk adjusts the carrying amount of the hedged item and is recognised in profit or loss.

3. Fair value hedge accounting is discontinued prospectively if
   - the hedging instrument expires or is sold, terminated or exercised,
   - the hedge no longer meets the five conditions we described above,
   - the entity revokes the designation.
4. Where hedge accounting is discontinued, adjustments to the carrying amount of a hedged financial asset for which the effective interest rate is used are amortised to profit or loss.

Accounting for cash flow hedges

1. The part of the gain or loss on the hedging instrument that is determined to be an effective hedge is recognised in the statement of other comprehensive income. The ineffective part of the gain or loss on the hedging instrument is recognised in profit or loss.
2. The hedge may result in the recognition of a financial asset or a financial liability. In this case, the associated gains or losses that were recognised in other comprehensive income are reclassified from equity to profit or loss as a reclassification adjustment.
3. Where the hedge results in the recognition of a non-financial asset or a non-financial liability, the standard permits the entity to select from a choice of accounting policies.
4. Cash flow hedge accounting is discontinued prospectively if
   - the hedging instrument expires or is sold, terminated or exercised,
   - the hedge no longer meets the five conditions,
   - the forecast transaction is no longer expected to occur,
   - the entity revokes the designation.

Accounting for hedges of a net investment in a foreign operation

Hedges of a net investment in a foreign operation, including a hedge of a monetary item that is accounted for as part of the net investment, are accounted for similarly to cash flow hedges.

The part of the gain or loss on the hedging instrument that is determined to be an effective hedge is recognised in equity and the ineffective part is recognised in profit or loss.

The gain or loss on the hedging instrument relating to the effective portion of the hedge that has been recognised in the statement of other comprehensive income is reclassified from equity to profit or loss as a reclassification adjustment on the disposal of the foreign operation.

IFRS 7 Financial Instruments: Disclosures

The IASB issued IFRS 7 to bring disclosure requirements up to date with what has been happening in practice. The techniques entities adopt for managing exposure to risks arising from financial instruments had developed in recent years. Entities have been introducing new techniques and the IASB decided that a standard was required to deal with these developments. It recognised that users need information about risk exposure and how the entity manages it. The objectives of IFRS 7 are to require disclosures regarding financial instruments that enable users to evaluate

1. their significance for the entity's financial position and performance,
2. the nature and extent of risk to which the entity is exposed during and at the end of the reporting period and how the entity manages those risks.

The standard is wide in scope and includes a list of the financial instruments in its remit. The standard applies to all entities: those with only a few financial instruments and those with many. The amount of disclosure required depends on the range and number of financial instruments held.

The standard is divided into two distinct sections: The first section covers quantitative disclosures about the numbers in the balance sheet and the income statement. The second section deals with qualitative risk disclosures. These are the management's objectives, policies and processes for managing those risks. The quantitative disclosures provide information about the extent to which the entity is exposed to risk, based on information provided internally to the entity's key management personnel. The standard identifies the different types of risk to which the entity may be exposed; these are credit risk, liquidity risk and market risk.

The nature and size of a company will be relevant to disclosures. We show in the following part of the financial instrument disclosures made by Lloyds Bank PLC. This is taken from their annual report 2021 which is downloadable. We would add that their annual report is almost 350 pages and that their website covers many aspects of the company's operations.

(1) Financial instruments measured at amortised cost.
Financial assets that are held to collect contractual cash flows where those cash flows represent solely payments of principal and interest are measured at amortised cost. A basic lending arrangement results in contractual cash flows that are solely payments of principal and interest on the principal amount outstanding. Where the contractual cash flows introduce exposure to risks or volatility unrelated to a basic lending arrangement such as changes in equity prices or commodity prices, the payments do not comprise solely principal and interest. Financial assets measured at amortised cost are predominantly loans and advances to customers and banks together with certain debt securities used by the Group to manage its liquidity. Loans and advances are initially recognised when cash is advanced to the borrower at fair value inclusive of transaction costs. Interest income is accounted for using the effective interest method (see (D) above). Financial liabilities are measured at amortised cost, except for trading liabilities and other financial liabilities designated at fair value through profit or loss on initial recognition which are held at fair value. Where changes are made to the contractual cash flows of a financial asset or financial liability that are economically equivalent and arise as a direct consequence of interest rate benchmark reform, the Group updates the effective interest rate and does not recognise an immediate gain or loss.

IFRS 9 Financial Instruments

IFRS 9 is a lengthy standard. It addresses the weaknesses of methods of accounting for financial instruments revealed by the 2007/2008 financial crisis. It also incorporates in one standard the three major activities of accounting for financial instruments: classification and measurement, impairment and hedge accounting. The standard establishes requirements for reporting financial assets and financial liabilities so that users are better able to determine the amounts, timing and uncertainty of an entity's future cash flows.

The standard is structured into four main accounting issues: recognition and derecognition, classification and measurement. In each of the first three sections, the treatment of both financial assets and liabilities is set out. In this section, we discuss first the accounting treatment of financial assets, second, the treatment of financial liabilities and finally, hedge accounting.

Financial assets

In considering financial assets, we are considering the acquirer of the financial instrument and whether it is an asset and appears as such on the balance sheet. Financial assets can include debt instruments where the entity expects to be repaid the loan it has made and equity instruments (shares) where the entity has ownership interest in the residual net assets of another entity. This division is important as we look at classification and measurement of financial assets.

The recognition and derecognition of financial assets have certain conditions but the main requirements are logical. An entity recognises a financial asset in its statement of financial position when, and only when, the entity becomes party to the contractual provisions of the instrument. An entity derecognises a financial asset when either the cash flows from the financial asset cease or it transfers the financial asset. What constitutes a transfer has many conditions but the essence is that the transfer must involve either transferring the right to receive the cash flows or the entity has to pay the cash flows to one or more recipients.

We explain several terms before looking at the accounting requirements:

Amortised cost: The amount at which the financial asset or financial liability is measured at initial recognition minus the principal repayments, plus or minus the cumulative amortisation.

The effective interest method is used for any difference between that initial measurement and the maturity amount and, for financial assets, adjusted for any loss allowance.

Effective rate method: The rate that exactly discounts estimated future cash payments or receipts through the expected life of the financial asset or financial liability to the gross carrying amount of a financial asset.

Fair value through profit or loss (FVTRL): Financial assets at fair value through profit and loss are carried in the consolidated balance sheet at fair value with gains or losses recognised in the consolidated statement of income.

The accounting approach considers that the classification and measurement of the debt instrument are linked. Debt instruments can be classified either at amortised cost or at Fair Value Through Profit or Loss (FVTPL). If the debt instrument meets two simple tests, it is subsequently accounted for using amortised cost.

The two tests are the Business Model (hold to collect model) and the Cash Flow Test (hold to collect and sell model). The business model test is satisfied where the entity holds the asset for the contractual cash flows rather than selling it before maturity. The cash flow test is satisfied when the contractual terms result in receipts of cash flows on specified dates of either the principal or interest.

If a debt instrument satisfies these two tests, the initial measurement is at fair value plus transaction costs. Subsequent measurement is at amortised cost. If a debt instrument does not satisfy these two tests, the default requirement is that initial and subsequent measurement is at FVTPL with any gains and losses shown in the Income Statement.

Equity investments must be measured at fair value in the statement of financial position. An entity can decide at inception that equity investments are irrevocably classified and accounted as Fair Value Through Other Comprehensive Income (FVTOCI). Any gains and losses are recognised in other comprehensive income, but dividend income is still recognised in income. Such an election cannot be made if the equity investment is acquired for trading.

It is possible that an entity decides to change its business model for financial asset. Instead of holding the asset for the contractual cash flows until maturity, it could decide to sell it before maturity or vice versa. If the business model objective for its financial assets changes so its previous model no longer applies, then other financial assets can be reclassified between FVTPL and amortised cost, or vice versa. The entity cannot restate any recognised gains, losses or interest. In other words, it is a prospective action. However, once an equity investment has been classified as FVTOCI, it cannot then be reclassified.

The impairment of financial assets is a new requirement and the regulations are lengthy and complex. In this section, we concentrate on the basic principles and the definitions of specific terms. The objective of requiring the impairment of financial assets stems from the concept of recognising expected losses in the financial statements. The standard is wide in its scope and the same impairment model applies to all types of financial assets covered by the standard. There are exceptions for purchased or originated credit-impaired financial assets.

IFRS 13 Fair Value Measurement

The standard is applied when another standard either requires or permits fair value measurements or disclosures about such measurements apart from the following:

- share-based payment transactions under IFRS 2 Share-based payments (see Chapter 5),
- leasing transactions under IAS 17 Leases (see Chapter 10).

Some methods of measurement have the attributes of fair value but do not satisfy the accounting requirements. Examples are the use of net realisable value (IAS 2 Inventories) and value in use (IAS 36 Impairment). The aim of the standard is to improve the consistency and comparability in fair value measurements contained in some standards. To achieve this aim, the standard has developed a three-level fair value hierarchy. This is based on the inputs that entitles use to estimate the fair value, and there are the following three approaches:

Level 1: Quoted prices in active markets for identical assets and liabilities that the entity can access at the measurement date.
Level 2: Inputs that are not the quoted market prices in level 1 but are observable for the asset or liability either directly or indirectly.
Level 3: Inputs that are unobservable inputs for the asset or liability.

Some of the terms used require the following definition:

- Active market is a market in which transactions for the asset or liability take place with sufficient frequency and volume to provide pricing information on an ongoing basis.
- Exit price is the price that would be received to sell an asset or paid to transfer a liability.

- Fair value is the price that would be received to sell an asset or paid to transfer a liability in an orderly transaction between market participants at the measurement date.
- Highest and best use is the use of a non-financial asset by market participants that would maximise the value of the asset or the group of assets and liabilities (e.g. a business) within which the asset would be used.
- Most advantageous market is the one that maximises the amount that would be received to sell the asset or minimises the amount that would be paid to transfer the liability, after taking into account transaction costs and transport costs.
- Principal market is the one with the greatest volume and level of activity for the asset or liability.

An entity attempting to make a fair value measurement must estimate the price for an orderly transaction to sell the asset or to transfer the liability. It is assumed that the transaction would take place between market participants at the measurement date under current market conditions. In making the fair value measurement, an entity must decide the following:

- the particular asset or liability that is the subject of the measurement (consistently with its unit of account),
- for a non-financial asset, the valuation premise that is appropriate for the measurement (consistently with its highest and best use),
- the principal (or most advantageous) market for the asset or liability,
- the valuation technique(s) appropriate for the measurement, considering the availability of data with which to develop inputs that represent the assumptions that market participants would use when pricing the asset or liability and the level of the fair value hierarchy within which the inputs are categorised.

A critical criterion for the hierarchy is the separation of observable and unobservable inputs. Observable inputs consist of publicly available information about actual events or transactions, for example, securities traded on stock exchanges. Unobservable inputs consist of management's assumptions that cannot be corroborated with observable market data, for example, internal forecast of cash flows from intangible assets.

Both Level 1 and Level 2 of the fair value hierarchy consider the use of observable inputs. These are inputs where there is publicly available information about actual events or transactions.

Level 1 inputs are quoted prices (unadjusted) in active markets for identical assets or liabilities that the entity can access at the measurement date. One example is when the asset is a share actively traded on a stock exchange — the quoted price is for an identical asset, so it would be categorised as Level 1.

Level 2 inputs are defined as inputs other than quoted prices included within Level 1 that are observable for the asset or liability, either directly or indirectly. If the price for an identical asset or liability is not available, an entity can use a quoted price for an asset or liability that is similar to the asset or liability being measured.

Level 3 inputs is concerned only with unobservable inputs. These are inputs for which there is no market data available. These inputs must be developed by the entity using the best information available about the assumptions that market participants would use when pricing the asset or liability. The measurements therefore depend on the reporting entity's own view on the assumptions that market participants would use.

Entities must make extensive disclosures in the financial statements regarding fair value measurements.

IFRS 13 requires extensive disclosures related to fair value measurements. We emphasise that IFRS 13 applies not only to financial instruments but also to all assets and liabilities where the relevant standards either require or allow fair value measurements.

There are a few instances where the standard requires entities to comply with the measurement requirements but not have to make disclosures. These exceptions are as follows:

- defined benefit plan assets measured at fair value under IAS 19,
- retirement benefit plan investments measured at fair value under IAS 26,
- assets tested for impairment using fair value less costs to sell under IAS 36.

Where an entity must make disclosure, examples of key items are as follows:

- fair value at end of reporting period,
- the level within hierarchy,
- a description of valuation technique,
- quantitative information about significant unobservable inputs.

An entity that uses valuation IFRS 13 requires extensive disclosures related to fair value measurements.

Company practices

Companies are normally forthcoming on foreign currency and we show in the following an extract only from a lengthy note given by Unilever plc in its Annual Report and Accounts which is in total 199 pages and very informative"

Unilever plc 2021

Foreign currency

The consolidated financial statements are presented in euros. The functional currency of PLC is pound sterling. Items included in the financial statements of individual group companies are recorded in their respective functional currency which is the currency of the primary economic environment in which each entity operates. Foreign currency transactions in individual group companies are translated into functional currency using exchange rates at the date of the transaction. Foreign exchange gains and losses from settlement of these transactions, and from translation of monetary assets and liabilities at year-end exchange rates, are recognised in the income statement except when deferred in equity as qualifying hedges. In preparing the consolidated financial statements, the balances in individual group companies are translated from their functional currency into euros. Apart from the financial statements of group companies in hyperinflationary economies (see below), the income statement, the cash flow statement and all other movements in assets and liabilities are translated at average rates of exchange as a proxy for the transaction rate, or at the transaction rate itself if more Monetary assets and liabilities denominated in foreign currencies are translated into functional currency at the rates of exchange quoted at the balance sheet date. Non-monetary items that are measured in terms of historical cost in a foreign currency are translated using the exchange rates as at the dates of the initial transactions. Day-to-day transactions in a foreign currency are recorded in the functional currency at an average rate for the month in which those transactions take place, which is used as a reasonable approximation to the actual transaction rate. Translation differences on monetary items are taken to the consolidated income statement. A number of subsidiaries within the Group have a non-sterling functional currency. The financial performance and end position of these entities are translated into sterling in the consolidated financial statements. Balance sheet items are translated at the rate applicable at the balance sheet date. Transactions reported in the consolidated income statement are translated using an average rate for the month in which they occur. The differences that arise from translating the results of foreign entities at average rates of exchange, and their assets and liabilities at closing rates, are dealt with in a separate component of equity. On disposal of a foreign entity, the deferred cumulative amount recognised in equity relating to that particular foreign operation is recognised in the consolidated income statement. All other currency gains and losses are dealt with in the income statement.

Chapter Review

Although the IASB has made considerable efforts to answer the criticisms of accounting for financial instruments, we suspect that we have not reached the final stage. For preparers, users and auditors, the mix of standards regulating different aspects of financial instruments, with various effective dates and a significant number of amendments and revisions over the years, the regulatory framework is difficult to understand. In defence of the IASB, one can argue that the complexity of the accounting regime is a result of the many and rapid changes by companies in the use, and abuse, of financial instruments. The convergence project with the Financial Accounting Standards Board in the United States also involved considerable discussions that did not achieve agreement.

Unfortunately, we suspect that accounting for financial instruments will remain a major topic for the IASB. The complete solution may not rest in the power of the standard setters but in the strength of the legal requirements established by various governments. The 2007/2008 financial crisis was not only due to defects in accounting regulations but also due to the methods that some entities adopted in the use of financial instruments.

An examination of corporate financial statement demonstrates that they are attempting to make comprehensive disclosures but it is a difficult task. We show in the following a very, very small extract from the lengthy 2021 financial report of Legal and General Group plc.

The group holds financial investments and investment property to back insurance contracts on behalf of policyholders and as group capital. The group classifies its financial investments on initial recognition as held for trading (HFT), designated at fair value through profit or loss (FVTPL), available-for-sale (AFS) or loans and receivables. Initial recognition of financial investments is on the trade date. In general, the group's policy is to measure investments at FVTPL. Financial investments held by the group are designated as FVTPL as their performance is evaluated on a total return basis, consistent with asset performance reporting to the Group Investment and Market Risk Committee and the group's investment strategy. Assets designated as FVTPL include debt securities (including lifetime and retirement interest only mortgages) and equity instruments which would otherwise have been classified as AFS and reverse repurchase agreements within loans which would otherwise be designated at amortised cost. Assets backing non-participating policyholder liabilities are designated as FVTPL. The group's non-participating investment contract liabilities are measured on the basis of current information and are designated as FVTPL. All derivatives other than those designated as hedges are classified as HFT. Financial investments classified as HFT and designated at FVTPL are measured at fair value with gains and losses reflected in the Consolidated Income Statement. Transaction costs are expensed as incurred. Certain other financial investments classified as AFS are measured at fair value with unrealised gains and losses recognised in a separate reserve within equity. Realised gains and losses, impairment losses, dividends, interest and foreign exchange movements on non-equity instruments are reflected in the Consolidated Income Statement. Directly attributable transaction costs are included in the initial measurement of the investment. Financial investments classified as loans are either designated at FVTPL or initially measured at fair value plus transaction costs and subsequently measured at amortised cost using the effective interest method. The designated at FVTPL classification currently only applies to reverse repurchase agreements.

CHAPTER 9 Financial Instruments

Review Questions

1. Which one of the following is not a financial instrument?
   a. Cash
   b. Inventory
   c. Derivatives
   d. Accounts payable

2. Which best describes a swap?
   a. An agreement between two parties to exchange cash flows in the future.
   b. The transfer of staff from one company to another.
   c. The date of a swap is not fixed.
   d. A SWAP is not a form of derivatives.

3. What are short-term financial markets?

4. What are long-term financial markets?

5. What is the formal definition of "financial instruments"?

6. What is meant by the term "hedging"?

7. What is the meaning of the term "derivative"?

8. What is "hedging"?

Chapter 10

Short Standards

Structure of Chapter 10

Section title
IAS 10 Events after the reporting period
IAS 12 Income Taxes
IAS 16 Property, Plant and Equipment
IAS 19 Employee benefits
IAS 23 Borrowing Costs
IAS 33 Earnings per share
IAS 34 Interim financial reporting
IAS 40 Investment Property
IAS 41 Agriculture
IFRS 6 Exploration for and evaluation of mineral resources
IFRS 16 Leases
Chapter Review

In this chapter, we explain several short standards.They refer to specific economic transactions, activities and events not covered by the standards we have discussed in earlier chapters.The brevity of our explanation does not detract from the importance of these standards in the context in which they are applied.Students tend to think of accounting standards applying to large manufacturing companies.That is not the case and we include in this chapter examples from non-manufacturing companies, such as agriculture and investment property. We also explain those standards that apply to a certain event or procedure.

IAS 10 Events after the Reporting Period

The compiling and processing of financial information at the year end take a substantial amount of effort.There are also the examinations by the auditors that can take several weeks. The time the main financial statements are received by shareholders and made public can take considerable time, and in that period, the company is still in operation. An entity cannot issue its financial statements before the Directors sign (authorise) them. This delay before authorisation can give rise to problems.

First, there is the issue of important information about an earlier event not becoming available until after the year end but before the directors authorise the financial statements.The other possibility is that very significant events occur after the year end but before the directors authorise the financial statements. The question is what action the directors should take.

It is possible for many events to take place between the date of the year end and the signing of the financial statements.In addition, some events of substance initially occur before the year end, but the entity does not know the full financial consequences for some considerable time later. IAS 10 establishes the proper accounting treatment for events that occur, or information becoming available, after the end date but before the directors authorise the financial statements. In some circumstances, the financial statements will need to be adjusted in other instances they will not need to be adjusted.

Adjusting event

Adjusting events give new evidence on conditions as of the date of the balance sheet. Where an entity has an adjusting event, it must alter the financial statements to show this new information before its authorisation. For example, the balance sheet may record the company's closing stockat a carrying amount of £150,000. Shortly after the year end, an independent valuator informs them that this valuation is incorrect and it is only valued at £12,000 at the balance sheet date. Evidence has therefore become available that shows the original valuation to be incorrect and the financial statements must be restated before they can be authorised.

Typical examples of adjusting events are as follows:

- discovery of fraud or errors,
- information about the value or recoverability of an asset at the year end,
- settlement of an outstanding court case i.e. a case that was in court before the year end has been settled after the year end.

Non-adjusting event

This event takes place after the balance sheet date but is of such significance that the question arises as to whether the shareholders should be informed. The amounts shown on the financial statements are correct for the financial period, so there is an argument that there is no need to inform the shareholders. However, the standard takes the position that the financial statements are correct and no change is required, but, if the events are significant, the entity should inform shareholders. For example, premises correctly valued at the year end but subsequently severely damaged by floods before the authorisation date is a non-adjusting event. The financial statements are correct as of the year end and do not have to be restated. However, a non-adjusting event has occurred that is of significant importance and disclosure should be made. An entity would include this information in its Notes to the Accounts in its Annual Report.

Examples of non-adjusting events are as follows:

- fire after the balance sheet date destroying or damaging non-current assets,
- announcements of a major restructuring plan,
- major purchases of items, such as property, plant and equipment,
- purchase of another entity,
- major disposal of property, plant and equipment.

It is critical that entities correctly identify adjusting events and non-adjusting events. The former changes the financial statements for the reporting period. Non-adjusting events appear as a note. In determining the appropriate classification of the event, it is necessary to consider all the surrounding circumstances. For example, the reduction in value of a property after the balance sheet date but before the authorisation date is usually identified as a non-adjusting event. However, information received after the balance sheet date that demonstrated that the property had lost its value before the balance sheet date is an adjusting event.

The standard also requires that an entity should not prepare financial statements on a going concern basis if events occur between the balance sheet date and the date of authorisation that indicate the entity is not a going concern. Entities should disclose the authorisation date for financial statements. It is essential that users know this date as the financial statements and disclosures will not report any events occurring after the authorisation date.

The critical aspect of this standard is the timing of the event and the date of authorisation of the financial statements.The standard offers the following guidance:

1. An entity may have to submit its financial statements for approval after the issue of financial statements to shareholders. It is usual for the board to authorise the financial statements for issue prior to submitting them to the shareholders.The date of issue will be the date of authorisation and not the date of the shareholders' approval.
2. The management of an entity may have to issue its financial statements to a supervisory board (made up solely of non-executives) for approval.The financial statements are authorised when the board issues them to the supervisory board.

IAS 12 Income Taxes

A brief summary of the standard as the complication of tax requires another book by itself. As we are dealing with taxes that are paid to the government, it is not surprising that IAS 12 is very careful with the definitions which are as follows:

Accounting profit is profit or loss for a period before deducting *tax expense*.

Taxable profit (tax loss) is the profit (loss) for a period, determined in accordance with the rules established by the taxation authorities, upon which income taxes are payable (recoverable).

Tax expense (tax income) is the aggregate amount included in the determination of profit or loss for the period in respect of *current tax* and deferred tax.

Current tax is the amount of income taxes payable (recoverable) in respect of the *taxable profit (tax loss)* for a period.

For a large company, tax can be a substantial amount and the calculation of it can be complex.The objective of IAS 12 Income Taxes is to set the accounting treatment for income taxes. This includes all domestic and foreign taxes calculated on taxable profits. The standard also deals with transactions and other events of the current period that are recognised in the financial statements.These are as follows:

- recognition of deferred tax assets arising from unused tax losses or unused tax credits,
- the presentation of income taxes in the financial statements,
- the disclosure of information relating to income taxes.

Tax is a complex matter and the standard uses certain terms that have specific meanings.These terms are as follows:

- *Temporary difference*: A difference between the carrying amount of an asset or liability and its tax base.
- *Taxable temporary difference*: A temporary difference that will result in taxable amounts in the future when the carrying amount of the asset is recovered or the liability is settled.
- *Deductible temporary difference*: A temporary difference that will result in amounts that are tax deductible in the future when the carrying amount of the asset is recovered or the liability is settled.

The difference between accounting profit and tax profit arises from both permanent and temporary differences. Permanent differences are one of the differences due to certain transactions not being taxable.These differences affect only one period.They do not give rise to deferred tax. Temporary differences give rise to deferred tax and are the difference between the current tax expense and the adjusted figure. The main differences between the taxable "profit" and the entity's reported profits are as follows:

- the depreciation calculated under IAS 16 for reporting purpose differs from the allowances accepted by the tax authorities,

- employee expenditure recognised when incurred for accounting purposes and when paid for tax purposes,
- costs of research and development charged in the income statement in one period for accounting purposes but allowed for tax purposes in another period.

Users may misinterpret the reported profit without knowing that the entity has enjoyed significant tax relief.To remedy this, the entity must inform the user of the deferred tax as a deferred tax liability as this amount becomes an actual tax liability in future periods. An entity should recognise a deferred tax liability in full for all tax differences unless it arises from the following:

- goodwill for which amortisation is not deductible for tax purposes,
- the initial recognition of an asset/liability that is not part of a business combination and affects neither the accounting nor the taxable profit at the time of the transaction,
- investments where the enterprise is able to control the timing of reversal of the tax difference and it is probable that the reversal will not occur in the foreseeable future.

The standard requires entities to disclose the tax from ordinary activities on the face of the Statement of Comprehensive Income. An entity should also disclose the separate components of tax separately and these are as follows:

- current tax expense for the period of account,
- any tax expense recognised in the current period of account for prior periods,
- the amount of any benefit arising from a previously unrecognised tax loss, tax credit or a temporary difference of a prior period that is used to reduce the current tax expense,
- the amount of tax expense (income) relating to those changes in accounting policies and fundamental errors that are included in the calculation of net profit or loss, such changes are in IAS 8.

IAS 16 Property, Plant and Equipment

The objective of IAS 16 is to set out the accounting treatment for most types of property, plant and equipment. Non-current assets meeting the

PPE definition should be recognised if it is probable that there will be future economic benefits and the cost of the item can be measured reliably. Although IAS 16 has the title "Property, Plant and Equipment", the standard does not apply to all PPE and there are standards referring to specific items which we explain in other chapters in this book.

One particular feature of IAS 16 is the requirement for measurement to be originally at cost, but subsequently, the asset can be carried at either cost or a revalued amount.The revalued amount arises when a company adds to the original PPE item or replaces part of it. Service costs that improve the asset leading to additional economic benefits can be recognised but not normal servicing costs. For example, a major overhaul of a piece of machinery to obtain greater efficiency would lead to economic benefits. The cost of the major overhaul can be capitalised.

Examples of cost for items of PPE are as follows:

Land: Purchase price, legal fees and preparation of site for intended use.

Buildings: Purchase price and costs incurred in putting the buildings in a condition for use.

Plant and machinery: Purchase price, transport and installation costs and testing costs.

Abnormal costs such as rectifying installation errors, design errors, wastage and idle capacity are not part of the original cost of the asset but a charge to the profit or loss account. Unless the property, plant and equipment are used to develop or maintain these assets, IAS 16 does not apply to the following:

- PPE held for sale under IFRS 5,
- Non-current Assets Held for Sale and Discontinued items,
- Biological assets under IAS 41,
- Agriculture Assets under IFRS 6,
- Exploration for and Evaluation of Mineral Resources Investment property under IAS 40.

In calculating the cost, an entity cannot add the following items to the carrying amount of the item. These items include:

(i) Initial operating losses, if any. For example, an entity may not be enjoying economic benefit until it achieves a certain level of production. The losses it initially makes cannot be capitalised.

(ii) Costs incurred whilst waiting to bring the item into full use. For example, a hotel may be ready for opening but incurs security costs before the first guests arrive.

(iii) Costs incurred in relocating or reorganising part or all of an entity's operations. For example, a factory may be reorganised to move some heavy machinery so that it fits better into the production flow. This cost cannot be added to the value of the machinery.

(iv) Incidental operations that are not relevant to an item being at the location and in a fit condition for operations. For example, with the introduction of new machinery, a company may decide to move its storage facilities of raw materials. It cannot add this cost to the cost of the new machinery. With some items, it is possible that, when the activity has reached the end of its useful economic life, the entity will be obliged to dismantle the equipment and restore the site to its original state. These expected future costs can be included in the original cost of the asset.

Revaluation

IAS 16 permits the revaluation of non-current assets but whether a revaluation should take place is at the discretion of management who decide whether to revalue, when to revalue and, with some restrictions, which assets to revalue. One might suppose that, where an asset has increased in value, an entity would be keen to demonstrate this. It would reveal financial strength and an ability to meet claims and, possibly, prevent a hostile takeover. However, relatively few entities use the option in IAS 16 to revalue some of their assets. There are three reasons for this: First, by revaluing their assets, the ratio known as return on assets declines, and users might interpret this as a decline in company performance. Second, the revaluation is likely to result in an increased depreciation charge. Which could have a negative effect on profits. The third reason for entities not rushing to revalue assets is that, if they choose to do so, they must comply with the following regulations:

- Revaluations should be carried out regularly so that the carrying amount of an asset does not differ materially from its fair value at the balance sheet date.

- The entire class of assets to which that asset belongs should be revalued. A class of PPE is a grouping of assets of a similar nature and use in an entity's operations. Examples are buildings, machinery, motor vehicles, furniture and fixtures. An entity must revalue all buildings and not just a few.
- Depreciation is charged in the same way as under the cost basis.
- Increases in revaluation value should be credited to equity under the heading of "Revaluation surplus". If the increase is a reversal of a revaluation decrease of the same asset previously recognised as an expense, it should be recognised as income.
- Decreases as a result of a revaluation should be recognised as an expense to the extent that it exceeds any amount previously credited to the revaluation surplus relating to the same asset.
- Disposal of revalued assets can lead to a revaluation surplus which may be either transferred directly to retained earnings or left in equity under the heading "Revaluation surplus".
- The revaluation model can only be used if the fair value of the item can be measured reliably. The requirement to review revaluations regularly can apply annually or at least when there are indications that there have been changes in the prices in the market.

For most companies property, plant and equipment is a major item, and we show in the following the note made by Whitbread plc annual report and accounts 2020/2021.

Property, plant and equipment acquired separately from a business are stated at cost or deemed cost at transition to IFRS, less accumulated depreciation and any impairment in value. Gross interest costs incurred on the financing of qualifying assets are capitalised until the time that the assets are available for use. Property, plant and equipment acquired as part of a business combination are recognised at fair value. Depreciation is calculated on a straight-line basis over the estimated useful life of the asset as follows: › freehold land is not depreciated; › freehold and long leasehold buildings are depreciated to their estimated residual values over periods up to 50 years; and › plant and equipment is depreciated over three to 25 years. The residual values and estimated useful lives are reviewed annually. Profits or losses on disposal of property, plant and equipment reflect the difference between net selling price and carrying amount at the date of disposal and are recognised in the consolidated income statement.

IAS 19 Employee Benefits

This standard covers all forms of consideration given in exchange for services supplied by an employee.The consideration may be cash bonuses, retirement benefits and private health care.When studying this standard, we are considering **all** forms of consideration given by a business in exchange for services provided by its employees in a financial period. These include the following:

- short-term benefits becoming due within 12 months of services being given e.g. wages, salaries, bonuses and non-monetary benefits,
- post-employment benefits e.g. pensions and continued private medical health care,
- other long-term benefits e.g. long-term disability benefits and paid sabbaticals,
- termination benefits i.e. when an employee leaves.

The standard identifies the various types of benefits to which it applies. Some examples are as follows:

- wages and salaries,
- profit-sharing plans,
- bonuses,
- medical and life insurance benefits during employment,
- pension benefits,
- post-employment medical and life insurance benefits.

The accounting dilemma is whether the employee benefit is a liability or an expense.The general principle is that the cost of providing employee benefits should be recognised as an expense in the period where the employee earns the benefit, rather than when it is paid or payable.

With pensions, the employer receives the benefits of the employee's service now but does not pay the pension until the employee retires.The employer must pay the future pension and will classify it as a liability.

Short-term benefits

Short-term employee benefits are those payable within 12 months after service is provided. This includes vacations, paid sick leave and other acceptable absences where the benefits are still payable.The cost is an expense in the period that service is provided and is charged to the income statement.

Post-employment benefits

Post-employment benefits, also known as retirement benefits, cause the greatest accounting problems.There are two main types of retirement schemes: the defined contribution plan and the defined benefit plan. For defined contribution plans, the employing entity recognises contributions as an expense in the period that the employee provides service. In many schemes, the employee and the employer both agree to contribute specific amounts to the plan.

The amount paid into the defined contribution plan is fixed and the payments are invested to build up a "fund" for the particular employee. The disadvantage of the defined contribution plan is that the amount of the final fund relies heavily on the success of the investments.

Defined benefit plans are not calculated on contributions but the amount of pension an employee is guaranteed to receive on retirement. The pension is usually calculated by using a formula that takes into account the employee's length of service and salary.

To operate the scheme, an employer needs to know now the amount of contribution that they must make each year to pay for the final pension.Imagine that a company has an employee starting on 1 January 2015 and will retire in 2055.To determine the contribution that must be invested annually until the employee retires, the employer must assess the following:

- Whether the employee will leave or die before they are due to retire?
- How many years' service will they actually have?
- What will their final salary be?
- What will be the investment return on the contributions made each year?
- How long will the employee live after retirement because the pension will have to be paid until the employee dies?

Our comments on pension plans have been concentrated on the accounting issues. It is the laws of a country that regulate the nature, operation and regulation of pension plans. Companies must comply with the national laws.We have explained briefly the two schemes in the UK. The actual operation and regulation of pension plans for employees must comply with the laws of the countries in which they operate.This may add complications in some countries to the application of IFRS 19.

IAS 23 Borrowing Costs

The standard defines borrowing costs as the interest and other costs that an entity incurs in connection with the borrowing of funds. Some entities will purchase their non-current asset and others may construct their own. Those entities that construct assets themselves may borrow money to do so.The question arises whether the interest on the borrowings is part of constructing the asset and thus is capitalised on the balance sheet or, as with other interest payments, it goes to the profit or loss account as an expense.

The objective of IAS 23 is to set out the appropriate accounting treatment for borrowing costs that are directly attributable to the acquisition, construction or production of a "qualifying asset". A non-current asset that takes a substantial time to get ready for its intended use or sale is a qualifying asset.The borrowing costs for a qualifying asset are included as part of the cost of the asset. Borrowing costs, which do not meet the requirements of the standard, are recognised as an expense in the profit or loss account.

The standard does not apply to the following:

- qualifying assets measured at fair value, such as biological assets accounted for under IAS 41 Agriculture,
- inventories that are manufactured or, otherwise produced, in large quantities on a repetitive basis and that take a substantial period to get ready for sale (e.g. maturing whisky).

IAS 23 requires that borrowing costs, which are directly attributed to the acquisition, construction or production of a qualifying asset, must be capitalised as part of the cost of the asset. The Basis for Conclusions explains the use of the term Borrowing Costs rather than

Interest Costs.The term Borrowing Costs reflects the broader definition in IAS 23, which encompasses interest and other costs. Examples of qualifying assets include manufacturing plants, power generation facilities and investment properties. In some industries, entities can take a long time before they are in a saleable condition.The regulation is that such borrowing costs can be capitalised.This does not apply to inventories manufactured on a routine basis or produced in large quantities on a repetitive basis over a short time.

There are restrictions on the amount that a company can capitalise. The main rule is that capitalisation is the actual costs incurred less any income earned on the temporary investment of funds.Where the borrowings are one part of a general pool, the capitalisation rate is the weighted average of the borrowing costs for the general pool. In calculating the amount to be capitalised, it is important to identify the date that the project commences and the date that it finishes. The capitalisation of borrowings occurs on major, long-term projects, which can lead to situations where work is temporarily ceased. Capitalisation must then be suspended.

Timing of activity starting and continuing and the interest to be paid raises problems. In some circumstances, entities may have to secure the loan and pay interest before construction starts. A project may be suspended part way through but the interest still has to be paid. Finally, the company may not repay the loan until sometime after the project is completed, but it will still be required to pay the interest.The rules are as follows:

1. Interest paid prior to the activity commencing is charged as an expense to the profit or loss account.It cannot be capitalised.
2. Where a project is suspended for an extended time, interest cannot be capitalised.
3. If there is a temporary suspension of activity, interest can be capitalised.
4. At the cessation of the project, if the company does not immediately repay the loan, any subsequent interest cannot be capitalised and must be charged as an expense to the profit or loss account.
5. The amounts of borrowing costs eligible for capitalisation are the actual borrowing costs incurred on that borrowing during the period less any investment income on the temporary investment of those borrowings.

Worked Example 1 — Capitalisation and cost of asset

Dingdong Co takes a loan of £3 million at 5% per annum on 1 January 2021 for the construction of a qualifying asset.The work is completed on 31 December 2021.The company is able to repay the loan in full on 30 June 2022.

Construction cost of asset	£3,000,000
Capitalisation of interest for one year	£150,000
Total cost of asset on balance sheet	£3,150,000

Interest not capitalised and charged to profit or loss account
£3 million × 5% × 6 months = £75,000

IAS 33 Earnings per Share

This standard is of particular interest as it is a potential guide to investors on the dividend they may receive.The standard requires companies to calculate and disclose the basic earnings per share EPS on the face of their income statement and to disclose the following information:

- details of basic and diluted EPS on the face of the income statement,
- the amounts used for profit or loss for ordinary shareholders in calculating the basic EPS,
- the weighted average number of ordinary shares used in calculating the ratios,
- a description of the ordinary share transactions or potential ordinary share transactions that occurs after the balance sheet date and would have significant effect on the EPS.

The annual report of the Legal and General Company plc is extremely useful and with a very informative piece on its EPS.We show in the following a very short extract from an informative piece on their EPS:

> *The basic EPS is calculated by dividing the profit or loss attributable to ordinary equity holders of the parent equity by the average number of ordinary shares held currently. The resulting number serves as an indicator of a company's profitability. It is common for a company to report EPS that is adjusted for extraordinary items and potential share dilution.*

IAS 34 Interim Financial Reporting

Most stock exchanges around the world require their listed companies to issue interim financial reports to produce timely and reliable information. The stock exchange may require companies to issue these at the six-month stage (half-yearly) as in Canada and the UK or to issue them every three months (quarterlies) as in Australia and the USA.

Where the stock exchange regulations are for half-yearly interims, entities should issue interims for the first six months of the financial year but not for the second six months as the entity will be producing annual reports. For quarterly interims, the stock exchange normally requires entities to produce interim financial statements for the first three quarters of the year. There is no requirement for fourth quarter interims as an entity issues the annual financial statements.

IAS 34 specifies the content of an interim financial report that conforms to International Financial Reporting Standards. The standard does not state which entities must publish interim financial reports or how frequently. National governments, securities regulators, stock exchanges and accountancy bodies decide these requirements. The standard is essentially about the accounting treatment for the contents of the document.

Timing problems

The requirement for entities to produce annual financial statements may not reflect the timing of their activities. Some entities may be in retailing where there is a rapid turnover in stock daily. Others may be involved in heavy manufacturing with jobs lasting over 12 months. Some may have revenue and costs peaking at different times in the same financial year. If we consider agriculture, timing may be even more variable.

Standard setters and entities have been able to resolve most of the issues for annual reporting.When we come to half-yearly reporting, the recording and measurement of some transactions and events can become very difficult.We describe three scenarios to highlight them.

Scenario 1

A company has a year end on 31 December. An **annual** maintenance programme in the factory takes place on 1 September at a cost of £60,000. How should the company account for this?

(1) Ignore it at the half year as the event has not taken place.
(2) Charge £30,000 in the interim report as the charge of £60,000 reflects the maintenance charge for the entire year.

Scenario 2

A company's financial year begins on April 1st. It intends to launch a large advertising campaign in April 2015.The company plans for the campaign to last for 6 months.The total cost will be £500,000. It is anticipated that the benefits of increased revenues will last until 31 March 2016. How should the company account for this?

(1) Charge the full cost of the campaign in the interim statement on 30 September 2015 because the expenditure is incurred in that period.
(2) Spread the total cost over the 12 months as the benefits are for the full year. This would mean that £250,000 would show in the interim statement.

Scenario 3

A company manufactures Christmas decorations. Manufacturing occurs throughout the year but the main sales only take place in November and December. Consequently, the company has costs for the six months to June but very low sales figure. How should the company account for this? Would it be useful to users for the company to make a prudent proportional estimate of the sales it anticipates making for the year in the interim statement?

We can generalise from these three examples and identify the transactions and events that give rise to accounting dilemmas at the half year:

(a) seasonal fluctuations of revenue,
(b) substantial fixed costs in some periods but applying to the full year,
(c) costs/expenses incurred at infrequent intervals during the year which relate to a full year's activities,
(d) infrequent or unusual events or transactions that have a more substantial effect on the results of operations for an interim period.

There is also the basic problem of assembling information. There is a limited time to obtain the information for the interim period, which leads to numerous estimates. Entities must rectify any misleading estimates in subsequent periods. This may distort the year-end results.

The main decision for the regulators when developing a standard was whether to use a discrete, integral or composite approach (a mixture of the two) for interim reporting (1).The differences in the approaches are significant as follows:

- With the discrete approach, an entity treats each half-yearly or quarterly period as a self-contained period. Costs and revenues are matched in each period and the same accounting policies and treatments are used for the interim period as for the annual accounts.
- With the integral approach, an entity treats each shorter period as part of the longer period. This approach recognises that business activity may be cyclical with profits generated unevenly throughout the year. The integral approach attempts to match planned costs and profits on a basis relating to the year as a whole.
- The composite approach considers the nature of the transactions and events to determine the appropriate accounting treatment.

There are criticisms of all three approaches.The discrete approach can lead to successive six-month periods becoming distorted. Large fluctuations in revenues and expenses in one period can be misleading. For example, an annual charge for maintenance will appear in one six-month period, although the entire year has benefited. The discrete approach may not provide information for the user to predict what the results will be for the full year.

The integral approach also has its weaknesses.The spreading of costs to different periods can be misleading. It is a judgement that management is making.This could be incorrect by design or accidentally. There is also the danger that management is making adjustments based on its prediction of operations for subsequent periods.These predictions may be wrong.

The composite approach permits managers to determine whether they should use the discrete or integral approach for transactions.This method appears to reflect the weaknesses with both of the other methods.

Given these conceptual challenges, the standard setters decided to require the same accounting policies for the interim financial statements as for annual financial statements.This represents a "discrete period" approach to interim reporting. This pronouncement leads to conflicts with certain transactions. At the end of this section, we list the standard's guidance for specific transactions.

Main requirements

IAS 34 Interim Financial Reporting prescribes the minimum content for an interim financial report and the principles for recognition and measurement in complete and condensed financial statements for an interim period. The standard has been effective since 1 January 1999. The IASB made the latest amendment as a consequential amendment of IAS 1 (2007) Presentation of Financial Statements. These changes impacted terminology, the titles and the layout of the financial statements. The standard encourages entities to provide interim financial statements at least at the end of the first six months of their trading year and to make these statements available no later than 60 days after the end of the interim period. The standard only encourages and a country's legislation or stock exchange determines whether a company should publish interim reports and whether this should be quarterly or half-yearly.

Interim financial reports must show each of the headings and the subtotals as illustrated in the most recent annual financial statements and the explanatory notes as required by IAS 34. Additional line items should be included if their omission would make the interim financial information misleading. The notes to the interim financial statements are essentially an update. They include disclosures about changes in accounting policies, seasonality or cyclically, changes in estimates, changes in outstanding debt or equity, dividends, segment revenue and result, events occurring after balance sheet date, acquisition or disposal of subsidiaries and long-term investments, restructurings, discontinuing operations, and changes in contingent liabilities or contingent assets.

Interim reports are not usually subject to a full audit. Nevertheless, entities frequently desire some seal of approval and we show in the following an extract from the 2022 interim report of WPP plc. We emphasise that this is only an extract of some of the headings and the full report is 33 pages. We show the information on page 33 and the full report is easily accessible on the Internet.

WPP Interim Results 2022 (issued 5 August 2022).

33 Pass-through costs comprise fees paid to external suppliers where they are engaged to perform part or all of a specific project and are charged directly to clients, predominantly media costs. Pro forma

("like-for-like") comparisons are calculated as follows: current year, constant currency actual results (which include acquisitions from the relevant date of completion) are compared with prior year, constant currency actual results, adjusted to include the results of acquisitions and disposals, the reclassification of certain businesses to associates in 2021 and the restatement of agency arrangements under IFRS 15 for the commensurate period in the prior year. Both periods exclude results from Russia. The Group uses the terms "pro forma" and "like-for-like" interchangeably. Revenue less pass-through costs Revenue less pass-through costs is revenue less media and other pass-through costs.

Employer payroll taxes and insurance contributions

It is usual for an employer to estimate payroll taxes or contributions to government-sponsored insurance on an annual basis. If this is its normal practice, it should recognise related expense in interim periods.The method for making this estimate is to use an estimated average annual effective payroll tax or contribution rate. Even if an entity makes an actual payment of a large proportion in the first six months, it must still make an estimated average for the interim report.

There is an exception to this requirement and that is where an event has caused the entity to have a legal or constructive obligation. For example, the entity may have a leasing contract to use some expensive machinery. The contract may contain a clause that the entity must carry out annual maintenance: a legal obligation. The mere intention or necessity to incur expenditure related to the future is not sufficient to give rise to an obligation.

Provisions

If a company is aware that it will incur some costs in the not too distant, IAS 34 requires a provision to be made when the company has no realistic alternative but to transfer economic benefits because of an event that has created a legal or constructive obligation. The standard requires an entity to apply the same criteria for recognising and measuring a provision at an interim date as it would at the end of its financial year. The existence or non-existence of an obligation to transfer benefits is not a function of the length of the reporting period. It is a question of fact.

Year-end bonuses

In some organisations, employees may receive a bonus at the year end based on the profitable performance of the entity or some other measures of performance. Some entities may grant bonuses based on continued employment during a time. These may be purely discretionary, contractual or due to years of historical precedent. An entity can anticipate a year-end bonus only if

- the bonus is a legal obligation or past practice would make the bonus a constructive obligation and the entity has no realistic alternative but to make the payments,
- a reliable estimate of the obligation can be made.

Contingent lease payments

Contingent lease payments are an example of a legal or constructive obligation that, under IAS 34, an entity recognises as a liability. For example, a retailer may lease premises and the lease payments depend on the level of sales achieved annually. If this is the case, an obligation can arise in the interim period of the financial year before the achievement of the required annual level of sales. However, if that required level of sales is expected to be achieved, the entity has no realistic alternative but to make the future lease payment.

Intangible assets

Entities cannot defer expenses at the interim stage in the belief (or hope) that these expenses will meet later the criteria to permit capitalisation as an intangible asset. An entity should recognise intangible assets when they meet the recognition criteria.

Irregularly occurring and discretionary costs

An entity may budget to incur such costs as charitable donations and training of employees at some time during the financial year. Although the entity may plan and intend to incur these costs, they are usually discretionary and an entity can avoid them if it decides not to make the payments. An entity cannot recognise at the end of the interim period that it intends to make these payments later in the year.

Volume rebates

A company may purchase a substantial quantity of materials from another company in a financial period. Frequently, the cost charged to it is lower than the normal cost.This is known as a volume rebate and is frequently made at the year end. An entity can anticipate these rebates in the interim financial statement where they are contractual in nature, not discretionary, and it is probable that they earned or will take effect.This is contrary to what you may have thought would be the position but one suspects that these practices were established long before the standard was issued. The IASB may well have decided that it was not worthwhile to change established normal business practice.

Inventories

An entity measures inventories for interim financial reporting using the same principles as at financial year end. The recognition and measurement criteria are stated inIAS 2 Inventories. The valuation of inventories is a large task and to save cost and time, companies often use estimates to measure inventories at interim dates. IAS 34 explains the method for applying estimates in different situations.

Impairment of assets

IAS 34 requires at the interim stage to conduct the same procedure for impairment of assets as it would at the year end. However, entities are relieved of making detailed calculations. It should review indications of significant impairment since the end of the most recent financial year. If it appears that impairment has taken place, the entity must make detailed calculations.

IAS 40 Investment Property

It is not unusual for a company to invest in another business. The standard defines investment property as land, a building, part of a building held by the owner or, if there is a finance lease, by the lessee to earn rentals or for capital appreciation or both. The standard makes a clear distinction between property that an entity acquires for its own use and one the entity acquires for investment purposes. The standard sets out appropriate accounting treatment and disclosures required so that the user can gain a better understanding of the financial statements. In the following table, we show the types of property that are NOT investment property. Other standards regulate their accounting treatment.

Type of non-investment property	**Accounting standard**
Intended for sale in ordinary course of business, usually by a construction company	IAS 2 Inventories
Property being constructed on behalf of others	IAS 11 Construction contracts
Owner-occupied property	IAS 16 Property, plant and equipment
Property being constructed/developed as an investment property	IAS 40

There are two criteria for the recognition of investment property. They are that the property

- should be recognised as an asset when it is probable that the future economic benefits that are associated with the property will flow to the business,
- and the cost of the property can be measured reliably.

An entity can record investment property at either

- fair value: this is the amount where the property could be exchanged between knowledgeable and willing parties in an arm's length transaction or
- cost less accumulated depreciation and any accumulated impairment losses as prescribed by IAS 16.

If an entity selects the cost model, it must also disclose the fair value of the properties, usually in the Notes to the Accounts. If the entity cannot determine the fair value, then it must give

1. a description of the investment property,
2. explanation why fair value cannot be determined reliably,
3. if possible, range of estimates for fair value.

Certain conditions are in force if an investment entity selects fair value and these are

- all investment property held must be at fair value,
- gain or loss due to change in fair value to Income Statement,
- fair value must reflect market conditions at balance sheet date,
- transfers to and from Investment Property only when there is a change in use.

It is possible that the fair value of the investment property changes over time. The entity must recognise these changes in the fair values in the profit or loss for the period in which they arise.The standard does not specify where any gains and losses on changes in fair value should appear in the statement of comprehensive income. Of course, an entity may have an investment property but then decide to use the premises itself. Alternatively, it may own and use a property and then decide to vacate it and rent it out. If such a change in use takes place, a different standard applies. Following are three common scenarios demonstrating the change of use and the change in standard:

1. An entity has been renting office space to a third party but now intends to occupy the space itself. This is a change from IAS 40 to IAS 16 Property, plant and equipment.
2. An entity originally owned a building intended for sale but decides to rent it to a third party. The building now comes under IAS 40 Investment property.
3. An entity has been occupying a building but has decided to vacate it and let to a third party.This would have been under IAS 16 but now comes under IAS 40 Investment property.

On disposal or permanent withdrawal from use, a property should be derecognised. The gain or loss on derecognition should be calculated as the difference between the net disposal proceeds and the carrying amount of the asset. The gain or losses should be recognised in the income statement.

IAS 41 Agriculture

Definition: Agricultural activity

The management by a business of the biological transformation of biological assets for sale into agricultural produce or into additional biological assets.

In previous chapters, we have considered a range of different industries and the application of accounting standards.The agricultural industry is different from other industries.Unlike other business activities, agriculture is highly reliant on the climate. Thus, we have an industry-specific standard. Agricultural activity, particularly in some countries and regions, is a significant part of the economy. There is a range of dissimilar activities that come under the heading of Agriculture and the standard IAS 41 establishes the accounting treatment, financial statement presentation and disclosures for agricultural activity.

The standard applies to biological assets and agricultural products only. It does not deal with the process of turning agricultural produce into products e.g. grapes into wine, as this process comes under other standards. It specifically scopes out bearer plants, agricultural produce at the point of harvest and government grants related to these biological assets, land related to agricultural activity, intangible assets related to agricultural activity, government grants related to bearer plants and bearer plants.

Bearer plants are living plants that

1. are used in the production or supply of agricultural produce,
2. are expected to bear produce for more than one period,
3. have a remote likelihood of being sold as agricultural produce, except for incidental scrap sales.

We can explain biological assets by using an everyday perspective by looking at the products we eat and drink. Calves, cows, pigs, sheep, vines and fruit trees are all examples of biological assets as they are living animals and plants.The agricultural produce is the wool from the sheep, the milk from the cows and the fruit from the trees.Some produce will need processing after the harvest and examples are cheese from the milk, clothes from the wool and wine from the grape.

As far as recognition of biological assets is concerned, the standard has the following criteria:

- they should be recognised only where there is control of the asset because of past events,
- it is probable that future economic benefits will flow to the entity,
- the fair value or cost of the asset can be measured reliably.

The standard assumes that fair value is a reliable method for measuring a biological asset. On initial recognition and subsequently, an entity should recognise biological assets at fair value less estimated point-of-sale costs, if it can measure fair value reliably. The measurement method for agricultural produce is at fair value less estimated point-of-sales costs at the point of harvest. Point-of-sales costs include commissions, levies and transfer duties and taxes.

If there is a gain on initial recognition of biological assets at fair value and changes in fair value of biological assets during a period, the entity shows this in the income statement for that period. A gain on initial recognition of agricultural produce at fair value should be included in the income statement for the period in which it arises.

Students tend to ignore the agricultural industry when looking for examples.That is a mistake! We show in the following an extract from Arla Foods plc which is a significant agricultural company in Europe. It has over 10,000 employees, an excellent and very informative website and their annual report states:

> "*The ESG report focuses on presenting our ESG data and corresponding methodologies and accounting policies in detail*".

IFRS 6 Exploration for and Evaluation of Mineral Resources

Definition: Mineral resources

The search for mineral resources, including minerals, oil, natural gas and similar non-regenerative resources after the entity has obtained legal rights to explore in a specific area, as well as the determination of the technical feasibility and commercial viability of extracting the mineral resource.

To explain mineral resources, it is helpful to focus on the oil and gas industry as it is large and complex. Looking at the entire process, we have entities involved in finding, extracting, refining and selling oil and gas. There are also the refined products and related products.The operations require substantial capital investment and have long lead times. A critical issue is which costs the entity should capitalise and show on the balance sheet and those costs that it should expense on the income statement.

The industry is large and important with independent companies having diverse industrial practices so it is not surprising that IFRS 6 permits entities to continue to use their existing accounting policies. However, accounting policies must comply with IAS 8 Accounting Policies, Changes in Accounting Estimates and Errors.The requirement to comply with IAS 8 means the accounting policies must provide information that is not only relevant, but reliable, to the economic decision-making needs of users. Entities can, if they choose, change their accounting policies for exploration and evaluation expenditures if the change makes the financial statements more relevant and reliable.

Under the standard, we have two occasions for the measurement of assets: the initial measurement and the subsequent measurement. At first recognition in the balance sheet, the standard requires entities to measure exploration and evaluation assets at cost. Entities can set their own consistent policies on what should be included in cost and IFRS 6 lists the following as examples of expenditures that might be included in the initial measurement of exploration and evaluation assets (the list is not exhaustive):

- acquisition of rights to explore and topographical, geological, geochemical and geophysical studies,
- exploratory drilling, trenching, sampling and activities in relation to evaluating the technical feasibility and commercial viability of extracting a mineral resource,
- an entity can incur obligations for removal and restoration through the exploration for and evaluation of mineral resources.

After the initial recognition, entities can apply either the cost model or the revaluation model to exploration and evaluation assets. As there are likely to be both tangible and intangible assets, entities will apply the requirements of IAS 16 Property, Plant and Equipment and IAS 38 Intangible Assets.

Identifying impaired assets can cause problems because of the difficulty in obtaining the information necessary to estimate future cash flows from exploration and evaluation assets. IFRS 6 makes the process more practicable by identifying where impairment has taken place. A detailed impairment test is required in two circumstances:

1. when the technical feasibility and commercial viability of extracting a mineral resource become demonstrable, at which point the asset falls outside the scope of IFRS 6 and is reclassified in the financial statements,
2. when facts and circumstances suggest that the asset's carrying amount may exceed its recoverable amount.

The reference to facts and circumstances seems vague but the standard offers some examples:

- The period for the right to explore in the specific area has expired during the period or will expire in the near future and is not expected to be renewed.
- Substantive expenditure on further exploration for and evaluation of mineral resources in the specific area is neither budgeted nor planned.
- Exploration for and evaluation of mineral resources in the specific area have not led to the discovery of commercially viable quantities of mineral resources, and the entity has decided to discontinue such activities in the specific area.
- Sufficient data exist to indicate that, although a development in the specific area is likely to proceed, the carrying amount of the exploration and evaluation asset is unlikely to be recovered in full from successful development or by sale.

IFRS 16 Leases

The IASB added a new project to its agenda in 2006. It declared the intention to develop a new international accounting standard that remedied the deficiencies in existing regulations for accounting for leases. In August

2014, the IASB issued a Project Update. This document provided an update on the most important tentative decisions reached on the Leases project during the first half of 2014, explaining the IASB's reasons for reaching those decisions and the remaining work to be undertaken. In February 2015, the IASB issued another document entitled Leases: Definition of a lease.The document gave the following definition:

> *"A lease is defined as a contract that conveys to the customer the right to use an asset for a period of time in exchange for consideration."*

It may have taken many investigations and discussions but there is now a standard IFRS 16 Lease which sets out the criteria for recognising, measuring, presenting and disclosing and leases it holds. This is a specific and somewhat technical standard. However, the standard provides a single lessee accounting model which means that the leaseholders must recognise assets and liabilities for all leases. If the lease term is 12 months or less or the underlying asset has a low value, then the lease should be classified as an operating lease. The standard does not make for easy reading but it is clear that the intention is to make certain that lessees recognise assets and liabilities for their major leases.

Chapter Review

In this chapter, we have explained several accounting standards.The number of standards we have covered and the brevity of our explanations does not detract from their importance. Companies in the industries that we have identified must comply with the relevant standard otherwise they will not receive a clean auditor's report. IAS 16 Property, Plant and Equipment and IAS 34 Interim Financial Reporting are applicable to all companies regardless of the industry in which they operate. If you are studying one particle industry, we recommend that you obtain company's annual report so you can appreciate how the relevant standard is applied.

CHAPTER 10 Short Standards

Review Questions

1. Which of the following applies to Interim Financial Reporting Statements?
   a. Statements are not required by the stock exchange.
   b. The standard IAS 34 does not state how frequently the statements should be issued.
   c. The standard defines the companies that should issue statements.
   d. The statements must show each of the headings and the sub-totals as illustrated in the most recent annual financial statements.

2. Why is an adjusting event important?

3. What is the difference between identifying adjusting events and non-adjusting events?

4. If a company has borrowing costs, which are directly attributed to the acquisition, construction or production of a qualifying asset, what is the accounting treatment?

5. What is a volume rebate?

6. Is property being built on behalf of others treated as investment property?

7. Does IAS 41 Agriculture apply to the process of turning agricultural produce into products e.g. grapes into wine?
   a. Yes
   b. No

8. A fire at a company occurred after the balance sheet date which damaged non-current assets. Is the fire an adjusting or non-adjusting event?

Chapter 11

Equity and Liabilities

Structure of Chapter 11

Section title	Main content
Who owns the company?	An introduction to the notion of company ownership.
Identifying economic resources	This section is based on the information that should be disclosed in a company's Statement of Financial Position (balance sheet).
Share Capital (Equity)	Not a difficult topic but there is the distinction between ordinary shares and preference shares.
Capital reduction and share buyback	A process that shareholders may appreciate and is not too complex.
Statement of changes in equity	This is required by IAS 1 and discloses changes over a financial period in the reserves of the owners' equity.
Statement of comprehensive income	An important reporting requirement as the statement recognises both realised and unrealised gains and losses that have increased or decreased the owners' equity.
Financial Analysis	The collection and perusal of corporate financial information is only useful if a thorough financial analysis is conducted. In this section, various approaches of financial analysis are explained.

Efficiency and Financial Examination	An explanation of the use of the analysis of the financial reports of a company to assess its performance.
Chapter Review	Equity, liabilities, gains, losses, comprehensive income and financial analysis are explained.

In this chapter, we start by explaining equity and this is followed by an explanation of non-current liabilities. Equity and non-current liabilities have caused some problems for the standard setters. The line items that fall under the heading of equity are share capital and reserves of various types. Examples of non-current liabilities are items such as long-term borrowings, corporate income tax and provisions. In discussing equity and non-current liabilities, we refer to the requirements under the UK Companies Legislation and accounting standards. Our review of the regulations demonstrates that the legislators intend to protect the respective interests of shareholders and creditors. There is an emphasis on capital maintenance. The regulations ensure shareholders do not remove their capital thus leaving the creditors at risk. To ensure capital maintenance, the profit earned by an entity is not always available for distribution to the shareholders. This gives rise to various types of reserves with strict control over their use.

IAS 1 introduced a new financial regulation in 2007 that relates to equity. The statement of changes in equity informs the users of financial statement of the factors that cause a change in the owners' equity over the accounting periods. This statement is of particular interest to shareholders wishing to assess the size of their financial interest in the entity. Non-current liabilities are, in most respects, far simpler to understand than equity. It is simply that the entity owes money to various parties, but these are not due for payment in the 12 months following the date of the balance sheet. There are some complications with non-current liabilities such as tax and provisions which we discuss in this chapter.

As with some other aspects of accounting, sometimes terminology can be fluid. This is particularly true in respect of the terms capital and equity that, sometimes, are used interchangeably. The word equity refers to the share capital and all reserves held by the entity. In other words, the assets minus all liabilities, both current and non-current. The term capital refers strictly to investment made by interested parties by purchasing and holding shares in the entity.

Who Owns the Company?

When we are looking at large companies listed on the stock exchange, it is highly unlikely that it is owned only by the employees. The Directors may have some shares but they are also employees and they are answerable to the shareholders. A company may have a scheme which encourages employees generally to hold shares. Mostly, shareholders will have invested in the company by buying shares on the market and they will be seeking a financial return paid out of the profits. They can both be any dividend the company pays to those holding shares or the share price can rise and the holder of the shares can sell them at a higher price than they paid for them. In the UK, the main shareholders are usually large institute investors, such as pension funds, insurance companies, mutual funds or similar foreign organisations. The shareholders have considerable powers and, if they are dissatisfied with the dividend they receive on the shares or the price that it is fetching on the stock market, they can sell their shares. They also have such powers as removing the director.

If we rank the top UK companies by market capitalisation which is the value of a company that is traded on the stock market, calculated by multiplying the total number of shares by the present share price, the top companies are as follows:

- AstraZeneca industry is a research and manufacturing company and it is the largest medicine manufacturer in the UK.
- Shell is a global group of energy and petrochemical enterprises.
- Linde is a leading global industrial gases and engineering company.
- Unilever makes the following products in the UK: Marmite and Bovril, Pot Noodle, PG Tips and Colman's Mustard.
- HSBC is a well-known name in the UK and it is owned by the Hongkong and Shanghai Banking Corporation Limited.

If we rank the top UK companies by the number of employees (worldwide), they are as follows:

- Compass Group 478070,
- Tesco 367321,

- HSBC Holdings 219000,
- Unilever 148000,
- J Sainsbury 189000.

Companies are large and essential to society. They provide products and services we require and also employ many people. It is important to understand how they are financed and the statistical methods we can use to assess their performance. When ranking companies by the number of employees, it is important to remember that the nature of the business determines the employment level. If you have a number of stores selling different products, the company needs a large number of shop assistants.

Identifying Economic Resources

The statement of financial position, or balance sheet, shows the economic resources of the entity and the claims on those resources. The recipients of this information use it to assess the entity's financial strength. The use of offsetting by entities, generally, is not permitted. Offsetting is the use of one account to reduce the balance in another. The regulations prohibit the deduction of a liability account from an asset account, or vice versa. There are some exceptions to this rule. A standard may permit offsetting in specific circumstances. It is also possible that the basis of a particular transaction incorporates offsetting.

IAS 1 establishes the minimum information a company should disclose in regard to its economic resources. In practice, companies usually provide much fuller information, both in the financial statements and in the accompanying notes. The terms that you are likely to encounter are shown in the following. We have divided it into the headings of equity and non-current liabilities.

Equity is the residual interest in the assets of the entity after deducting all its liabilities.

Called-up share capital is the total amount shown on the balance sheet of the share capital shareholders still owe the company and have not yet paid:

- capital redemption reserve,
- cash flow hedging reserve,
- currency translation reserve,
- merger reserve,
- non-controlling interests,
- other reserves.

Non-current liabilities

- bonds and bank loans,
- borrowings,
- corporate income tax,
- derivative financial instruments,
- other payables,
- retirement benefit obligations,
- provision for liabilities and charges,
- trade and other payables.

Determining which items fall under the heading of equity is usually evident. It is mainly the contributions from shareholders. With liabilities, the division between current and non-current liabilities is less obvious than with assets. Some types of liability can fall into either category. IAS 1 differentiates by stating which liabilities are current. The basic points in identifying current liabilities are as follows:

1. The entity expects to settle the liability in its normal operating cycle. For example, your suppliers would expect to be paid promptly.
2. The entity holds the liability primarily for the purposes of trading,
3. The liability is due to be settled within 12 months after the reporting period. These liabilities are often related to large, long-term contracts.

Point 1 refers to the normal operating cycle. In some industries, this may exceed 12 months and may extend the recognition of current liabilities. With point number 3, if the entity is able to defer payment of a liability later than the 12 months, that liability is non-current. IAS 1 applies the default definition to identify non-current liabilities. If a liability does not meet the criteria as a current liability, it must be non-current. Fortunately, public limited companies are well aware of the detailed requirements of the standard and the classifications on their balance sheets are clear.

The ratio of total equity to non-current liabilities varies considerably. Each entity has its own pattern of non-current liabilities, but usually, borrowings are a substantial part. The source and nature of borrowings can change considerably from year to year. The user will be looking at these shifts and see how they correspond to the activities of the company. For example, if a company has commenced a large expansion project lasting 5 years, you could anticipate this would be reflected in the borrowings. In addition to the source of borrowings, the user is interested in what proportion of funding for the entity comes from shareholders and what comes from non-current liabilities.

In looking at the relationship of equity and other forms of funding, such as long-term borrowings, we are considering two groups: the lenders and the shareholders. Both groups are interested in the financial performance of the company, but possibly for different reasons. Shareholders will be interested in the profit the company makes, as that is the source of dividends. A healthy profit may also increase the share price leading to a capital gain for shareholders. Lenders will be looking for evidence that they will receive the interest on the funds that they have lent and that the company will repay the loan when it falls due.

Share Capital (Equity)

This term, *share capital*, usually refers to the amount that shareholders have invested in an entity by purchasing shares which the entity has issued. The amount of share capital can increase if an entity issues new shares to the public in exchange for cash. Any price differences arising subsequently from price increases or decreases on the stock exchange are not reflected in the balance sheet. In simpler terms, the value of the shares shown on a balance sheet is very unlikely to be the same as the current price being shown on the stock exchange. As with other values we discuss in this chapter, accounting is not good at identifying current values.

Essentially, there are two groups of investors: individuals and institutional investors. Individual investors are those who are sufficiently wealthy and knowledgeable to purchase shares directly. Institutional investors are any non-banking organisations or persons that qualify for special treatment and less regulation on their activities. An institutional investor is an investing entity with a very substantial sum for investment. Some examples of institutional investors are endowment funds, mutual funds, investment banks, brokerages, pension funds and insurance companies. The Universities Superannuation Scheme is a pension scheme in the United Kingdom with over £80 billion under management. It has over 400,000 members, made up of active and retired academic and academic-related staff (including senior administrative staff) mostly from those universities. If you have any funds with these organisations, your money is most likely invested in shares. Shareholders provide an essential source of capital investment to companies and have substantial powers in the control of the company. At the end of 2020, shares in quoted UK-domiciled companies listed on the London Stock Exchange (LSE) were worth a total of £2.17 trillion. A very substantial sum and, generally, increasing each year. However, the rest of the world holds over 50% of the value of the UK stock market.

You can understand that the shareholders that we have listed above want a good return on their investment. They expect to receive healthy dividends and hope that the price of the shares increases on the stock market. With these objectives, you can appreciate that other issues such as damage to the environment are not usually their main interest. They would expect that the company issuing shares takes appropriate action on any environmental issues.

The issuers of shares that interest us are those companies quoted on the London Stock Exchange. Those companies are subject to the regulations of International Financial Reporting Standards. Entities, generally, have two types of shares: ordinary and preference. Ordinary shares are referred to as common stock in the US. The main attributes of ordinary and preference are shown in the following table:

Ordinary equity shares	**Preference shares**
Carry the main risk	Usually a fixed rate of dividend
If there are no distributable profits, no dividend is paid	Dividend is paid before any dividend to ordinary shareholders
Holders of ordinary shares can vote at Annual General Meetings	Preference shareholders have no voting powers
Holders receive residual profit in the form of dividends after deduction of any fixed interest, preference dividend and tax	Cumulative preference shares accrue the dividends if there are insufficient profits and pay them in a more successful year
If entity stops trading, ordinary shareholders receive any net assets after creditors' paid	Redeemable preference shares allow the entity to redeem the shares at a set future date and price
Entities, usually, have a dividend policy that determines the share of profit paid to shareholders and the share of profit retained	Convertible preference shares can be converted into ordinary shares at a set date and price

There are shares that do not have all of these attributes. For example, there may be non-voting shares where the holders cannot vote at Annual General Meetings. Shares may be divided into type A shares and type B shares with differing rights and responsibilities. There can be a combination of the two types of shares in the form of convertible preferred shares. These allow the holder of the preference shares the option to convert them to ordinary shares at a particular date. The terms of conversion for such shares specify the date when the conversion takes place and the conversion rate i.e. the number of ordinary shares that will be exchanged for a specific number of convertible preference shares. The option to convert normally belongs to the holder, although some entities may hold the right to force a conversion. Remember that the purchaser of shares, whether an individual or some type of organisation, is looking for a financial return on its investment. This may be a dividend or it could be an increase in the value of shares on the stock exchange so that they can be sold at a profit.

Reserves

Reserves are that part of the shareholders' equity excluding the amount of the basic share capital. They are generally of two types: distributable and non-distributable. The entity's own memorandum and articles can impose certain restrictions on the reserves that can be distributed to owners in the form of dividends.

Total equity

If the share capital amount is added to the aggregation of all the reserves, this gives the shareholders' equity. Non-controlling interests are added to give the total equity. Non-controlling interests are minority interests where the shareholder owns less than 50% of outstanding shares. The basic structure of the amount of total equity is as follows:

	£
Share capital	XX
Add Reserves	XX
Shareholders' equity	XX
Non-controlling interests	XX
Total equity	XX

The total equity consists of the shareholders' equity i.e. the sum of the share capital and reserves *plus* the non-controlling interests which can be defined as the equity in a subsidiary not attributable, directly or indirectly, to a parent. For example, one entity may own 90% of the shares of another entity. The owners of the other 10% in that entity would have a non-controlling interest as they do not have sufficient power to influence decision-making.

To illustrate the above discussion, we show a section of the balance sheet of GlaxoSmithKline for 2021 which shows their non-current liabilities. We would add that this extract comes from an annual report which has a total of 312 pages and is easily accessible on the Internet.

Notes	**2021 £m**	**2020 £m**	
Non-current liabilities			
Long-term borrowings	29	(20,572)	(23,425)
Corporation tax payable	14	(180)	(176)
Deferred tax liabilities	14	(3,556)	(3,600)
Pensions and other post-employment benefits	30	(3,113)	(3,650)
Other provisions	31	(630)	(707)
Derivative financial instruments	3	(1)	(10)
Contingent consideration liabilities	32	(5,118)	(5,104)
Other non-current liabilities	33	(921)	(803)
Total non-current liabilities	(34,091)	(37,475)	
Total liabilities	(57,761)	(59,623)	
Net assets	21,342	20,808	
Equity share capital	36	1,347	1,346
Share premium account	36	3,301	3,281
Retained earnings	37	7,944	6,755
Other reserves	37	2,463	3,205
Shareholders' equity	15,055	14,587	
Non-controlling interests	6,287	6,221	
Total equity	**21,342**	**20,808**	

When perusing this statement, you should remember that we are looking at £ million. They are large amounts! This statement is supported by notes with the relevant page number given in the first column. If you were conducting a full analysis of the financial statement, you may wish to look at the results for the last five years.

Capital maintenance

Capital maintenance has two aspects: a legal one as included in the Companies Act and a conceptual one. The legal requirements for capital maintenance are to ensure that all creditors have some protection against shareholders withdrawing from the total shareholders' funds and leaving insufficient to pay creditors. The total shareholders' funds are the share capital, share premium and capital redemption reserve. To pay dividends to shareholders, first, an entity must have a distributable profit. Of course, a distribution of profits means paying out cash and an entity may wish to retain cash to maintain and expand the business and to pay creditors when the debt falls due. It is therefore unlikely to pay out all its distributable profit to shareholders.

Capital Reduction and Share Buyback

Capital reduction is the process of decreasing an entity's shareholder equity through share cancellations and share repurchases, in other words, buying back shares. Doing this results in any profit being shared among fewer shareholders and, hopefully, this makes them happy. Having been so careful to maintain the amount of share capital, it is hardly surprising that there are restrictions on entities that, for various reasons, wish to reduce it. For example, a listed public company may wish to improve the amount of profit that is attributable to each share. It can do this by reducing the number of shares in issue. It may also wish to demonstrate that the amount of net assets attributable to each share is higher. In these scenarios, the entity wishes to emphasise its financial worth to shareholders. It can do so by reducing the number of shares in issue. The fewer the number of shares, the higher the profit per share and the value of net assets per share. These two factors make shareholders happy. There are two methods for reducing share capital: a capital reduction or a share buyback.

One solution to lack of profit is to write off accumulated losses to the share capital account. This involves opening a capital reduction account. The debit balance (i.e. loss) on the retained earnings account is transferred to the capital reduction account by a credit to the retained earnings account and a debit to the capital reduction account. The capital reduction account is credited and the share capital account is debited. Capital reduction is more common with private entities than public entities. The latter can only reduce their share capital by special resolution following confirmation by the court.

Another strategy followed by an entity is share buyback. This reduces the number of shares in the market place and the entity may be able to pay a larger dividend on the remaining shares if its profit is sufficient. Research indicates that when entities announce their intention to buy back their shares, the market reacts positively with an increase in share prices. This occurs although the announcement is not necessarily a firm commitment. The shares purchased by the entity are usually referred to as treasury shares and receive no dividend. Treasury shares should not be confused with treasury bonds, gilts or stock issued by governments which pay a fixed rate of interest.

Statement of Changes in Equity

A statement of changes in equity is a financial statement, sometimes referred to as Statement of Retained Earnings in US GAAP, which discloses changes over a financial period in the reserves comprising the owners' equity. IAS 1 requires such a statement as it assists users of financial statement in identifying the factors that cause a change in the owners' equity over the accounting periods. The statements provide information about equity reserves which is helpful in understanding any movements that occur. A comparison is required with previous years. The standard requires disclosure of the following information:

- total comprehensive income for the period, showing separately amounts attributable to owners of the parent and to non-controlling interests,
- the effects of any retrospective application of accounting policies or restatements made in accordance with IAS 8, separately for each component of other comprehensive income,
- reconciliations between the carrying amounts at the beginning and the end of the period for each component of equity, separately disclosing the following:
  - profit or loss,
  - other comprehensive income and an analysis of other comprehensive income by item must be presented either in the statement or in the notes.
  - transactions with owners, showing separate contributions by and distributions to owners and changes in ownership interests in subsidiaries that do not result in a loss of control.

The following amounts may also be presented on the face of the statement of changes in equity or in the notes:

- amount of dividends recognised as distributions,
- the related amount per share.

As you can imagine, the complexity of the statement of changes in equity depends on many factors, including the size of the entity, the type of industry and the activities in which it engages. It is impossible to comprehend fully the statement without reference to the other financial statements and the notes to the accounts. As an example of the type of note that companies give, we show in the following a very small extract from the 255 page of Vodafone plc 2022 annual report:

> *Accounting policies Other investments comprising debt and equity instruments are recognised and derecognised on a trade date where a purchase or sale of an investment is under a contract whose terms require delivery of the investment within the timeframe established by the market concerned, and are initially measured at fair value, including transaction costs. Debt securities that are held for collection of contractual cash flows where those cash flows represent solely payments of principal and interest are measured at amortised cost using the effective interest method, less any impairment. Debt securities that do not meet the criteria for amortised cost are measured at fair value through profit and loss. Equity securities are classified and measured at fair value through other comprehensive income, there is no subsequent reclassification of fair value gains and losses to profit or loss following derecognition of the investment.*

The company's annual report is very comprehensive and not only expresses the financial progress of the company but also provides an insight into the policies of the company. The following is a small example from their annual report, and similar comments can be found in the annual reports of other companies:

> *Our investors include individual and institutional shareholders, as well as debt investors. We maintain an active dialogue with our investors through our extensive investor relations programme. Vodafone plc*

Statement of Comprehensive Income

The development of global business has resulted in many entities being involved in various forms of relationships with other entities in different countries. These may include transactions conducted with foreign buyers or sellers or participation in foreign operations and, in these circumstances, foreign currencies are involved. Entities require guidance to account for these currency transactions in a consistent manner.

The IASB made a significant amendment to IAS 1 in 2011. A completely new Statement of Comprehensive Income replaced the existing profit or loss account or income statement. This was not merely a change in title but a change in content. Comprehensive income recognises both realised and unrealised gains and losses that have increased or decreased the owners' equity in the business. The items that appear in a comprehensive income statement that were not reported in the traditional profit or loss account are such transactions as revaluations of non-current assets. Two other items are gains and losses from translating the financial statements of a foreign operation (IAS 21) and remeasurement of defined benefit plans (IAS 19). We explained the requirements of both these standards in earlier chapters.

There has been considerable debate on the purpose of the statement of comprehensive income and its conceptual basis. Some argue that it is difficult to understand and provides little information of value to the users. Others claim that it has information value and preparers and users of financial data need time to become accustomed to it. Ignoring these differences in opinion, we briefly review in this chapter the two standards that are related to the Comprehensive Income Statement but also have a broader agenda. The standards are IAS 21 The Effect of Changes in Foreign Exchange Rates and IAS 19 Defined Benefit Plan. Both of these were issued long before the requirement for a Comprehensive Income Statement.

The main requirements of IAS 21 are as follows:

- transactions in foreign currencies must be expressed in the entity's reporting currency,
- the financial statements of foreign operations must be translated into the entity's reporting currency.

IAS 19 is concerned with the entire spectrum of employee benefits. Your first response may be that employee benefits are just wages and salaries and there are no problems. There are, however, different types of benefits from company to company and country to country. Possibly the most complex, from an accounting viewpoint, is the payment of pensions and other benefits such as health care. The standard sets out requirements for accounting for pensions. Depending on the nature of the scheme and the assumptions concerning the payment of future benefits, the standard requires certain gains and losses to be shown in other comprehensive income.

One important definition is given in IAS 1 which states:

> *Profit or loss is the total of income less expenses, excluding the components of other comprehensive income.*

The above definition focuses on the calculation of profit or loss. It is possible to calculate profit in two different ways. We can take our revenues, deduct the expenses and the result will be a "profit" as defined above. This calculation is the accruals method and relies on conventions that have developed over many years. Our definitions and the identification of income and expenses determine what profit is. An alternative method is to take the difference between how wealthy the entity is at the beginning and the end of the financial period. The owners' equity can be used as the measure of wealth, assuming there have been no direct transactions with shareholders, such as payment of dividends during the financial period. If the owners' equity has declined over the period, there is a decrease in wealth. If the owners' equity has increased, there is an increase in wealth. This ignores any direct transfers to or from equity.

Profit, as we have measured it, originally tells part of the story but the statement of comprehensive income gives a fuller picture. It captures the gains and losses, both realised and unrealised, that increase or decrease the owners' equity. One example of a non-realised gain leading to a gain in equity is a revaluation of non-current assets. An entity owns property that was purchased for £1 million. Due to the location of the property and a buoyant property market, the property has been revalued to £1.25 million. The entity is wealthier and using the accounting equation of assets − liabilities = capital, the shareholders are wealthier. If we have increased the assets by quarter of a million pounds, capital must have increased by the same amount.

This can be considered good news for the shareholders, but the gain has not been realised. The entity has not sold the property, and until it does, the gain will not be realised in the form of cash. The question arises as to what information should be given to shareholders and how it should be given. From the user of financial statements, the term "profit" has some deficiencies:

- It is transaction based. It only records profits that have been realised. An entity may own land or buildings that have increased in value. The impact of that increase is not recognised until the asset is sold and the gain realised.
- It is historical and does not reflect the impacts of inflation. Even over the period of 12 months, if inflation is high, the financial statements do not reflect this.
- It is not possible to compare the actual profit for the period with the predictions of managers. It is difficult to judge whether the entity has been as successful as managers anticipated.
- Depreciation is only an allocation on a fairly arbitrary basis of the original historic cost of an asset.
- The definition from IAS 1 emphasises that the profit or loss excludes comprehensive income, in other words, the income statement does not capture all transactions that may impact shareholder equity.
- It is not conceptually based and applies accounting conventions that sometimes do not have any conceptual basis.

These deficiencies have been identified by the Conceptual Framework of the IASB which states that Income increases in economic benefits during the accounting period in the form of inflows or enhancements of assets or decreases of liabilities that result in increases in equity, other than those relating to contributions from equity participants. It also encompasses both revenues and gains. Revenue arises in the course of ordinary activities of an entity and is referred to by a variety of different names including sales, fees, interest, dividends, royalties and rent. A Statement of Comprehensive Income is therefore defined as the change in equity during a period resulting from transactions and other events, other than those changes resulting from transactions with owners in their capacity as owners. Total comprehensive income comprises all components of "profit or loss" and of "other comprehensive income".

Companies can choose whether to provide the information either in a single statement or in two statements. A single statement incorporates all items of income and expense. In other words, it is a statement of total comprehensive income. With a two-statement presentation, the first statement discloses income and expenses recognised in profit or loss, and the second statement begins with the amount of profit or loss from the first statement. It then shows all items of income and expense that IFRSs require or permit to be recognised outside profit or loss. In other words, other comprehensive income.

We show in the following an extract from the annual report and accounts of the Unilever Group plc 2022. We emphasise that to illustrate the nature of the information provided, we are showing only the descriptions and not the financial amounts:

Other comprehensive income
Items that will not be reclassified to profit or loss, net of tax: Gains/(losses) on equity instruments measured at fair value through other comprehensive income
Remeasurement of defined benefit pension plans
Items that may be reclassified subsequently to profit or loss, net of tax:
Gains/(losses) on cash flow hedges
Currency retranslation gains/(losses)
Total comprehensive income
Attributable to: Non-controlling interests
Shareholders' equity

Financial Analysis

Basic analysis

The first step in an analysis is to carry out an initial review. This can be conducted very easily and give you some understanding of the business in which you are interested. The following three approaches are simple and quick to apply:

1. Trend analysis which looks at changes over a period of time and puts hard numbers on them. The period may be as simple as comparing this year with last year or includes several years. Usually, two main items are selected to do the analysis and sales and profit are frequently the most interesting ones.
2. Vertical analysis is where you may only take one component, such as sales or profit, but conduct an analysis over several years. This will

signal whether the activity is steadily increasing or decreasing over a period of time.

3. Comparative analysis is simply comparing the results of one company with another over a period of years. If available, you can make the comparison with the industry average where this information is available. This can be linked to a trend or vertical analysis. Clearly, it is best to compare companies that are in the same industry or related industries.

Trend analysis

The purpose of this analysis is to find out whether the amount shown on the financial statements for the present financial period is better or worse than in previous financial periods. We are examining data for particular financial activities or results either by a simple comparison with the previous year or over an extended period. This could be years, months, or even weeks if the data is available. Needless to say, the results most of us are interested in are sales, usually referred to as revenue, and profits.

In the following simple example, we compare the present year with the previous year for both revenue (sales) and profit. There are sometimes several types of profits referred to on the Income Statement, which we explain later in this chapter. The comparison is the current year to the present year. To demonstrate the international aspect of investments in shares, we show the change in dollars and percentages.

Year-to-year analysis

	Current year	**Previous year**	**Change**	**% Change**
Sales	£3,000	£2,600	£400	15%
Profits	£460	£420	£40	10%

The above is a simple analysis where we are comparing only two years. We have taken the amount of change and divided it by the previous year's amounts of sales and profit to give the percentage change. We have calculated only the main amounts and not calculated the percentage points as the differences are insignificant. If you can only find differences by working to the percentage point, you may wish to consider whether the difference is only a slight sneeze and not a terminal disease.

The obvious question we need to answer is the reason that revenue increased by an appreciable percentage but profit did not. If we analyse the results of a real company, we would usually find that the directors provide an explanation for this anomaly in their annual report and accounts. One possible reason we can suggest for the trends is that costs have increased but it was not possible to increase the selling prices of the products. Another reason may be that the company has purposely decreased the selling price of its products to enter new markets. If the data you have analysed is for a company you own or you are an employee, it should be possible to ascertain the reason.

A comparison of this year's data with the previous years can be revealing, but it is much more useful if you can compare the data for at least five years and possibly more. In the following example, we have the amounts for five years for the revenue and the total costs. Most companies have on their websites the annual report and accounts for many years, so obtaining the data should not cause a problem. You should be aware that accounting regulations are amended from time to time. This includes both International Financial Reporting Standards and US regulations.

If you are conducting an analysis of organisational performance over several years, you should check if there have been any changes in the financial regulations. This includes charities and other types of organisations. In the following example, we show the revenue and total costs of a fictitious company over a five-year period.

Trend analysis of revenue and costs in £000 for five years

	2017	**2018**	**2019**	**2020**	**2021**
Revenue	110	112	114	113	112
Total costs	80	85	87	87	88

We could now calculate the percentage changes, but even the basic figures show significant differences that require further investigation. Over the five-year period, revenue peaked in 2019 but has declined again. Over that period, costs have gradually increased. Further investigation would be required to find out the reasons. One may be that the market has tightened so the company has had to reduce its selling price per item. However, the costs of production may have increased for other reasons but cannot be passed on to customers. In the annual report, the Directors usually explain changes in the economic environment that have impacted their activities.

Some managers find that a line graph of the trend pinned on their office notice board is a helpful tool for focusing attention when it is needed. If the data are available on a weekly or monthly basis, the graph visually demonstrates possible problems and assists you as a manager in making financial decisions.

Same size or vertical analysis

This analysis is usually conducted by calculating all the costs over several years and calculating them as a percentage of the sales figure. You may find that a company has already provided this information in its annual report. The following example uses the profit and loss account to demonstrate the calculations for one year:

Vertical analysis for one year

	2020		**2021**	
	£000	**%**	**£000**	**%**
Sales	200		250	
Materials	80	40.0	110	44.0
Wages	50	25.0	70	28.0
Overheads	25	12.5	25	10.0
Transport costs	15	7.5	20	8.0
Depreciation	5	2.5	5	2.0
Profit	25	12.5	20	8.0

It is impossible to draw any firm conclusions from the above analysis but it does focus on the investigations one can usefully make. Usually, with such a substantial drop in sales over one period, you would anticipate the profit also is dropping, but in this example, it has increased in absolute terms. A closer examination shows that materials and wages have both decreased in absolute terms.

With a decrease in sales, one would anticipate this but the decrease in percentage terms is higher than one would expect. This requires closer investigation. Overhead and depreciation costs have remained the same in absolute terms. As these are usually fixed in nature, regardless of changes in activity, it is not surprising that the percentage figures have increased in 2021.

The first step therefore is to determine the reason for the decline in the sales figure. Is the same volume being sold and the company has reduced its selling price or has there been a decrease in the volume sold? At this stage of the investigation, we would favour the former, but further analysis is required.

Comparative analysis

You can easily conduct a trend or vertical analysis for one company and draw conclusions. However, the knowledge you can gain from analysing one company can be greatly improved with comparators. This can be a comparison with one or more companies or comparison with industry averages. You can do the calculations yourself but there is a substantial amount of information on the website which provides substantial information.

You will find it is best, at least as a starter, to concentrate on companies in the same industry. Different industries have different profiles. For example, a car manufacturer will have very different revenues and costs than a chain of hotels. If you search the Web, you will find that there are numerous sources of ratios for specific industries. These averages are extremely helpful as they provide a guide to competitor's performance. Compare their own data figure with those averages, and it will help you to draw conclusions. You will find that a visit to the website will provide numerous guides to industry averages.

Errors and frauds

In conducting an analysis of an organisation's financial statements, some degree of caution should be exercised. Capturing all of an organisation's activities in financial terms and explaining them in a structured manner are difficult tasks. There is always the possibility of errors occurring and, in some cases, fraud. We suggest some simple examples in the following:

Imagine you have a worker who is paid £20 per hour. At the end of the month, you look at his time sheet and it states 100 hours worked. You therefore show in your financial accounts the cost of wages as

£2,000. However, suppose the worker made an honest error in its recording and he worked more or less hours. Your financial statements are incorrect.

You need to pay for the electricity for the period but the invoice has not yet arrived despite the requests you have made. You make your best estimate but it may be somewhat later before you know the actual amount. Another possible example is when a customer is refusing to pay the full amount for the service she has received and wants a £500 discount. The matter is unresolved. What do you put in your financial statements at the end of the financial period?

Accountants have to make the best estimates in these circumstances and are guided by the requirements of financial accounting standards. This does mean that the financial statements that you examine may not have the 100% accuracy that you believe. Taking a company's activities and describing them in financial terms have difficulties and errors may occur.

Information quality

Your analysis will depend on the quality and accuracy of the financial statements. You must check that the financial statements have been properly audited and there should be confirmation by independent auditors of this accompanying the statements. Even this is not always a guarantee on the quality of the statements. Although accounting standards set out the procedures for accounting transactions and the information to be disclosed, there can be errors and sometimes deliberate misinformation.

One type of fraud that is extremely difficult to identify is that by an outside entity against an organisation, sometimes with the collusion of that organisation. These minor collusions by an organisation with outside parties do not usually impact the financial statements although there are financial benefits to those doing them.

One should not conclude that most companies' financial statements are questionable. We do not wish to overemphasise the possibility of error or fraud. The major frauds that have been discovered over the years hit the headlines but undiscovered errors or fraud can be present. Our advice is if the types of analysis we explain in the following chapter give results that do not seem credible, you check your calculations carefully and with any decisions you are making, you proceed with caution.

Efficiency and Financial Examination

A scrutiny of a company's profits is important, but it is essential to understand how rich or poor it is. A poor company could become bankrupt! Even a company that appears to be successful in making profits can have financial difficulties. You may have conducted your profitability analysis and be satisfied with the financial performance of the company but you need to go further. In this section, we give a broad introduction to the conduct of a financial analysis and a full explanation for the calculation of detailed financial ratios and their interpretations are given in the Appendices at the end of this book.

One important question is whether the company can manage its cash. Remember that profit and cash are different measures. A company can appear very profitable but may go bankrupt because of poor cash management. We need to look in detail at how a company manages its cash position. We list in the following the ratios that help you determine whether it is managed efficiently:

- working capital ratio,
- current test,
- inventory (stock) turnover,
- debtor collection period,
- creditor payment period.

We demonstrate the method for calculating these ratios in the following examples. None of the calculations is complicated, but you do need comparisons either over a period of time or with other companies. This enables you to judge whether the company you are investigating is improving or not. Without comparisons, you are unable to draw any conclusions. Useful information can be obtained from the following sources:

- the financial statements for the same company for previous years,
- the financial statements of similar companies,
- industry ratios,
- comments in the financial press,
- the website of the company, if there is one.

Working capital ratio

This is a ratio that captures both liquidity and efficiency. Working capital is calculated by deducting current liabilities from current assets. The equation is as follows:

$$\text{Working capital} = \text{Current assets} - \text{current liabilities}$$

A company must be alert to the amount of investment made in non-current assets, such as buildings and machinery. It needs to be even more alert to the money it is using in its daily operations. This is known as the investment in working capital. Insufficient working capital can cause a company to become bankrupt. The use of ratios assists a company to manage its working capital. It also reveals to investors the immediate financial health of the company. The following ratios explore the different aspects of liquidity.

Current test

This is a liquidity ratio that shows the relationship between the business's liquid (current) assets and its current liabilities. In other words, it shows whether the company looks able to pay its current debts without seeking loans. Inventory (stock) is a current asset, but it has to be sold before you can turn it into cash. It is therefore normal practice to use current assets minus the value of stock when calculating the current test. Similarly, we normally only take the creditors that have to be paid within the next 12 months as this is our present concern. If we have creditors we have to pay after 12 months, this is a separate and less urgent consideration. The calculation is as follows:

$$\frac{\text{Current assets} - \text{inventory}}{\text{Creditors: amounts due within one year}}$$

As you can see from the equation above, all the figures you want should be found on the balance sheet. The calculation can either show the percentages or the times figure. You need to remember that the accounts are prepared on a prudent basis and that the amounts owed to current creditors at the end of the financial year will be due at different times in the next financial year. However, most analysts would agree that the ratio should not fall below 1:1. If it does, it means that the company owes more money to its current creditors than it can collect from its current debtors.

It is difficult to generalise on what the levels of liquidity should be. However, if you do the analysis for several years and the ratio is declining, the obvious worry is whether the company will be able to continue to pay its debts.

Inventory (stock) turnover

This is an efficiency ratio that measures the average number of times stock has been sold and replaced during the year. There is the reasonable assumption that quick stock turnover is the mark of an efficient company. The turnover rate will depend on the type of product and the nature of the industry. What one does not want to see is the factory pressing on with production if the sales team cannot find customers. The formula for the ratio is as follows:

$$\frac{\text{Cost of sales}}{\text{Average inventory}}$$

You need to look at the profit and loss account to obtain the figures for the average inventory. If they are disclosed, you can use the following formula:

$$\frac{\text{Opening inventory} + \text{Closing inventory}}{2}$$

However, if a figure for opening stock is not provided, you can use closing stock for the previous year as the proxy.

Debtor collection period

This is an efficiency ratio that gives an indication of the effectiveness of the management of working capital. It measures the average time trade debtors (customers) have taken to pay the business for goods and services bought on credit over the year. The debtor collection period in days is calculated using the following formula:

$$\frac{\text{Trade debtors}}{\text{Turnover}} \times 365$$

If a breakdown of debtors is not given in the balance sheet, it is likely that the figure for trade debtors is given in the notes to the accounts.

Creditor payment period

This is an efficiency ratio that measures the average time that the business has taken to pay its trade creditors. The creditor payment period in days is calculated using the following formula:

$$\frac{\text{Trade creditors}}{\text{Purchases}} \times 365$$

Although some people do not like debts and prefer to pay invoices and statements soon as they receive them rather than wait until they are due, this is not always a good way of managing cash. Receiving goods on credit is the equivalent of having an interest-free loan. If the supplier does not give credit, the business may have to go into overdraft to pay cash for the goods. This does not mean that a business should wait until it receives a solicitor's letter or risk supplies being cut off, but from a financial point of view, management should take the maximum time allowed to pay trade creditors while at the same time collect payment from trade debtors as quickly as possible.

The premise underpinning these ratios is that companies should be able to pay their current liabilities from their current assets. If they are unable to do this, they must seek more finance. This can be difficult if the economy is in decline or its future strength uncertain. However, not all countries may have the same approach so you must examine what is normal practice in a particular country.

In the course of your career, it is quite likely that you may be asked to conduct a ratio analysis. This could be for a department, the company itself, a competitor that you may try to acquire or even a complete industry. In this section, we will provide a guide as to the steps you should take and also offer caution on the limitations of ratios.

We outline in the following a process for conducting an analysis that can be applied to most situations:

Accounting ratio analysis and interpretation

1. Acquire financial statements for several years, preferably a minimum of three years although five years would be preferable. This should include annual and interim financial statements. If you are able to obtain any internal financial documents it would be helpful.
2. Take a quick scan of all the documents to see if there have been any significant changes over a period of time. Putting the key figures for the main figures such as revenue and earnings on a spreadsheet helps the comparison. It is also useful to include aggregations such as total assets, net current assets and working capital
3. If you have the published documents you must review the notes. You are looking for any note that calls your attention to unusual events e.g. after the financial period, provisions, contingent liabilities and impairments.
4. Examine the balance sheet, income statement and cash flow statement without calculating ratios. Your objective is to detect any items that look particularly large or unusual.
5. Identify and calculate the ratios that you consider to be the most important for your task and relevant to the company you are investigating.
6. If possible, obtain the ratios for a competitor and the industry averages. These are usually available in most libraries or on the Internet. Ensure that the definition of terms and method of calculation is comparable to your own.
7. Analyse and interpret the ratios using all the information you have collected. The process of interpretation may reveal additional information you require to complete your task.
8. If the management of the company has discussed their financial results and in an annual report they will have done so, compare it to your own interpretation. If there are differences, investigate them.

Put in wider context

1. Review the company's products and services and their long-term prospects.

2. Assess the strengths and weaknesses of senior managers of the company.
3. Evaluate the company's markets by product and region.
4. Assess the economies and political stability in the regions where the company operates.
5. Compare your findings with competitors.
6. Revisit your ratio analysis and interpretation and re-evaluate your findings within the wider context.
7. Write your report remembering to define the terms you have used and to present the calculations in a tabular format.

Despite the great value of ratio analysis properly conducted, there are deficiencies. Some of these we have already commented on but we repeat them here for the benefit of completeness.

- There are no agreed definitions of terms, so ratios based on different definitions cannot be compared. You must ensure that your comparisons with data obtained from other sources are valid.
- Ratio analysis is only useful if comparisons are made and the choice of analysis depends on the user and the availability of data:
  - If data are not disclosed, less precise alternatives will have to be used (but look first in the notes to the accounts).
  - Comparative data may not be available for trend analysis (e.g. a new business has no track record) or for inter-company comparison (e.g. if company operates in a niche market or there are no industry benchmarks).
- Figures in financial statements can be misleading:
  - If there is high inflation or if window dressing, unscrupulous manipulation or an unusual accounting treatment has been used. Window dressing is where companies present results in such a way that is favourable to the company but could mislead the unwary user.
- Financial statements do not take account of non-financial factors, such as the following:
  - Are there sound plans for the future? Does the company have a good reputation, strong customer base, reliable suppliers and loyal employees? Does it have obsolete assets, strong competitors and poor industrial relations or operate in a high-risk industrial sector?

Types of analysis

There are other methods for analysing and presenting ratios and we will consider them in this chapter with the full explanation of the calculations given in the appendices. The main methods used are as follows:

- trend analysis,
- common size statement analysis,
- vertical analysis,
- horizontal analysis.

Year-to-year change and trend analysis

With this technique, we are looking at data either with a simple comparison with the previous period or over an extended period of time. This could be years, months, weeks or even hours and minutes. The change could be for one item only or it could be for several items. In the following presentation, we are looking at the sales figure for one company. The comparison is the current year to the present year with the change being shown in dollars and percentages.

Year-to-year change — Example 1

	Current year	**Previous year**	**£Change**	**% Change**
Revenue	£70,150	£59,287	£ + 10,863	+18.3%

On a trend analysis, it is often more informative to take two or three key items and compare them over several years to reveal the changes in their relationship. For example, one could take the revenue each year and compare it to the profit before interest and tax as in the following example.

Comparison PBIT to revenue for 8 years — £000s

	2015	**2016**	**2017**	**2018**	**2019**	**2020**	**2021**	**2022**
Revenue	96	102	112	105	108	110	115	118
Gross profit	56	60	72	65	70	65	62	55

The above tables demonstrate the trend, but it is often far more helpful for the user to show the data in the form of a chart.

Revenue analysis

The following example is sometimes referred to as a same size analysis or a vertical analysis. Revenue is considered as 100% and all the costs and the profit are expressed as a percentage of that amount. We could express all the separate assets on the statement of financial position as a percentage of the total assets or the separate liability accounts as a percentage of total liabilities. These presentations and analyses of data are much more helpful if comparative figures are given, the figures for the previous financial period if they are available.

	Income statement for 2009	
	£	%
Revenue	500	100
Cost of sales	375	75
Salaries	30	6
Rent	10	2
Admin	9	1.8
Depreciation	20	4
Interest	5	1
PBT	51	10.2

This has been a brief introduction to the different forms of analysis and presentation you can make. These approaches are often best presented as a chart to assist the user in understanding the relationship of the data.

Chapter Review

The debate on the nature and definition of profit has encouraged the IASB to require a statement of total comprehensive income. Their reasons for doing so did not receive overwhelming agreement from the providers of financial information. However, as familiarity with the statement of comprehensive income increased, doubts and uncertainties on its usefulness have been mostly dispelled. We do not anticipate any significant changes being made to the present requirements.

However, the financial details of many of the statements we have explained are only useful if we have some way of analysing them. The analysis of financial statements has also demonstrated the importance of reliable data. In this chapter, we have demonstrated the use of data analysis. We have explained the frequently used terms and everyone has their own favourites. When making comparisons with other data, it is important to ensure that you are using the same formats.

Understandably, the International Accounting Standards Board has been responsible for accounting issues, but now society is questioning whether human activity needs to be reassessed. The discussion is now not about how we account financially for our business activities but the damage that is done to the environment. In the following chapter, we discuss sustainability.

CHAPTER 11 Equity and Liabilities

Review Questions

1. Market capitalisation is
   a. the value of a company that is traded on the stock market, calculated by multiplying the total number of shares by the present share price
   b. the amount that directors have invested in the company
   c. the total value of the assets less the total amount of liabilities
   d. the total value of the goods and services that a company has sold within one year

2. Ordinary shares
   a. usually give a fixed rate of dividend
   b. do not give voting powers to the holders
   c. allow the entity to redeem the shares at a set future price and date
   d. do not pay a dividend if there is no profit

3. What is meant by the term "equity"?

4. If a company reduced the number of shares it has in issue, will this improve the amount of profit that is attributable to each share?

5. What are reserves? How many types are there usually?

6. What is meant by the term "Capital Reduction"?

7. When conducting an analysis of a company's financial progress, what is meant by the term "trend analysis"?

8. What are the differences between the terms "equity" and "capital"?

Chapter 12

Accounting for Sustainability

Structure of Chapter 12

Section title
A slow beginning
Expanding the information
Accounting developments
Want more — Get more
The UK regulations
Financial accounting issues
Sustainability
Chapter Review

This final chapter briefly reviews the issues in financial reporting that we discussed in previous chapters. This prepares the past and present financial reporting issues. The main part of the chapter focuses on sustainability. The previous chapters have explained the present position with financial reporting standards. In doing so, we have emphasised that not all countries have adopted international accounting standards but use their own regulations. For example, the US has not adopted international standards but use their own standards. Islamic countries have their own accounting and reporting regulations and there are other countries which have decided to develop on their own approach. Also, remember that "private" companies, that is, those not listed on a stock exchange, do not usually use international standards. This chapter explains where we are now with financial reporting with the cautionary note that changes are taking place. In recent years, there has been an increasing concern about the subject of "Sustainability". The accounting profession has shown a considerable interest in the subject of sustainability and we consider the background to this. In doing so, we reflect on some of the issues we discussed in previous chapters.

The international accounting standards that are currently in force deal with accounting issues and not the impact of companies on the environment. We would emphasise that although a number of "jurisdictions" have adopted international accounting standards, the companies in any one country may not follow the same standards as other countries. In this chapter, we will first consider the approach in the UK and then consider other developments. Although we use the term "company", in the UK, there are companies, particularly those quoted on the stock exchange, that follow International Standards but there are smaller UK companies that follow Financial Reporting Standards as issued by the Financial Reporting Council in the UK.

The number of organisations now involved in setting financial reporting standards and involved in the development of sustainability standards is substantial. Acronyms instead of the full names are mostly used in discussing their activities. The following list should assist in reminding you of the material we covered in earlier chapters:

- CCRA is Climate Change Risk Assessment.
- COP 26 Summit Glasgow 2021.
- CSR is Corporate Social Responsibility Reports.
- DEI is Diversity Equity and Inclusion.
- EFRAG is the European Financial Reporting Advisory Group that advises the European Commission on International Financial Reporting Standards in Europe.
- ESG is Environmental Social and Governance.
- FRC (Financial Reporting Council) is UK based and regulates auditors, accountants and actuaries. It also sets the UK's Corporate Governance and Stewardship Codes. In January 2022, it issued the present editions of UK and Ireland accounting standards.

- IASB (International Accounting Standards Board) is an independent group of individuals responsible for the development and publication of IFRS Accounting Standards, including the *IFRS for SMEs* Accounting Standards.
- IAS is International Accounting Standards which are still in force.
- IFRIC (International Financial Reporting Interpretations Committee Interpretations) was developed by the IFRS Interpretations Committee and was issued after approval by the International Accounting Standards Board (IASB).
- IFRS is International Financial Reporting Standards.
- IFRS Foundation is a not-for-profit, public interest organisation established to develop high-quality, understandable, enforceable and globally accepted accounting and sustainability disclosure standards. The standards are issued by two standard-setting boards, the International Accounting Standards Board (IASB) and International Sustainability Standards Board (ISSB).
- ISSB is International Sustainability Accounting Standards Board.

A Slow Beginning

In this section, we explain events in the UK starting in 1945 when the Board of Trade asked the Cohen Committee to review company law and the "safeguards afforded for investors and the public interest". For the first time, there was a stated duty for a Committee on Company Law to be aware of companies' responsibilities to society, instead of to investors and creditors only. In its final report, the Cohen Committee stressed the importance of information to shareholders and society in general and this sentiment was mirrored in the Companies Act 1948 which required the following:

- Only members of a recognised accounting body could act as auditors.
- The auditors have to state whether the balance sheet and income statement were in agreement with the books of the company and gave a full and fair view of the company's financial status and operating results.
- Consolidated accounts were required for the first time.

This tentative beginning for disclosure of corporate information was further advanced when, in 1967, an amending Act required Turnover (Revenue) to be disclosed and the Directors Report expanded.

A century of company legislation had reached the stage where several important concepts had been established:

- Limited liability gave protection to investors.
- Financial statements should give a full and fair view.
- Consolidated accounts were required.
- A balance sheet and a profit and loss account were required.
- Companies had a responsibility to society at large.

This was a start towards greater financial disclosures by companies and since 1948 there have been several more Companies Acts in the UK, and the legislative framework for corporate reporting was firmly established. However, the main recipients of a company's annual financial statements are the shareholders who have the authority at Annual General Meetings to question the Directors. One could argue whether the concepts of financial statements give a "full and fair view" of events. We have noted in previous chapters that accounting has not been able to resolve the problems of addressing inflation and identifying the present value of some assets thus reducing the information value of the financial reports which are issued. Companies and auditors report to shareholders who have made financial investments in the company. Whether companies have responsibilities to society for broader issues, such as sustainability, are still being debated. We would also question the role that accounting bodies have in regulating society.

Expanding the Information

It was not until the 1970s that, in various countries, standard-setting bodies and committees were established and the term *accounting standards* came into widespread use. The Accounting Standards Steering Committee (ASSC) in the United Kingdom was established in 1970. The US FASB succeeded the Accounting Principles Board (APB) on July 1, 1973. Two days later, the International Accounting Standards Committee was formed.

The demands and pressures of national political and economic environments largely formed the way that individual countries established their own standard-setting body. Standard setters work within a coalition of interests including reporting organisations, shareholders, the media, political groups and others. The powers of these interested parties differ, and the need and desire of the accounting standard setters to gain the support of particular factions also vary. For example, the United States is notable because of the considerable statutory authority of the Securities and Exchange Commission (SEC) to participate in the standard setting process and the extent to which lobbying takes place. In the United Kingdom, support is more indirect, with the legislation requiring organisations to comply with accounting standards but with little direct government influence in the development of standards, although there are signs of this approach changing.

The establishment of standards in a country greatly improved financial reporting in that country. Unfortunately, the output of the standards and the financial statements, issued by companies operating within one country, were difficult to compare with those of a company operating in another country. National accounting standards differed in several ways. In the latter half of the 20th century, there were some highly publicised examples of very profitable companies in Europe that wanted to list shares on the New York Stock Exchange (NYSE). In order to do so, the profitable company had to redraft those financial statements in accordance to US GAAP. In some instances, the previously declared profit for a financial year turned into a loss. Thus, a conceptual inconsistency exists as the activities of a particular company in a specific financial period can show either a profit or loss depending on which national accounting regime applies.

It is uncertain whether the International Accounting Standards Committee had, as its long-term aim, the achievement of standardisation with all accounting regimes being the same, or harmonisation where some differences are acceptable. In its early years, with scarce resources and little power, the IASC concentrated mainly on the harmonisation of financial reporting on a worldwide basis. One major factor in promoting the role of the IASC was the reaction of the emerging economies. Many were attempting to establish themselves in international trade or to move away from command economies. The IASC offered a quick and acceptable route for establishing an appropriate and acceptable accounting regime. The standards offered significant flexibility in developing financial statements thus easing the process of adoption. The other benefit was they carried none of the possible political implications from adopting the standards of any particular country.

A second factor assisting the IASC was the increased encouragement from several organisations and countries to pursue the goal of international harmonisation more rapidly and effectively. The European Union (EU) had for many years been seeking accounting harmonisation throughout the EU by issuing Directives that were binding on all member states. In 1978, the Fourth Company Law Directive dealing with the annual accounts of companies was passed. The Seventh Directive passed in 1983 extended this to the preparation of consolidated accounts. However, progress was slow and the process cumbersome. Towards the end of the 1980s, the European Commission gave increasing support to the efforts of the IASC. However, over recent years, the harmonisation of financial information has declined and although the IASC was successful in the core standards project, in retrospect, it is easy to see that the work it was attempting to undertake was impossible due to the way that the organisation was structured and resourced. The IASC recognised the problems confronting it. Although there was a desire to make progress, the question whether the IASC could achieve the goals remained. Either a complete overhaul of all aspects of the IASC was required or a new body formed. The latter was the course of action chosen and we now have the International Accounting Standards Board. The move to sustainability reporting standards was to follow and, at the time of writing this book, we wait to experience the first standards.

Accounting Developments

Accounting firms have shown a great interest in "sustainability reporting", but, at present, there are no clear agreements as to who should be setting standards, who should use them and who should be responsible for monitoring the process. In the UK, the accounting profession has made strong moves to be the promoter of sustainability. However, for any form of reporting the key questions are who is reporting, to whom and for what purpose. In this section, we address these issues with the cautionary note that there may be more changes in the parties connected with the development of sustainability reporting.

Before examining sustainability reporting, it is useful to consider the strengths and practices of financial reporting. Essentially, the financial reports are intended for shareholders who have invested money in a company by purchasing shares. The shareholders are generally most focused on the financial activities of the company. Accountants record the financial transactions of a company and these results, usually referred to as the financial statement, form reports to shareholders. It is assumed that the information will assist in the decision-making of current and prospective investors in the company. Although this may help investors, when we reach the stage of paying taxation, the tax authorities have their own rules as to what is taxable.

It is worth reviewing some of the weaknesses of financial reporting which we discussed in earlier chapters before questioning whether accounting organisations are the best body for sustainability reporting. The main flaws, we see in financial reporting as it is now used, are as follows.

Inflation: We all acknowledge that the money we spend today is worth less than the same sums we spent 5 years ago. Although the accounting profession has tried to resolve this issue, it has failed. A company can continue the same level of activity but the financial measure used to record them is weak. Companies can show an increasing profit over the years but have the same level of activity. Inflation has "inflated" the numbers with no change in the actual level of business activity.

Depreciation: The amount shown on balance sheet for the fixed assets of a company does not show the financial value of those assets in today's terms. A company may purchase expensive machinery that it considers will last for 20 years. It will usually calculate the annual depreciation of that machinery by dividing the cost by 20. Each year, it will treat the depreciation as a charge to the profit statement and the cost of the machinery less the depreciation charged will appear on the balance sheet. Both figures are fictitious. The annual depreciation charge does not show the loss in value of the asset and the amount shown on the balance sheet does not show the current value of the asset.

Land and buildings: These are usually shown on the balance sheet at their original cost. In some instances, the investment was made many years ago but they remain shown at their original cost. Their present values are usually many, many times that amount.

Intangible assets: These are identifiable non-monetary assets without physical substance. We explained these in earlier chapters.

Even with the commendable efforts of the accounting profession to provide annual financial information that is reliable, accurate and informs us as to what is actually happening, there are still weaknesses in financial reports. It has its flaws. It is possibly surprising that the accounting profession is seriously being considered as the collector and reporter of sustainability information. There is no denying that accountants have made progress in recording corporate financial activities but it is not immediately apparent they have abilities as the providers of sustainability information.

Their present role is that of reporting financial information to shareholders but it is reasonable that those who own shares in a company wish to know how sustainable its activities are. However, including this information in the financial reports issued by companies is not emphasising that the issues are in the mainstream public domain.

It is also not apparent what action should be taken to remedy any sustainability issues. Shareholders can decide not to deal in shares where there are sustainability problems but the public has little power to bring about change. Does the government have the resources or authority to take action against a company where the accountants (appointed by the shareholders) have identified sustainability problems? These are issues to be resolved but full credit must be given to those companies that are now providing sustainable information in their annual report.

Want More — Get More

Not surprisingly, the increase in the number of organisations requiring some specific disclosures has led to an increase in the size of the annual reports and accounts of companies. In the following we show the information on the annual reports of J Sainsbury PLC to demonstrate the growth of disclosures. In 2013, the company published 127 pages, and by 2022, it was 208 pages with both reports also adding a glossary. The increase in pages does not provide financial information in much greater detail but there are additional non-financial information items as shown by the following comparisons:

J Sainsbury annual report and accounts 2013
Business review

- 1 Financial highlights
- 2 Chairman's letter

Looking down this list, you will see the titles of the various activities of the business. We would first draw your attention to page 79 Notes to the Financial Statements. You will find that the discussions we have had in earlier chapters on the requirements of financial reporting are on these pages. In addition to all of the above information, there is a separate Strategic Report and we show the items in the following report:

J Sainsbury annual report and accounts 2022
Strategic Report

If you visit the company's excellent website, you will also have access to substantial information about the company and its products. There is also a section entitled "useful information" that includes the following:

About Sainsbury's

- Sustainability
- Our stories
- Shop with our brands
- Jobs
- Contact us

About our brands

- Sainsbury's groceries
- Argos
- Tu
- Sainsbury's Home
- Sainsbury's Bank
- Habitat

Useful information

- Modern Slavery Statement
- Privacy Policy
- Cookie Policy
- Cookie Settings
- Terms and conditions
- Accessibility
- Site map
- Alerts

Not only does the company provide useful information about its organisation and brands, but there is also information on sustainability and a Modern Slavery Statement which is 26 pages and explains their position and the decisions they are making. This not the only company providing significant information on "sustainability". The growth in the annual report and accounts is to some extent to meet the financial interests of the investors and other business contacts. However, in reading the company reports on sustainability, it is evident but also includes information that can be viewed as presenting themselves as a responsible organisation. This is not a criticism but acknowledges that the activities of companies can have a major impact on the world in which we live. We will expand on this in the later segment on sustainability.

The long-term effects of COVID-19 have become apparent this year, driving forward our commitment to support workers in our supply chains and build resilience into our business model.

The UK Regulations

In earlier chapters, we have explained the financial statements that companies produce and the operations of the International Accounting Standards and International Financial Reporting Standards that regulate the financial reports issued by a PLC which is a public limited company in the United Kingdom. A PLC has shares which are traded on the stock exchange. It is the equivalent of a US publicly traded company that carries the term Inc. or corporation designation. The importance of PLCs to our way of living cannot be ignored. As well as providing products and services, it has a major impact on employment and the environment in which we live. The main aspects of PLCs in the UK are as follows:

- PLC is a public limited company which can issue shares to the public.
- All of the companies listed on the London Stock Exchange are PLCs.
- Any retail investor may buy stock in a PLC.
- Unlike privately held companies, public companies must publish certain financial data and disclosures for the public at regular intervals.
- The financial statements must be audited.

The formal names of some familiar brands like Burberry and Shell include the suffix PLC.

PLCs and the role of auditors

A very important aspect of preparing and issuing financial reports is the role of auditors. In the first year of a company, the directors will appoint auditors, but in the following years, auditors are appointed by shareholders and are answerable to them. Remember, it is the shareholders who own the company. The main regulations apply to the appointment of auditors by public limited companies. Auditors are appointed at each annual general meeting. Their appointment usually holds until the close of the next annual general meeting. Usually, the same auditors will continue for each year unless the shareholders, for some reason, choose to vote for a change of auditors at the annual general meeting. There are several legal requirements on the role of the auditor the main ones being as follows:

- If, for some reason, there is a casual vacancy, the directors can appoint the auditors.
- If no auditor is appointed at the annual general meeting, the company can appoint an auditor until the next annual general meeting and fix the remuneration to be paid by the company for his services.
- The company must give notice in writing to an auditor of his appointment.
- Every company at a general meeting called for the purpose of removing an auditor before the expiration of his term of office and appointing another auditor in his stead for the remainder of his term.
- The auditor must conduct an examination of the company and report the findings to the members at the Annual General meeting.
- If the auditor cannot give a favourable opinion, the reasons must be stated.

The audit report is a lengthy document and we show in the following a part of the auditor's report for Shell plc:

In our opinion, the financial statements of Shell plc (the Parent Company) and its subsidiaries (collectively, Shell or Group):

- *give a true and fair view of the state of Shell's and of the Parent Company's affairs as at December 31, 2021 and of Shell's income and the Parent Company's income for the year then ended;*
- *have been properly prepared in accordance with UK adopted international accounting standards and International Financial Reporting Standards (IFRS) as issued by the International Accounting Standards Board (IASB); and*
- *have been prepared in accordance with the requirements of the Companies Act 2006.*

Financial Accounting Issues

In determining financial reporting standards, little attention is paid to the nature and process of accounting itself. International Accounting Standards 1 states in paragraph 9 the following:

> *The objective of financial statements is to provide information about the financial position, financial performance and cash flows of an entity that is useful to a wide range of users in making economic decisions. Financial statements also show the results of the management's stewardship of the resources entrusted to it.*

Innocuous as the above statement appears, many would dispute it, particularly on the notion of a wide range of users and on the inclusion of the stewardship statement. In addition, there are practical difficulties in accounting that are rarely discussed or resolved. The issue of what we should be measuring and how we should do it has not been examined in depth.

We may have been able to recognise our economic phenomena but the next question is whether we can measure it with reliability. Traditionally, accountants have used a method known as historical cost accounting to record the value of items in the accounts. The value of the economic phenomena at the time that it took place is the value that is used and, with some exceptions, stays at that figure in the records. This method has the great advantage of being very reliable (you know what was paid), but, unfortunately, this method has some weaknesses as your measure (money) has flexible values over time.

Imagine that you purchased a computer and a house on the same date five years ago. It is definite that the value of your computer will be a lot less than you paid for it as developments in technology will have made it redundant. On the other hand, it is likely that the value of the house has increased significantly if you have a booming housing market, which is extremely active with many buyers. In both cases, the historic cost is different from the present value of the items and, therefore, of little use for any decisions you wish to make now.

With some transactions and events, we may have great difficulty in measuring the value. For example, if you have purchased the right to drill for oil and you have struck lucky, how much is that oil worth? It is obviously worth less while it is still in the ground, but how much less? Another example of difficulties in measurement is with brand names. Many of us will purchase clothes or equipment because it has a "brand" name. If that name attracts us to buying the item, then that brand must have value for the entity that owns it. But how do we measure that value?

Inflation

This can be defined as a sustained increase in the general price level of goods and services over a period. Each unit of currency buys fewer goods and services. In other words, there is a reduction in the purchasing power per unit of money. Inflation causes substantial problems for companies in determining their financial strategy and the investors in assessing financial performance. The following example, although simplistic, demonstrates the issues and is a good basis to discuss the impact of inflation and the possible solutions.

Example

Moneybags Company raises £60,000 to purchase a small factory for £50,000 and intends to manufacture umbrellas. The materials cost of manufacturing one umbrella is £1.00. Any profits are distributed in full.

In the first three months, it buys materials for 10,000 umbrellas and sells them for £1.50 each. The profit is £5,000.

In the second three months, due to inflation, it is anticipated that the purchase price for materials has increased to £1.25 for an umbrella. As Quarter 1 profit has been distributed in full, the company has only £10,000 to purchase materials, which will be sufficient to manufacture 8,000 umbrellas. The company could pursue any one of the three strategies detailed in the following:

Possible scenarios — 8,000 pens

	Retain old selling price £1.50	**Pass cost increase on to buyers £1.75**	**Increase selling price to maintain profit level £1.875**
Sales	£12,000	£14,000	£15,000
Costs	£10,000	£10,000	£10,000
Profit	£2,000	£4,000	£5,000

There is pressure on the Directors to maintain profits but the question is whether the market will accept the selling price of £1.875 per umbrella. In view of inflation, the profit for Quarter 1 should not have been distributed fully, but the investors may object to this.

The other factor is the cost of the factory at £50,000. The return on assets in Quarter 1 is £5,000/£50,000 = 10%. Maintaining the profit level at £5,000 would maintain this performance but inflation may have caused the value of the factory to rise. If we assume there is a 25% increase, at current values, the factory is now worth £6,000. The return on assets with present values is therefore £5,000/£60,000 = 8.3%. A decline that will bring sorrow to the investors.

In earlier chapters, we have discussed the issues regarding the accounting professions' difficulties in accounting for inflation. A company's activities can remain exactly the same year after year but the financial reporting will change because of inflation. In case you believe that the inflation rates in the above example are unrealistic, we give in the following the annual inflation rates in the UK for the period 1974–1980:

1980	18.00%
1979	13.40%
1978	8.30%
1977	15.80%
1976	16.50%
1975	24.20%
1974	16.00%

Source: http://www.whatsthecost.com/historic.cpi.aspx.

Inflation data for a country are usually based on the Consumer Price Index or similar and within a country, there are likely to be significant variations. For example, in Canada, the inflation rate in 2013 was running below the 2% level. However, it is reported that in 2013 the price of farmland in Quebec in Canada rose by 19.4%. Nationally, Canadian farmland from coast to coast has risen by an average of 12% a year since 2008. In Australia, the inflation rate was under 3% in 2013, but house prices jumped almost 10% in 2013 with Sydney's property market rising by 14.5%.

These intra-country variations in inflation are of little interest to the accountant, but when the country's inflation rate hits double digits, as in the UK, there is a demand that accountants do something about it as the financial statements are misleading. What action will be taken, and by whom, if sustainability issues are identified?

Sustainability

The history

There have been several champions for sustainability reporting for many years and there has also been action from some. Bloomberg Philanthropies is a prime example and its aim is to develop better, longer lives for the greatest number of people around the world. It invests in 941 cities and 173 countries and in 2021 distributed $1.66 billion. It has for several years been involved in many activities including a great interest in the environment and has a Climate & Environment program aimed at preventing climate change and protecting the environment across several issues, from driving the transition to clean energy and supporting climate action in cities to preserving ocean ecosystems.

The Global Sustainability Standards Board (GSSB) sets worldwide standards for sustainability reporting. It issued the world's first accepted standards for sustainability reporting: the GRI Standards. GRI was founded in Boston in 1997 following public outcry over the environmental damage of the Exxon Valdez oil spill. GRI (Global Reporting Initiative) is the independent, international organisation that helps businesses and other organisations take responsibility for their impacts by providing them with the global common language to communicate those impacts. It claims to issue the world's most widely used standards for sustainability reporting. The GRI secretariat is headquartered in Amsterdam, Netherlands,

There is also the Sustainability Accounting Standards Board in the US which was founded as a non-profit organisation in 2011 to help businesses and investors develop a common language about the financial impacts of sustainability and to guide the disclosure of financially material sustainability information by companies to their investors. Available for 77 industries, the Standards identify the subset of environmental, social and governance (ESG) issues most relevant to financial performance in each industry.

The International Sustainability Standards Board (ISSB) was established on November 3, 2021. The ISSB is tasked with developing a comprehensive set of baseline sustainability standards for global use. It is claimed that such a set of standards would facilitate the harmonisation of sustainability disclosures across jurisdictions and replace the use of existing voluntary standards. The ISSB announcement came at the 26th United Nations Climate Change Conference of Parties ("COP26") that took place in Glasgow, Scotland. In 2021, the European Commission's proposal for a Corporate Sustainability Reporting Directive (CSRD) envisaged the adoption of EU sustainability reporting standards. The draft standards would be developed by the European Financial Reporting Advisory Group (EFRAG). EFRAG which has recently issued exposure drafts on the first set of Draft European Sustainability Reporting Standards (ESRS).

From the European viewpoint, there is EFRAG which is a private association established in 2001 with the encouragement of the European Commission to serve the public interest. EFRAG extended its mission in 2022 following the new role assigned to EFRAG in the CSRD, providing Technical Advice to the European Commission in the form of fully prepared draft EU Sustainability Reporting Standards and/or draft amendments to these Standards. Its Member Organisations are European stakeholders and National Organisations and Civil Society Organisations. EFRAG's activities are organised in two pillars: a Financial Reporting Pillar, influencing the development of IFRS Standards from a European perspective and how they contribute to the efficiency of capital markets and providing endorsement advice on (amendments to) IFRS Standards to the European Commission, and second, a Sustainability Reporting Pillar, developing draft EU Sustainability Reporting Standards and related amendments for the European Commission.

Many of the efforts made have been useful in bringing attention to the issues of sustainability, but there is sometimes an absence of information on the concepts of the organisations developing the sustainability standards and who is expected to benefit from reporting companies achievements. It would be fair to suggest that some of the efforts are less rigorous than one would expect on a subject that may be significant importance to all of us. There has also been a somewhat irritating process of name changing of the various bodies and it is not always evident whether the name change is "cosmetic" or demonstrates a change in their activities. However, in January 2023, it was announced that the ISSB is consulting with the European Commission and EFRAG toward an agreed objective of a framework for maximising the interoperability of their standards and aligning on key climate disclosures. If there is an agreed process for the development of Sustainability Standards, it will give clarity and support disclosures by companies.

Accountants involvement

The main movement towards action in the UK has come from the accounting profession which has shown a great interest in "sustainability reporting" and there are now very few companies that do not address the issues of sustainability in their annual reports. One may question the motivations of the accounting world in being so active in this area. Their record in determining the structure and content of reporting the financial activities of a company are well established, although we have identified weaknesses in earlier chapters. However, in any form of reporting, the key questions are to whom are you reporting and for what purpose. Although listed companies annual reports are freely available, the main audience is still the shareholders. If they judge that a company's business operations are not sustainable, they will not invest in a company. However, the more cynical among us will say that if the company is paying large dividends to shareholders; their enthusiasm for identifying sustainability problems may be dimmed.

Before examining sustainability reporting, it is useful to consider the strengths and practices of financial reporting. In earlier chapters, we have noted some "weaknesses" but it is useful to develop these. In this context, we are focussing on those companies that are listed on the Stock Exchange and provide financial reports. Essentially, the financial reports are intended for shareholders and are focused on the financial activities of the company. Accountants record the financial transactions of a company and these results, usually referred to as the financial statements, from reports to shareholders. It is assumed that the information will assist in the decision-making of current and prospective investors in the company. It is worth looking at a weakness of financial reporting before questioning whether accountants are the best body for sustainability reporting.

A major issue with financial accounting information is that it does not show the effects of inflation on the financial statements. Some would even argue that it makes no sense to prepare financial statements that ignore inflation as the information, over years, is useless for comparative purposes. Inflation rates can have a substantial impact on financial statements. The highest inflation rate in the USA was 3.8% in 2008. In the UK, 3.86% in 2011. Inflation rates can fluctuate significantly on an annual basis. In Saudi Arabia, the rate averaged 1.93% from 2000 until 2020, reaching a high of 11.10% in July of 2008 and a record low of −5% in December of 2018. There are over several countries currently with an inflation rate over 20%. These are general inflation rates, but different items within a country will show different rates. Fluctuations in inflation impact on the financial statements of companies that means that making any conclusions from financial statements must be taken with great care, particularly if making judgements based on several years of operation.

The impact of inflation leads to misinformation for the user of financial statements. If you examine a company's balance sheet, most fixed asset will be shown at their original cost less the cumulative depreciation. If the assets have been purchased at different times, the money measurement of cost may be different. Machinery purchased on one date with a life of 10 years may be replaced at the end of that period with similar machinery but the cost is likely to be higher. The amounts in the financial statements do not reflect the "present value" of machinery at any one particular moment. In fact, the depreciated value depends on the method of depreciation used by a company. Depreciation is simply a process of allocation of cost over the period an asset is used and not valuation of the asset at any particular date. One can argue that the impact of sustainability must be time relevant and sustainability standards must resolve this issue. But are accounting bodies able to achieve this?

Having concentrated on inflation, it is reasonable to mention the impact of stagflation. This can be regarded as a period of inflation combined with a decline in the gross domestic product and usually a high unemployment rate. The term was used when in the UK inflation rose in the 1960s and 1970 and the response by the government at that time led to a period of stagflation. One may argue that, both inflation and stagflation are government issues to resolve. That is accepted, but undoubtedly these fluctuations in the value of money impact on financial statements.

Another unresolved issue that is directly relevant to accounting standards is the mathematics of depreciation. It is easy to understand, but the value of the information is, at best of little use and the method, in respect of the issues of sustainability, is questionable. For example, a company buys expensive machinery for £5 million and it anticipates that it will last 10 years. It follows the normal practice of spreading the cost of the machinery over its useful life. This means that there will be a regular charge at the end of each year to the income statement of £500,000. At the end of the fifth year, the machinery will be shown on the balance sheet at £2,500,000. This does not show the market value of the machine. In fact, most items are depreciated, quite correctly using the prevailing accounting standards, but the machinery is, most likely, not worth the amount it shows on financial statements.

One could find fault with other publicly available financial information but our earlier chapters on financial reporting standards demonstrate that the accounting profession is endeavouring to provide understandable and useful information to the shareholders.

The problems

A broad definition of the term sustainability is the avoidance of the depletion of natural resources in order to maintain an ecological balance. In business and political contexts, limits to sustainability are determined by physical and natural resources, environmental degradation, and social resources. Accordingly, sustainable policies place some emphasis on the future effect of any given policy or business practice on humans, the economy, and ecology.

Although there are various organisations are attempting to address the issues of measuring and reporting sustainability by companies, there are many hurdles to be overcome. For example, despite many years of the development of international accounting, the US and many other countries have not adopted fully international accounting standards and companies comply with a country's own accounting standards. Despite the good work done by institutions such as the International Financial Reporting Standards Board, it remains difficult to assess how standards are set and the level of compliance internationally. Sustainability is an international issue, but, at this stage, it is difficult to predict how an international approach to the sustainability issues can be applied.

There has been tremendous growth in the concerns over the impact of organisational activities on our planet. The issue of sustainability has been of significant interest, but most countries also have their own sustainability weaknesses that can be traced back any years. For example,

North American forests have been permanently cleared of vegetation for agriculture and other uses, primarily within the last two centuries, and Australia has lost 27% of its rainforest, 19% of open forest, 11% of woodland forest and 28% of mallee forest since 1750.

A company is formed with the main purpose of financially benefiting the owners. In doing so, it will employ people and use any natural sources that it is legally able to do so. The company was not formed to protect the environment. If there are legal regulations set by the government with which it must comply, it will do so but the IFRSB and EFRAG have no apparent expertise in investigating sustainability issues. It is also difficult to determine the powers they have to take action when it detects sustainability issues.

There are other examples but, given the difficulty that financial accounting standards setters have experienced in attempting to identify, measure and record such issues as inflation and intangible assets and the disclosure of information on financial statements that would be of interest, there must be doubt about their involvement with sustainability. That has not prevented any established firm of accountants from claiming their expertise when there are issues of not only finance but also sustainability.

On a more personal level for students will the reporting of ESG by companies become the responsibility of accountants for approval and will this mean it is a subject to be studied by accounting students. There may also be the issue of "greenwashing". It is known that any disclosure of information may be affected by the giver who attempts to "whitewash" the information to make the situation better than it really is. Will we enter into a situation where companies "greenwash" their activities to persuade the users of the information that the company is actively ensuring sustainability?

Sustainability and corporate social reporting

Increasingly, the terms sustainability and corporate social responsibilities have been appearing in companies' annual reports and accounts, usually included either as part of the strategic report or in the corporate governance section. Other terms such as social and environmental reporting, social responsibility reporting and environmental accounting are also used. These disclosures attempt to bridge the possible divide between economic growth and protection of the environment or societal interests.

The World Commission on the Environment and Development as long ago as 1987 gave the following definition of sustainability. It stated that it was the development that meets the needs of the present without compromising the ability of future generations to meet their own needs. One would not disagree with the definition but it is difficult to see how the statements can be implemented, but, as we note in the following section, there are attempts to resolve the issue of sustainability.

In 2010, the European Commission renewed its efforts to develop Corporate Social Responsibility to encourage long-term employee and consumer trust. The Commission considered that environmental issues were a priority subject for greater disclosures. This is not a compulsory standard but a guidance document providing advice and recommendations to those organisations wishing to embrace CSR. It discusses the following subjects:

- organisational governance,
- human rights,
- labour practices,
- the environment,
- fair operating practices,
- consumer issues,
- community involvement and development.

There have already been initiatives in sustainability reporting. We have identified these earlier in the chapter, but as there are many institutions giving sustainability advice, it is useful to complete this chapter with a quick review of the current potion. The Global Sustainability Standards Board (GSSB) sets globally accepted standards for sustainability reporting and issued the world's first globally accepted standards. It oversees the development of the GRI Standards according to a formally defined due process reporting. It provides the world's most widely used standards for sustainability reporting. There is also the Sustainability Accounting Standards Board in the US which was founded as a non-profit organisation in 2011 to help businesses and investors develop a common language about the financial impacts of sustainability and to guide the disclosure of financially material sustainability information by companies to their investors. Available for 77 industries, the Standards identify the subset of environmental, social and governance (ESG) issues most relevant to financial performance in each industry.

International Sustainability Standards Board

The International Sustainability Standards Board was established on November 3, 2021, with the role of developing a comprehensive set of baseline sustainability standards for global use. It is claimed that such a set of standards would facilitate the harmonisation of sustainability disclosures across jurisdictions and replace the use of existing voluntary standards. The ISSB announcement came at the 26th United Nations Climate Change Conference of Parties ("COP26") that took place in Glasgow, Scotland.

In 2021, the European Commission's proposal for a Corporate Sustainability Reporting Directive (CSRD) envisaged the adoption of EU sustainability reporting standards. The draft standards would be developed by the European Financial Reporting Advisory Group EFRAG which has recently issued exposure drafts on the first set of Draft European Sustainability Reporting Standards (ESRS).

Due to the different use of terms used by the various groups, it is impossible to determine the extent and value of what can be identified as sustainability reporting at the international level. Although all the various organisations are attempting to address the issues of measuring and reporting sustainability by companies, there are many hurdles to be overcome. For example, despite many years of the development of international accounting, the US and many other countries have not adopted fully international accounting standards. Despite the good work done by institutions such as the International Accounting Standards Board which is the accounting standard-setting body of the IFRS Foundation, it remains difficult to assess the level of compliance internationally. There is not a specific legal requirement for companies to comply with the standards. However, we can assume that those organisations making investments internationally regards SASB Standards as essential information when purchasing the shares of a company.

The SASB has been very active and has issued standards relevant to 77 industries which not only are in English but translations can also be obtained in French, German, Japanese and Spanish. Standards are free to download for non-commercial use and standards for commercial purposes are available. The standards are industry based, and as an example, we have selected from the website the standards in the Chemical industry. The website provides the following information:

Chemicals industry transform organic and inorganic feedstocks into more than 70,000 diverse products with a range of industrial, pharmaceutical, agricultural, housing, automotive, and consumer applications. The industry is commonly segmented into basic (commodity) chemicals, agricultural chemicals, and specialty chemicals. Basic chemicals, the largest segment by volume produced, include bulk polymers, petrochemicals, inorganic chemicals, and other industrial chemicals. Agricultural chemicals include fertilizers, crop chemicals, and agricultural biotechnology. Specialty chemicals include paints and coatings, agrochemicals, sealants, adhesives, dyes, industrial gases, resins, and catalysts. Larger firms may produce basic, agricultural, and specialty chemicals, while most companies are specialized. Chemicals companies typically manufacture and sell products globally.

In previous chapters, we have explained in detail the requirements of International Financial Reporting Standards which are issued by the IFRS Foundation. IFRS Sustainability Disclosure Standards are developed by the International Accounting Standards Board (IASB) and the International Sustainability Standards Board (ISSB). The boards are overseen by the IFRS Foundation Trustees, who in turn are accountable to the IFRS Foundation Monitoring Board of public authorities with responsibility for corporate reporting.

There is clearly substantial pressure from many sources for Sustainability information to be made available. A brief review of annual reports illustrates that many companies are taking the developments very seriously and including sustainability details in the information they make public. One example which we show in the following is that of Diageo plc. We emphasise that this information is in addition to the annual "financial" report and ESG stands for **Environmental, Social and Governance**. The full report is 119 pages and is well illustrated:

This ESG Reporting Index aims to complement our integrated Annual Report by providing a broader range of ESG disclosures. Our Annual Report explains the wider context in which we operate and presents our ESG performance in relation to both our corporate performance and global sustainable development issues. Our ESG Reporting Index supplements the information provided in our Annual Report by providing detailed information about how we manage our most material issues.

We use three ESG reporting frameworks, including the Global Reporting Initiative (GRI), Sustainability Accounting Standards Board (SASB) and United Nations Global Compact (UNGC) Index. These frameworks allow us to provide information in a structured and consistent way, enabling our stakeholders to analyse our performance over time, and relative to other organisations. The purpose of each of these frameworks and information on how they should be used are described below, alongside our reporting boundaries and methodologies. Throughout this ESG Reporting Index we often refer to our Annual Report and website, where more information on our strategy, standards and policies can be found. Please note that each disclosure in this ESG Reporting Index can be read in isolation; the hyperlinked navigation at the top of each page enables readers to quickly move from section to section and works best when the report is downloaded to desktop. Section What is in this section and how to use it Introduction An overview of our reporting approach, our materiality assessment and a brief overview of our Society 2030: Spirit of Progress plan. GRI Index A broad and comprehensive set of disclosures on organisational impacts that are relevant to a wide range of stakeholders, in line with the GRI framework. Some topics are material to our supplier sites and some to the countries where we make and sell our products. Please see page 7 for information on how we have mapped the GRI standards to our Society 2030: Spirit of Progress plan. UNGC Index Our UNGC 'communication on progress' in line with our participant-level membership of UNGC. To avoid duplication, this section cross-references widely to the GRI Index disclosures. SASB Sector-specific disclosures for alcohol beverage companies that are financially material to our business, in line with the SASB framework. To avoid duplication, this section cross-references widely to the GRI Index disclosures. Reporting boundaries and methodologies Information about how we report on each of our Society 2030: Spirit of Progress targets and various other quantitative metrics. For each Society 2030: Spirit of Progress target we provide the key performance indicator, definitions, scope, baseline, and information on how we avoid double counting where relevant. Assurance statement Independent assurance is a key part of our approach to reporting. Again, this year, we engaged PricewaterhouseCoopers LLP (PwC) to provide limited assurance on some key ESG metrics. Within this report, information that is within PwC's limited scope is marked with the symbol Δ. PwC's assurance statement includes a list of metrics that have been assured and a description of the approach PwC took.

If we concentrate on the present actions of major companies, it raises some interesting questions. We do not intend to discuss them in this book, but our discussion on sustainability opens the questions as to the future of Corporate Social Responsibility (CSR). This is a concept which describes a company's commitment to carry out its business in an ethical way. This means that a company retains the objective of providing a financial return to its shareholders but also realises its social, economic and environmental impact, and human rights obligations. CSR can involve such activities as environmental management e.g. waste reduction and sustainability responsible sourcing. You will find that many companies are now making their approach to CSR on their websites and the issue of "sustainability" is part of a company's approach to corporate social responsibility.

Chapter Review

This chapter has discussed the notion of sustainability. Several accounting organisations have become active in suggesting that they can be the main force when it comes to reporting on sustainability. Much of the interest and action, however, has been with large companies listed on the stock exchange. However, accountants have failed to explain specifically their role and their knowledge in investigating and reporting sustainability. Much of the relevant information will not be financial in nature nor has the intended audience been identified. Importantly, there is no explanation of the type of action to be taken against perceived "offenders" and accountants have no authority to take action.

Imagine that the accountants produce a report that accepts the company's figures and a very good profit has been made. If the accountants are also responsible for the sustainability report, what do they do? They can report that the company has not met the sustainability targets but does this mean that the company will close? Will the company change its practices if it is making good profits and not carrying out any activities that are definitely illegal? The discussions and examples on sustainability have used mainly large companies that are quoted on the stock exchange. One suspects that there are many small, unlisted companies that are conducting activities that are not sustainable. At present, there are no suggestions on the best method to prevent their unsustainable activities.

From the notion of "sustainability," discussions have moved onto the broader notion of Corporate Social Responsibility. One view is that a company is still formed with the main purpose of raising money for the owners i.e. the shareholders. In doing so, it will employ people and use any natural sources that it is legally allowed to do so. The company was not formed to concern itself with protecting the environment. If there are legal regulations set by the government with which it must comply, it will do so. Firms of accountants and other "sustainability" organisations have been established but may have little expertise in investigate some sustainability issues. Neither do they have any authority to take action where it detects such issues. Presumably, the hope is that if their auditor's report mentions unsustainable activities the existing shareholders and others will close their business contacts.

The explanations, discussions and examples in our book have been focused on large companies. It may be that the notion of "sustainability" is only important for them because shareholders are interested in the financial and continuous success of the business in the form of dividends. There are many small companies which are not listed on the stock exchange. Their owners will be intent on resolving any tax issues and ensuring that the company continues in business as they are, and possibly a small number of employees rely on the company being "profitable".

There are many issues and questions regarding the issues of sustainability and corporate social responsibility. This leads to the discussions of what is legal or illegal and who is responsible for setting "standards". We believe that future discussions will lead to legal and political issues. However, these issues will have little or no impact on the financial reporting requirements we have explained in the previous chapters.

CHAPTER 12 Accounting for Sustainability

Review Questions

1. Sustainability reporting is
   a. required by the UK government
   b. Only needed for oil companies
   c. advocated by accounting organizations
   d. required only for partnerships

2. Accounting students do not study sustainability reporting because
   a. other accounting areas are more important
   b. there is no legal requirement to do so
   c. professors do not understand it
   d. only charities and the public sectors use sustainable reporting

3. Name two of the weaknesses in current accounting regulations that result in up-to-date information not being provided.

4. Who would, in the first year of business, usually decides who the auditors should be? Who makes the appointment in subsequent years?

5. What is meant by the term "stagflation"?

6. What is the Global Sustainability Standards Board (GSSB) and what does it do?

7. What is Corporate Social Responsibility?

8. What is the definition of sustainability given by the World Commission on Environment and Development?

Index

Printed in the United States
by Baker & Taylor Publisher Services